WORLD FILM LOCATIONS SÃO PAULO

Edited by Natália Pinazza and Louis Bayman

First Published in the UK in 2013 by Intellect Books, The Mill, Parnall Road, Fishponds, Bristol, BS16 3JG, UK

First Published in the USA in 2013 by Intellect Books, The University of Chicago Press, 1427 E. 60th Street, Chicago, IL 60637, USA

Cover photo: *Não Por Acaso* (2007) © Buena Onda, Fox Filmes do Brasil, Globo Filmes

Copy Editor: Emma Rhys

A Catalogue record for this book is available from the British Library

World Film Locations Series
ISSN: 2045-9009
eISSN: 2045-9017

World Film Locations São Paulo
ISBN: 978-1-78320-029-0
ePub ISBN: 978-1-78320-116-7
ePDF ISBN: 978-1-78320-115-0

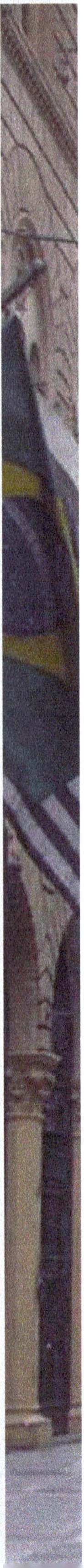

WORLD FILM LOCATIONS SÃO PAULO

EDITORS
Natália Pinazza and Louis Bayman

SERIES EDITOR & DESIGN
Gabriel Solomons

CONTRIBUTORS
Kyle Black,
Alessandra Soares Brandão,
Murilo Gabriel Berardo Bueno,
Reinaldo Cardenuto,
Maria Ignês Carlos Magno,
Márcia Carvalho,
Carolin Overhoff Ferreira,
Fabiana M. Ghiringhello,
Scott Jordan Harris,
Tatiana Signorelli Heise,
Tiago de Luca, Cecília Mello,
Maria Luiza Martins de Mendonça,
Gabriel Menotti,
Santiago Oyarzabal,
Michael Pigott,
Rafael Mendonça Lisita Pinto,
Renato Luiz Pucci Jr.
Daniel Serravalle de Sá,
Antônio M. da Silva,
Ramayana Lira de Sousa,
Alfredo Suppia, Fábio Uchôa

LOCATION MAPS
Joel Keightley

PUBLISHED BY
Intellect
The Mill, Parnall Road,
Fishponds, Bristol, BS16 3JG, UK
T: +44 (0) 117 9589910
F: +44 (0) 117 9589911
E: *info@intellectbooks.com*

Bookends: City view (Nicolas De Camaret)
This page: Photo by Paulo Silvestrini
and Carol Bandeira de Mello
Overleaf: Carandiru (Kobal)

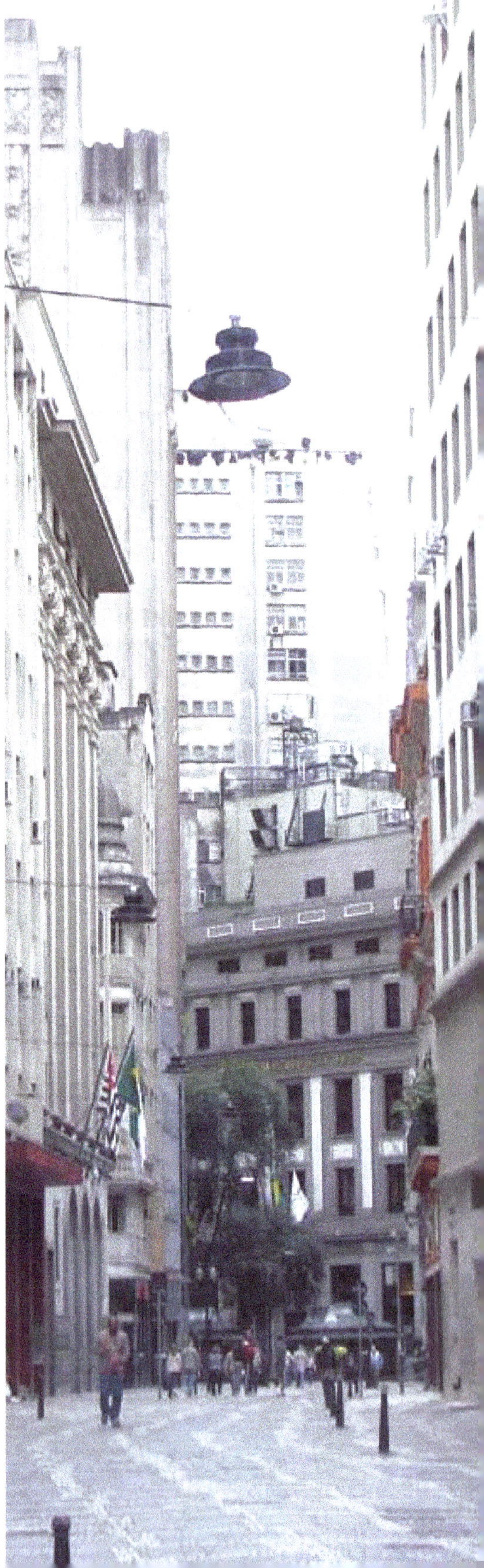

CONTENTS

Maps/Scenes

Essays

Backpages

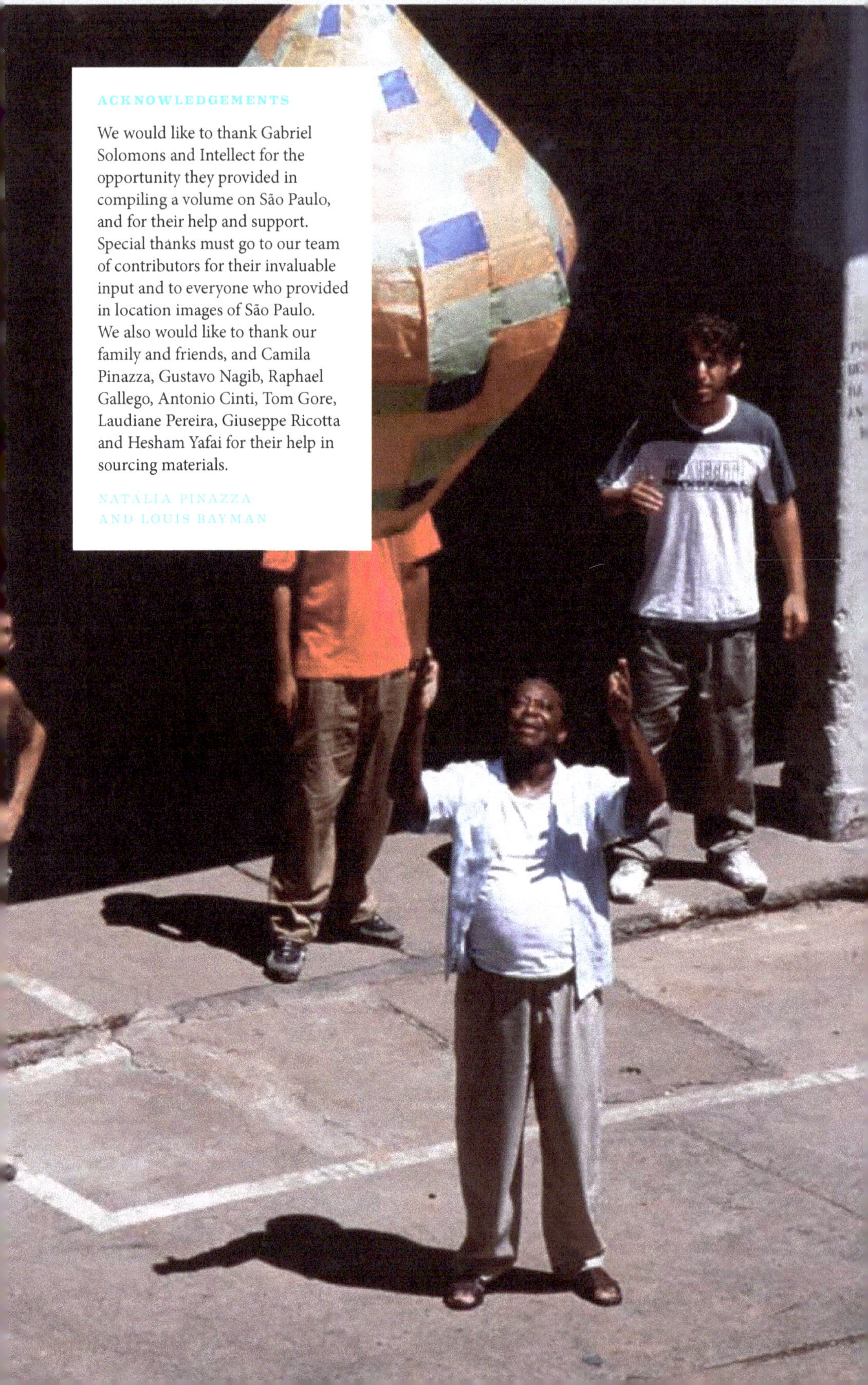

ACKNOWLEDGEMENTS

We would like to thank Gabriel Solomons and Intellect for the opportunity they provided in compiling a volume on São Paulo, and for their help and support. Special thanks must go to our team of contributors for their invaluable input and to everyone who provided in location images of São Paulo. We also would like to thank our family and friends, and Camila Pinazza, Gustavo Nagib, Raphael Gallego, Antonio Cinti, Tom Gore, Laudiane Pereira, Giuseppe Ricotta and Hesham Yafai for their help in sourcing materials.

NATALIA PINAZZA
AND LOUIS BAYMAN

INTRODUCTION

World Film Locations *São Paulo*

LOCATION IS A KEY FACTOR throughout the process of making a film. As well as being the environment in which events occur, it can occupy centre stage of dramatic and artistic focus. Cinema has, from its earliest years, displayed an interest in the spectacle offered by urban locations, bringing images from different cities around the world, contributing to the imaginative process of understanding urban conditions, and representing the dynamism – or the listlessness – of endlessly multiplying human relationships and the mechanisms and processes in which they occur. Given pre-production issues of viability and logistics and the unexpected events that can occur while filming, location can be an exciting and volatile factor in film-making, particularly in a number of the films analysed in this volume in which technological and financial restrictions as well as artistic choices necessitated an improvisational approach. Therefore, spectators can identify different ways of treating a location not only between films but also within a single film, making location a fascinating aspect to explore in cinema.

In centring on São Paulo, the largest city in South America and one which leads the emergence of the region as an economic centre, this volume of World Film Locations breaks away from the dominance of exoticism in the international imaginary of Brazil. Foregrounding São Paulo's position within film history, one finds a location which is a home to urban cultural phenomena from modernism to hip hop and trash. São Paulo is characterized by working environments, and is marked by histories of subversion, dictatorship, and the social consequences of the relentless urbanization present in every metropolis in the late-capitalist world.

This book is composed of a selection of 43 scene reviews from a variety of films set in São Paulo. These short reviews include images of the city from films that have gained worldwide distribution and that may be relatively well known to readers, as well as films that are not easily accessible either to the national or international public. As such the selection covers a variety of films that present São Paulo as a changing landscape. The fact that the films testify to the rapid changes that the city constantly undergoes has sometimes posed a challenge, since the locations of some of the scenes are no longer recognizable. Another element that makes São Paulo a challenging place to map in the cinema is that some areas are typical not of anything specific to São Paulo nor even to Brazil, but of a sprawling and often anonymous international city, a factor which is further discussed in the book. The globalized character of São Paulo is also shaped in terms of aesthetics and cultural trends adopted by films set there, in particular postmodern approaches to the city.

The scene reviews are complemented by a historical overview and six essays that introduce the reader to the key themes, trends, film-makers and movements that have shaped our understanding of the symbiotic relationship between São Paulo and cinema, offering many original insights into the topic. The collection also highlights how São Paulo's on-screen representation has been shaped by social-historical changes and the challenges that film-makers face in a city marked by contradictions. Although this treatment of the topic has no precedent in any English language publication, we make no claim that it is exhaustive. Instead, the book serves as an introduction for film enthusiasts, visitors and tourists to filmic representations of the city, while opening scholarly debates on global concerns such as marginalization and rapid urbanization.

World Film Locations: São Paulo is a book that uses the cinematic visions of a city that transcends national boundaries in the context of Brazil's changing economic and cultural landscapes. ⁜

Natália Pinazza and Louis Bayman, Editors

SÃO PAULO

City of the Imagination

Text by
REINALDO CARDENUTO

TO WRITE BRIEFLY ABOUT the presence of São Paulo in films is a complicated task. Confronting a city that at the beginning of the twentieth century was predominantly rural, but that entered the twenty-first century as one of the biggest and most complex megalopoli in the world, Brazilian cinema has constructed multiple approaches to stress the haunting feeling of being faced with a locus where historical and geographical changes happen in a vertiginous and at times violent way. In the cinema – and in the 'Paulistano' (São Paulo city dweller) – São Paulo evokes profoundly ambiguous feelings: a scary and overwhelming city of social and political contradictions that have become increasingly acute as the years have gone by, it is simultaneously a source of inspiration for its multicultural character, for the poetry extracted from the concrete, and for a cosmopolitanism that projects the city towards the outside world. Brazilian cinema has transited through this ambiguity, and it is not easy to provide an overview of the films that have represented the city over time. Nonetheless, it is with the pleasure of confronting my own memory as a cinephile that I present some of the subject's key aspects.

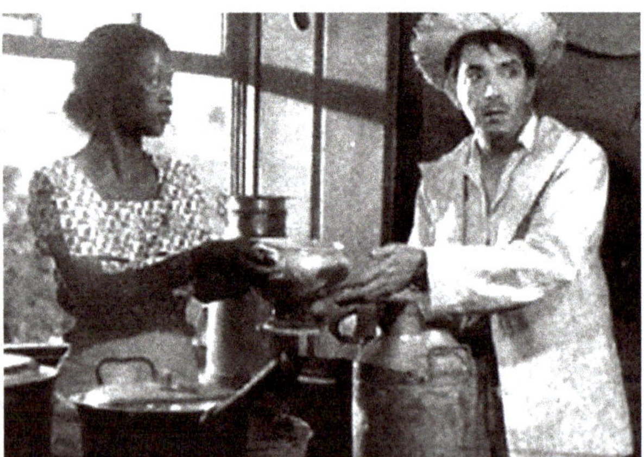

Overall, the tendency in Brazilian cinema in the first half of the twentieth century is to represent São Paulo as a city where a work ethic and economic growth were part of a project of modernization. In the rare films that remain from the 1920s, São Paulo appears as a metropolis destined to be an exemplar of bourgeois progress and virtues. In *Exemplo regenerador* (1919) and *Fragmentos da vida* (1929), both directed by José Medina, the characters' moral vices end up punished, for they display a lack of adaptation to a city aiming towards perfection. In *São Paulo, sinfonia da metrópole/São Paulo, a Metropolitan Symphony* (1929), a documentary made by Adalberto Kemeny and Rodolfo Rex Lustig, the most important element lies in the attempt to adjust a cinematographic language to a dynamic locus where the accelerated rhythm of life and work seemed to contain the expectation of a pleasing urbanization marked by social well-being.

Into the 1950s, some of the films made in Brazil remained inclined to record São Paulo as holding the promise of a possible modernity. In institutional films produced for the governing São Paulo City Councils or for the industrial sector, film-makers such as Benedito Junqueira Duarte (*Retificação do rio Tietê* [1940]) and Jean Manzon (*A Luta pelo transporte em* São Paulo [1952]), made propaganda documentaries that assigned power to public and private forces, thus leading the metropolis towards the desired progress. Although some fictional feature films started narrating social dramas lived in the city – such as the comedy *Candinho* (1953) by Abílio Pereira de Almeida and the realist film *O Grande momento/The Great Moment* (1958) by Roberto Santos – the tendency remained to represent the city as a symbolic space of conflicts that would eventually be resolved.

It was only in the 1960s that the cinematographic vision of São Paulo radically changed. Confronted with the failure of the

Opposite *Candinho* (1953) / Below *Eros* (1964)

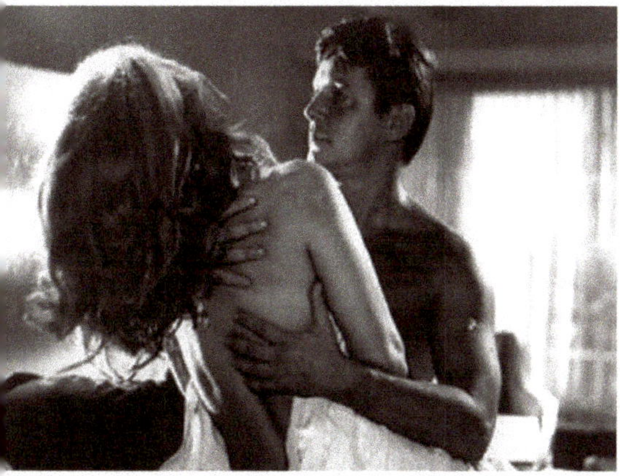

Above © 1964 Kamera Filmes, Vera Cruz Studios
Opposite © 1953 Vera Cruz Studios

desired modernization and a city whose social contradictions were increasing, Brazilian cinema started to take a critical distance towards the Paulista metropolis. In that decade, alongside documentaries such as *Viramundo* (1964–65), in which Geraldo Sarno exposes the drama of the north-eastern migrant facing under-employment and a lack of prospects in São Paulo, important films invested in aesthetic experimentation through which echoed contemporary metropolitan dissonances and crises. In *Noite vazia/Eros* (1964) by Walter Hugo Khouri the emptiness felt by two men bored with their bourgeois lives inspires a striking *mise-en-scène* that transforms the Paulistana dawn into an environment of profound existential agony. In *São Paulo Sociedade Anônima* (1965) by Luiz Sérgio Person, the city becomes a force that oppresses the protagonist, Carlos, and prevents him from breaking free from a life imprisoned in the mechanisms of capitalist work without hope of freedom.

From these works onwards, films which had a political tendency – making up a significant share of Brazilian cinema – generally continued with a dramaturgy that represented São Paulo as an agonizing space marked by acute conflicts, in which contradictions multiply and seem increasingly far from a solution. The drama of north-eastern migration, 'favelization' (the emergence of a number of *favelas*, slums) and the oppressed worker re-emerge as topics in *O Homem que virou suco/The Man Who Turned Into Juice* (1981) by João Batista de Andrade. A metropolis in which the popular classes live amidst violence with no escape from criminality or police corruption emerges in *Pixote: A lei do mais fraco/Pixote: Survival of the Weakest* (1980) and *Carandiru* (2003) both by Hector Babenco; in *Os 12 trabalhos/The Twelve Labours* (2006) by Ricardo Elias; or in *Linha de passe* (2008) by Walter Salles and Daniella Thomas. São Paulo is a city of social relations pushed to their limits, with a sort of continuous and endless tension, in films such as *Um Céu de estrelas/A Starry Sky* (1996) by Tata Amaral; *O Invasor/The Trespasser* (2002) by Beto Brant; *A Casa de Alice/Alice's House* (2007) by Chico Teixeira; or *Os Inquilinos/The Tenants* (2009) by Sérgio Bianchi.

Overall, the tendency in Brazilian cinema in the first half of the twentieth century is to represent São Paulo as a city where a work ethic and economic growth were part of a project of modernization.

Film-makers whose approaches differ from the realism mentioned in the previous paragraph have made films in which some of the constituent elements of modern São Paulo – cacophony, cosmopolitanism, existential fragmentation and the 'concrete' – form a poetic representation of the anguish of contemporary urban men. Without abdicating readings of the city as a violent dystopia, but inspired by the city's contradictions to create extremely intriguing aesthetic experiences, are counter-culture films such as *O Bandido da luz vermelha/The Red Light Bandit* (1968) by Rogério Sganzerla; *Zézero* (1974) by Ozualdo Candeias; and *Filme demência* (1986), by Carlos Reichenbach, the last one a loose adaptation of Goethe's *Faust* (1772-1829) in São Paulo.

The emptying of a social and political critique alongside the fascination with the modern metropolis refers to the creation of the practices of a postmodern perspective, in a polyphonic style which includes parody and that worships the pop and electronic cosmopolitanism of São Paulo in the 1980s, in feature films such as *Cidade oculta/Hidden City* (1986) by Chico Botelho; *Anjos da noite/Night Angels* (1987) by Wilson Barros; and *Beijo 2348/72* (1990) by Walter Rogério. More recently, Lina Chamie's *A Via Láctea* (2007) departs from the naturalism that has marked contemporary Brazilian cinema, in a film that contributes to the multiplicity of gazes turned on São Paulo with a non-linear narrative consisting of audio-visual fragments of the city to mirror a shattered subjectivity in the chaos of the urban universe.

SPOTLIGHT

SÃO PAULO ON THE BIG SCREEN

Text by ALFREDO SUPPIA

Cinematic [Post]Modernity

AT 24 OR 30 FRAMES PER SECOND, the largest city in Brazil emerged as the most genuine face of national modernity throughout the twentieth century. A controversial face, given the ambiguity and contradictions of modernization in Brazil.

In early twentieth-century São Paulo, economic development demanded increasingly frequent cinematic records of events and 'modern touchstones'. Films like *Eletrificação da Companhia Paulista de Estradas de Ferro/Electrification of the Paulista Company of Railroads* (1923), and particularly *A Sociedade Anonyma Fábrica Votorantim/The Votorantim Company* (Armando Pamplona, 1922), approached modern motifs under an essentially descriptive aesthetics. *The Votorantim Company* illustrates the ambiguities of modernization in São Paulo and Brazil, in as much as it suggests curious contradictions between discourse and image, as shown in Ismail Xavier's analysis of industrial discipline vs the workers' spontaneity in the film (Xavier 2012: 58–59).

The dynamism of the metropolis, its frenzy of pedestrians, vehicles and industrial machines captured the attention of a number of film-makers. This is how *São Paulo, Sinfonia da Metrópole/São Paulo, a Metropolitan Symphony* (1929), by Adalberto Kemeny and Rodolfo Rex Lustig (Hungarian film-makers based in Brazil), appeared imbued with the spirit of films like *Berlin: Die Sinfonie der Großstadt/Berlin: Symphony of a Great City* (Walter Ruttmann, 1927), or *Человек с киноаппаратом/The Man with the Movie-Camera* (Dziga Vertov, 1929). Since then, magnetic investigations of the city have multiplied on-screen, such as Jean-Claude Bernardet's *São Paulo: Sinfonia e Cacofonia/São Paulo: Symphony and Cacophony* (1995) or Elie Politi's *Visão Paulista/Paulista Vision* (1972).

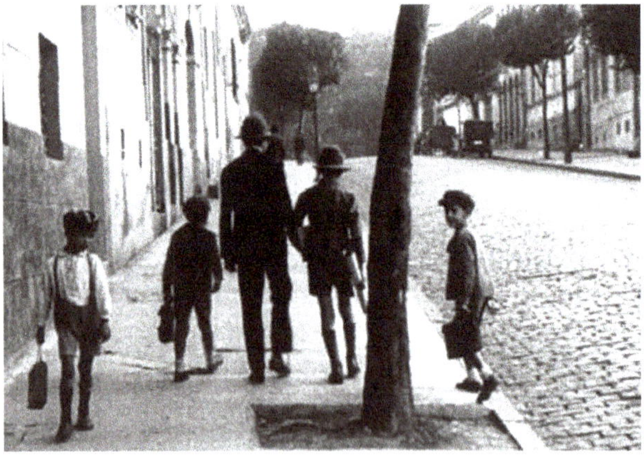

In the 1950s, São Paulo continued to capture national attention as an expression of modernity with the rise of Vera Cruz, the big studio funded by the bourgeois elite. However, it was Roberto Santos's independent film *O Grande momento/The Great Moment* (1958) which best depicted the more human and familiar face of '[a] city growing before our eyes, but seen from the little neighborhood, a place which remains warm and optimistic' (Barbosa 2012: 68). Later, Luiz Sérgio Person's *São Paulo S.A./São Paulo Co. Ltd.* (1965) portrayed a noisy and ruinous utopia, the existential collapse of a middle-class man oppressed by the vertical, monumental and profit-oriented metropolis.

The motif of São Paulo as a harsh mistress, guardian of both treasures and misfortunes to those who dream of the utopian metropolis, is reiterated in a series of films that revolve around the theme of migration, the inland worker seeking better living conditions in the big city – such as in Ozualdo Candeias's *Zézero* (1974) or João Batista de Andrade's *O Homem que virou suco/The Man Who Turned Into Juice* (1981).

In the 1980s, São Paulo recovered its status as a privileged landscape in film production, which was notably urban in terms of style and themes. It was time for the 'New Paulista Cinema' ('Novo Cinema Paulista'), well-illustrated by the 'São Paulo night

Opposite *São Paulo, a Metropolitan Symphony* (1929)
Below *A Dama do Cine Shangai/The Lady from Shanghai Cinema* (1988)

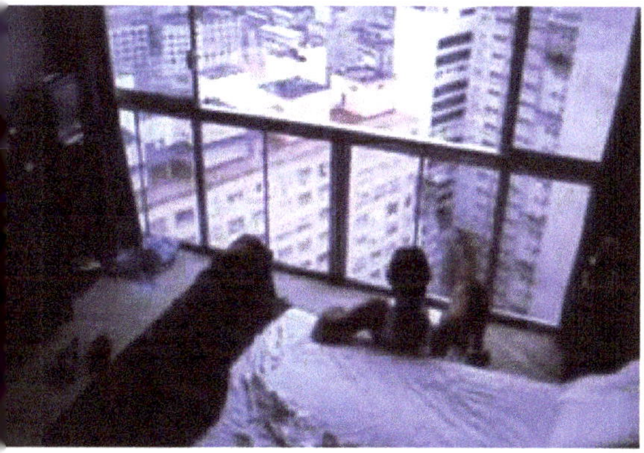

trilogy' ('trilogia paulistana da noite'): *Cidade oculta/Hidden City* (Chico Botelho, 1986), *Anjos da Noite/Night Angels* (Wilson Barros, 1987) and *A Dama do Cine Shangai/The Lady from Shanghai Cinema* (Guilherme de Almeida Prado, 1988). According to Andréa Barbosa,

> [a] gigantic city thus appears as one of the main features in these films. It is not just a backdrop, it is both a landscape and a character that interacts with other characters through its own form, its emptiness, its beauty, its misfortune. (2012: 101)

Rubens Machado notes that São Paulo seemed 'to have become a kind of fashion' in the 1980s, with a new 'cycle of cosmopolitan reaffirmation' in tandem with a certain 'depersonalization' of the metropolis (quoted in Barbosa, 2012: 21). This 'New Paulista Cinema' is the one Luiz Renato Pucci J. (2008) denominates 'neon-realism', the Brazilian postmodern film from São Paulo. According to Barbosa, the *cinema paulista* of the 1980s recreates São Paulo as '[a] nocturnal, blue and humid city, populated by angels and marginal people (or marginal angels) that wander amidst endless alleys and walls' (Barbosa, 2012: 102).

The motif of São Paulo as a harsh mistress, guardian of both treasures and misfortunes to those who dream of the utopian metropolis, is reiterated in a series of films that revolve around the theme of migration.

During the *Retomada* years (approximately 1995-2002), the architectural modernity and verticality of the borderless 'concrete jungle' - metonyms of a controversial modernizing utopia - gave way to more heterogeneous, 'subterranean' and 'fragmented' gazes. The streets of São Paulo re-emerge as a laboratory for investigations into the country's most acute contradictions. In this context, Beto Brant's *O invasor/The Trespasser* (2002) is a film that sharply criticizes the corruption and social violence so deeply rooted in Brazil. Unlike *São Paulo Co. Ltd.*, *The Trespasser* 'darkens' the tone, further exploring the labyrinthine character of the metropolis in a cruel and naturalistic approach to social inequality and widespread crime.

At the same time provincial and cosmopolitan, São Paulo continued to attract the gaze of foreign film-makers in the 2000s, including in Eric Eason's *12 horas até o amanhecer/Journey to the End of the Night* (2006) or Nelson Yu Lik-wai's *Dangkou/Plastic City* (2008). Although not explicitly, São Paulo's Octavio Frias de Oliveira Bridge helped to 'futurize' the imaginary city in Fernando Meirelles's *Blindness* (2008). Also, a myriad of spaces have marked films with São Paulo's unmistakable 'stamp'. The skyline of the city, with the presence of the Banespa building in the downtown area, appears several times as a kind of 'image-chorus' in Chico Botelho's *Cidade Oculta/Hidden City* (1986), whereas Rua Augusta has 'starred' in movies such as Carlos Reichenbach's *Esta Rua Tão Augusta* (1966–/9), or Francisco Cesar Filho's *Augustas* (2012). Avenida Paulista, the financial heart regarded as a pinnacle of modernity in Brazil, has hosted a variety of film sequences, like Phillipe Barcinski's formalist delirium in his short *Palíndromo/Palindrome* (2001), a metaphor for the modernizing vertigo that victimizes ordinary people.

In the 1990s and the 2000s, São Paulo offered a privileged stage for the most diverse cinematic investigations into corruption (Sérgio Bianchi's *Cronicamente Inviável/Chronically Unfeasible*, [2000]), social inequality and crime (Roberto Moreira's *Contra Todo*, [2003]; Walter Salles J.'s *Linha de Passe*, [2008]; Jeferson De's *Bróder*, [2009]), precarious labour (Caíto Ortiz's *Motoboys: Vida Loca*, [2004]; Ricardo Elias's *Os 12 Trabalhos/The Twelve Labours*, [2006]); and dehumanization, delusion and isolation imposed by the city (Heitor Dhalia's *O Cheiro do Ralo/Drained*, [2006]; Philippe Barcinski's *Não por Acaso*, [2007]). In all these films, one can notice different times overlapping in a kaleidoscopic metropolis, archaism and modernity amalgamated or in conflict, the city's dramatic role chiseled on its manifold 'skin'. São Paulo is both a maze and a metonym for a nation still in search of its true (modern) identity. ⁜

N

LOCATIONS MAP

SÃO PAULO

maps are only to be taken as approximates

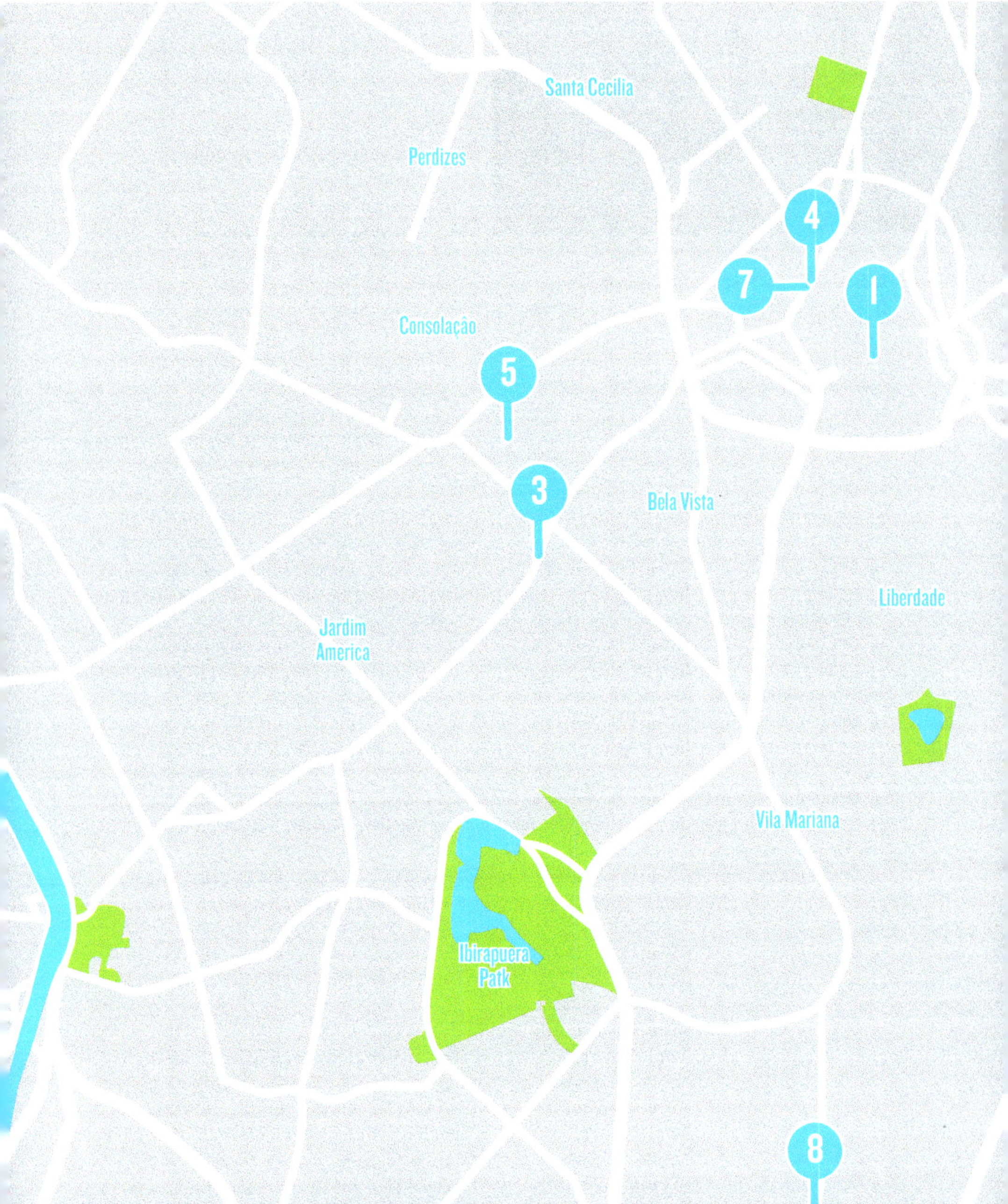

SÃO PAULO LOCATIONS
SCENES 1-8

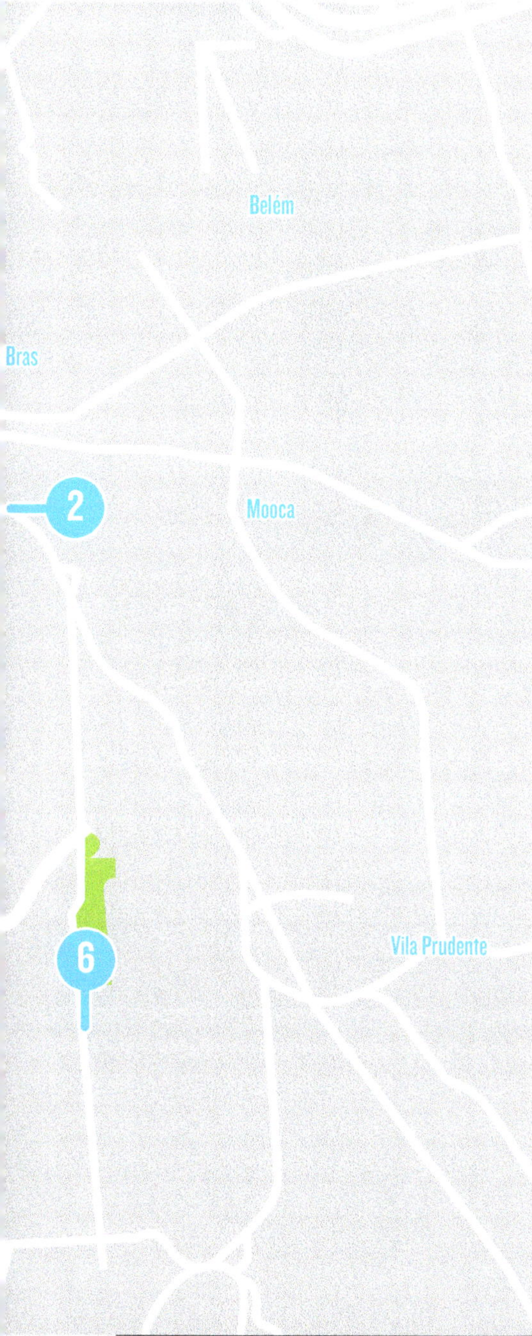

SÃO PAULO, A METROPOLITAN SYMPHONY/ SÃO PAULO, SINFONIA DA METRÓPOLE (1929)

LOCATION *Rua XI de Novembro*

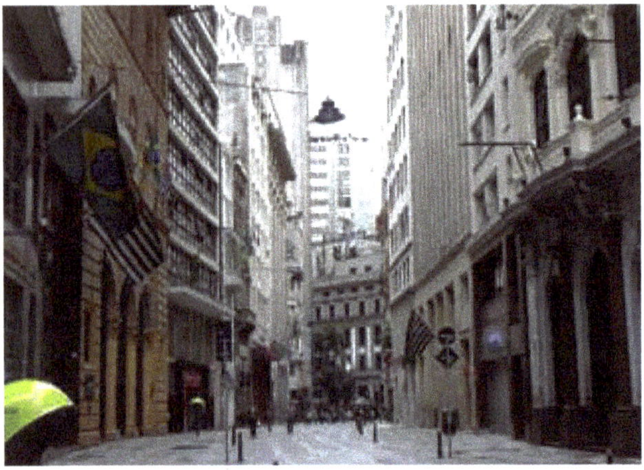

THE SÃO PAULO VERSION inspired by Walther Ruttmann's *Berlin: Die Sinfonie der Großstadt/ Berlin, Symphony of a Great City* from 1927, is less modernist than its German counterpart. However, it keeps pace with the earlier film by using the same structure: one day in the life of what was to become Brazil's and now South America's economic centre, starting with its awakening around the city centre at the School Yard, where the city was founded in 1554. Sào Paulo then numbered few more than one million inhabitants and the many views of the panning camera at its beginning show open spaces of what is today a densely populated and chaotically grown sky-scraping megalopolis. Famous sites of the city, such as the Anhangabaú Valley, the Luz Train Station or the Jockey Club, the financial headquarters on Rua XV de Novembro and the commercial district around School Yard appear as placid places. The two directors, immigrants Adalberto Kemeny and Rudolph Rex Lustig, opted for a more didactic approach by focusing on working people and students and by suggesting how their arduous labour was leading the city to 'order and progress', the motto of Brazil's flag. Educational buildings are filmed profusely, such as the Caetano de Campos School at Republic Square, the Butantã Institute, the Law Faculty at Largo Sào Francisco, and even an unknown kindergarten. Besides a single scene that draws attention to social inequality by means of a huge hand that takes from the rich in order to give alms to the poor, the film displays a rather overoptimistic patriotic attitude towards the city's growth. This uncritical fascination again compares *Sào Paulo* with *Berlin*. *Sào Paulo* is an impressive document that gives an idea of how modernization was taking shape and was being praised in the late 1920s in Latin America. ➺ ***Carolin Overhoff Ferreira***

Directed by Adalberto Kemeny and Rudolph Rex Lustig
Scene description: The city opens its eyes around the School Yard
Timecode for scene: 0:01:00 – 0:03:33

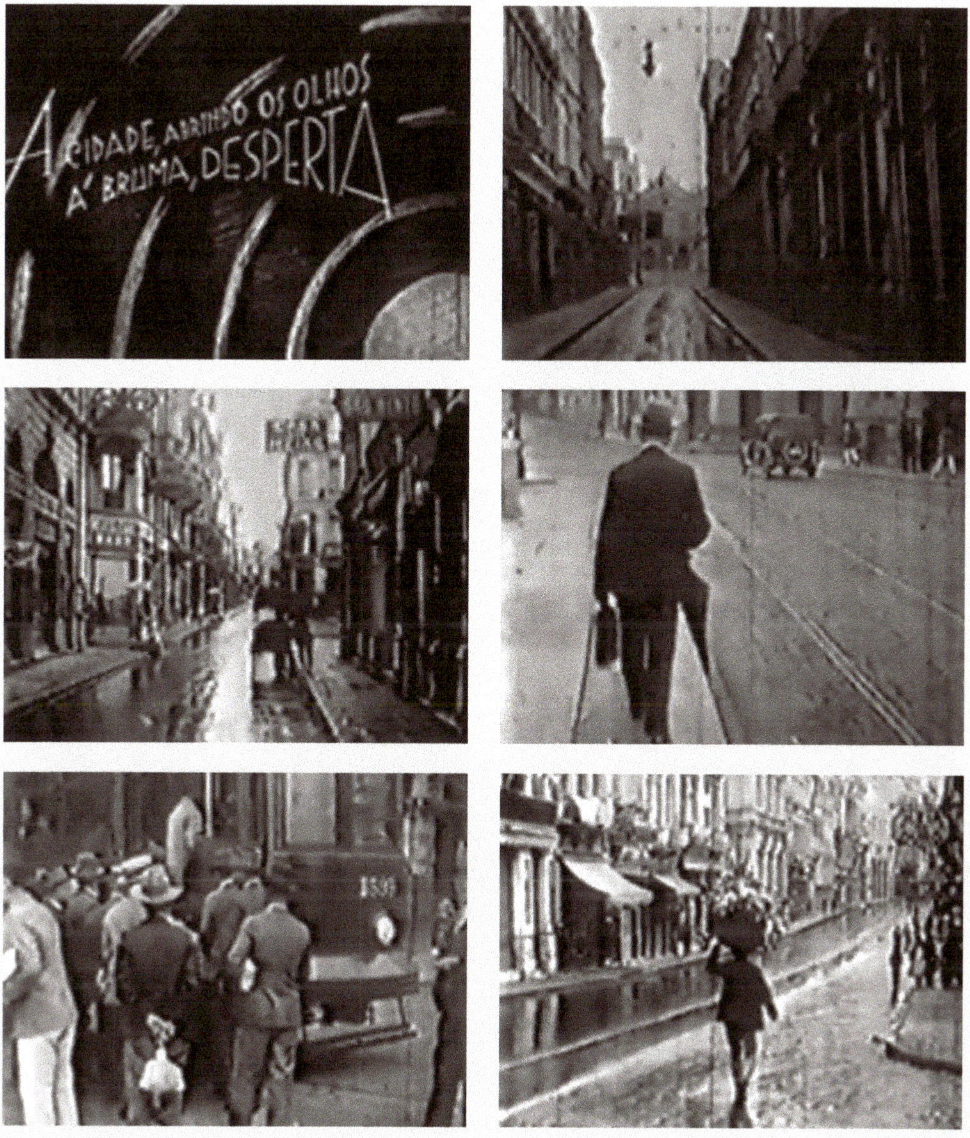

Images © 1929 Rex Filmes

THE GREAT MOMENT/ O GRANDE MOMENTO (1958)

LOCATION *Avenida do Estado, Cambuci*

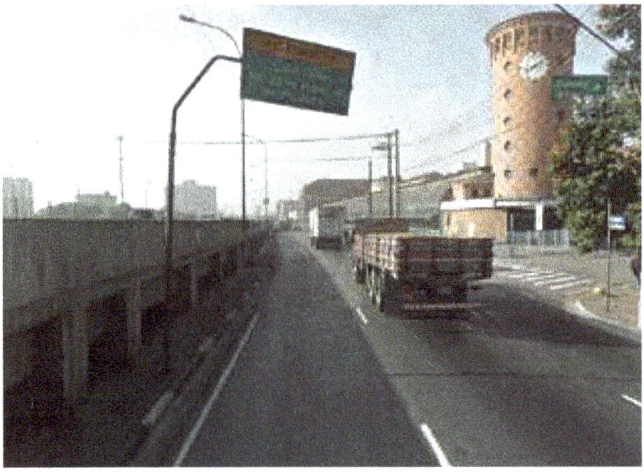

THE GREAT MOMENT is a landmark film for its focus on urban everyday life in São Paulo, and features the city's working-class districts of Brás, Mooca and Cambuci in a number of sequences shot on location. The 'great moment' of the title is Zeca's wedding to Angela. He is the son of a lower middle-class family of Italian immigrants, the Santini, who is struggling to make ends meet: on the big day he must find money to pay for his suit, the photographer, the flowers and the party, and thus the film develops almost like a comedy – albeit with sad overtones – in which a series of obstacles come between the protagonist and his ultimate goal. At some point Zeca has to make the difficult decision of selling his bicycle, but before letting it go he takes a farewell ride that cuts across the streets of Cambuci. He goes past Avenida Prefeito Passos and the now defunct Cine Itapura, and it is possible to glimpse in different shots the tower of Nossa Senhora da Paz on Rua do Glicério, where later he would be getting married, as well as the vertically built city centre and the dome of Sé Cathedral, contrasting with the then horizontally built working-class industrialized districts. The ride finishes in Avenida do Estado, where Zeca revels in his last bit of freedom. This is a memorable sequence in which, even if for just a fleeting moment, money and social imperatives seem to evaporate, liberating Zeca – and the film camera – to run free. ➾***Cecília Mello***

Photo © Google maps

Directed by Roberto Santos
Scene description: Zeca takes his bike for one last ride
Timecode for scene: 0:35:38 – 0:37:22

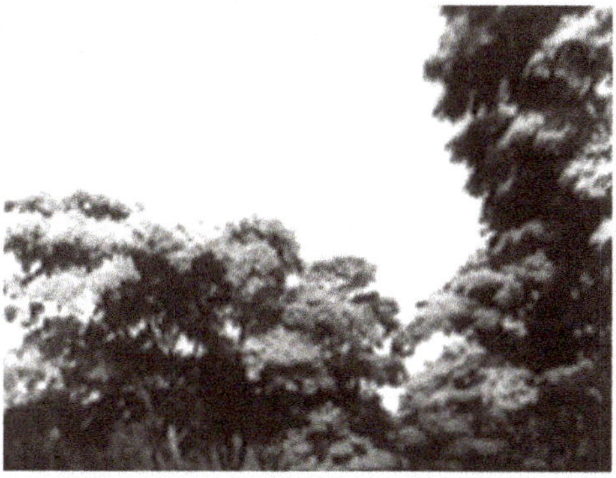

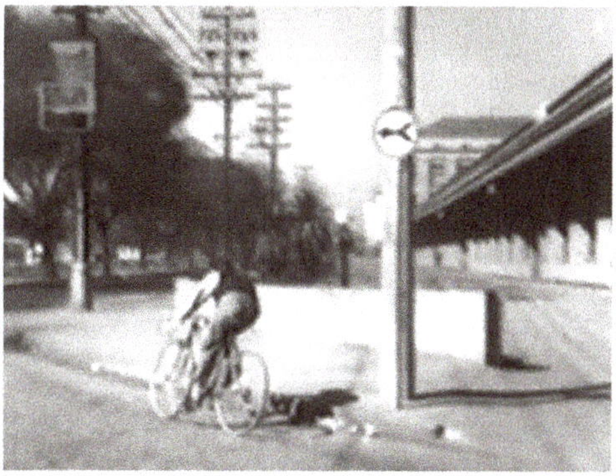

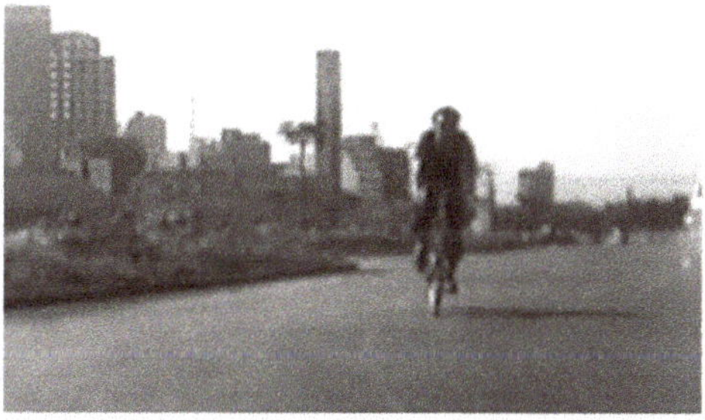

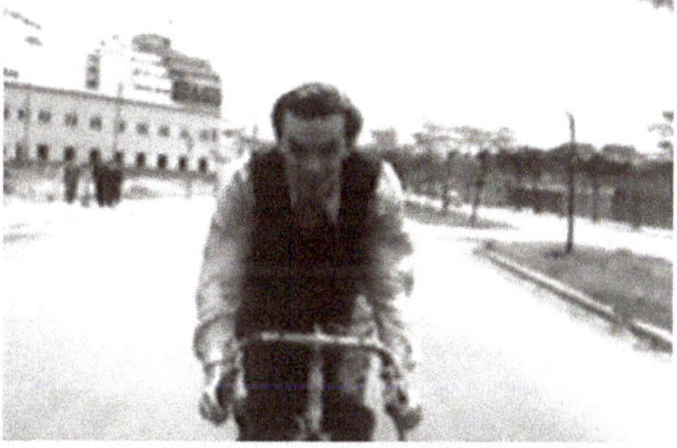

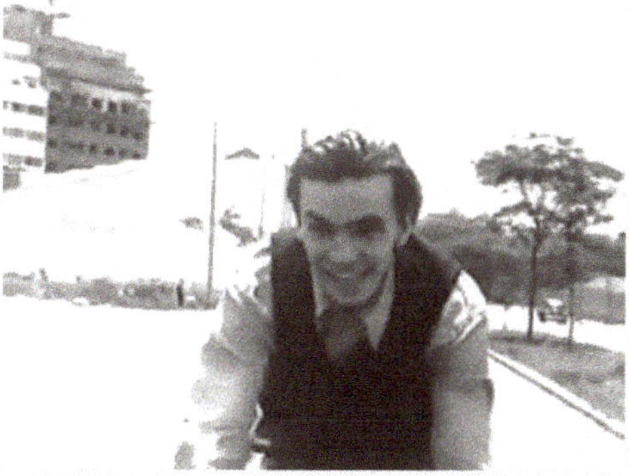

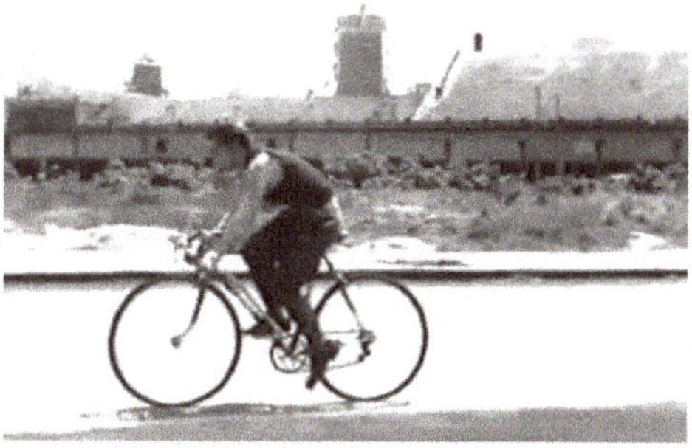

Images © 1958 Nelson Pereira dos Santos Produções Cinematográficas

EROS/NOITE VAZIA (1964)

LOCATION *Avenida Nove de Julho*

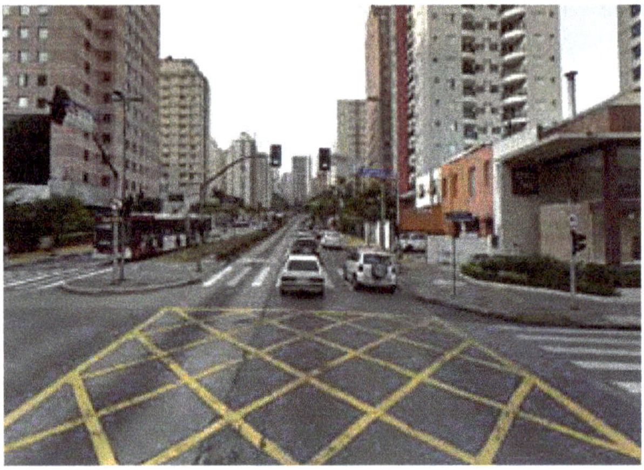

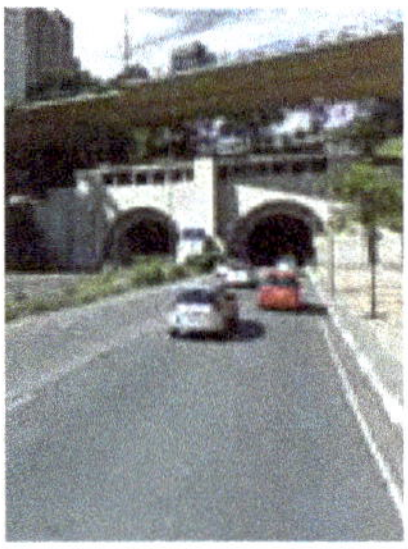

TWO ENTREPRENEURS go around the dance clubs in town. One of them, Luis, is married and has a bad character; the other, Nelson, is single, depressive and follows his friend's initiatives. They are looking for women to have new sexual experiences. Their search is repeated every night without success until they meet two beautiful prostitutes at a restaurant and take them to an apartment. After the first moments of physical contact, boredom takes over. One of the women wants their money whereas the other is naive and romantic. Despite many attempts to reach the desired feeling, nothing seems to work when existential problems and issues of social class emerge. Later on, Nelson and the romantic prostitute manage to reach a sort of mystical sexual relationship inspired by pictures of an Indian temple. However, they are soon interrupted by Luis. In the morning they drop the women off at a square and drive through the Avenida Nove de Julho, which links the decrepit downtown with other richer neighbourhoods. The number of buildings increases as the traffic passes, and Luis suggests that they should continue their hunt for sex in the evening. After entering the Nove de Julho tunnel, darkness takes over the screen. The sound of an electronic buzz suggests the existential hell in which they live. Their last conversation shows that they are stuck within the mechanisms of desire. The most celebrated film by director Walter Hugo Khouri, *Eros* ends with Nelson, the single character, up a leafy tree, which is a forlorn representation of nature within the urban jungle. ***Renato Luiz Pucci Jr***

Photo © Google maps

Directed by Walter Hugo Khouri

Scene description: A farewell at Praça Roosevelt and a road through Avenida Nove de Julho

Timecode for scene: 1:25:51 – 1:28:18

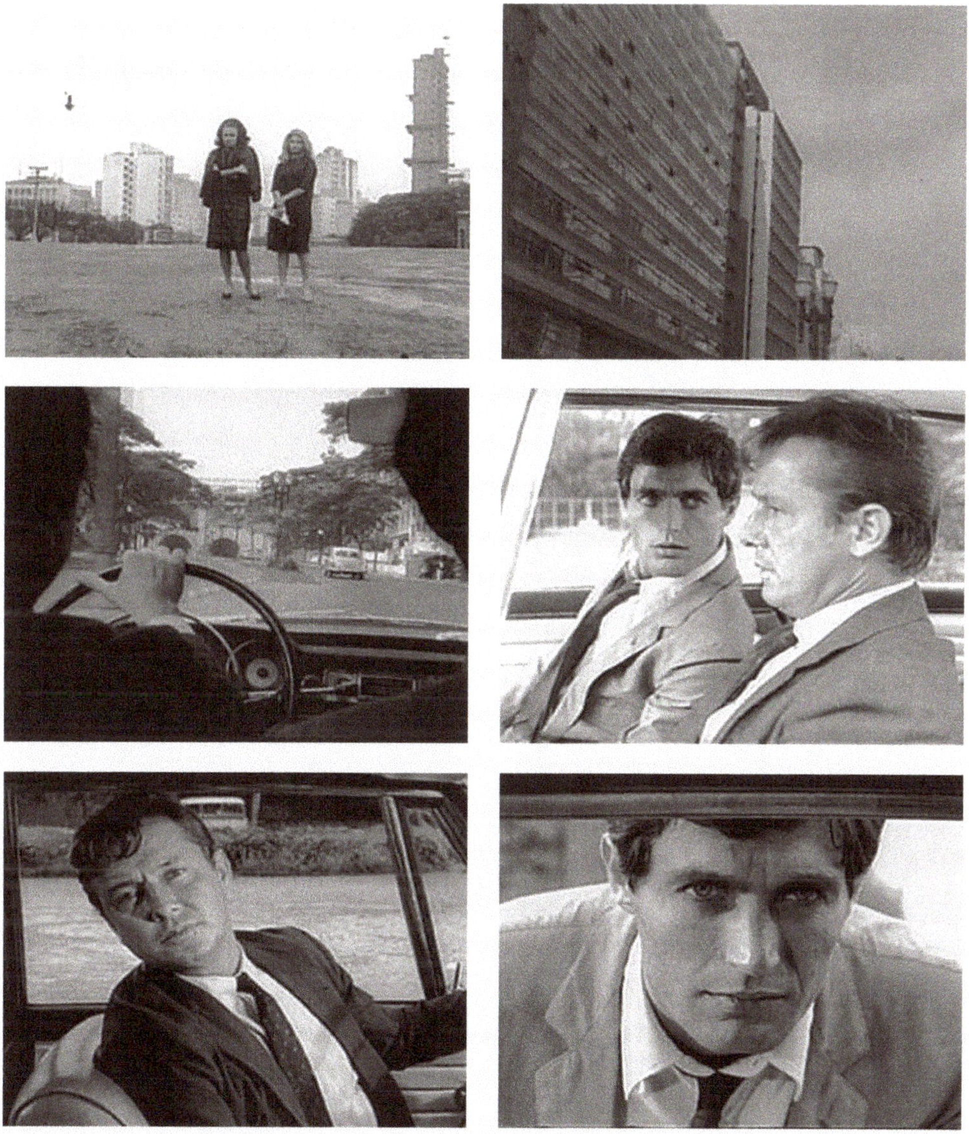

SÃO PAULO SOCIEDADE ANÔNIMA (1965)

LOCATION

Viaduto Do Chá, Sé

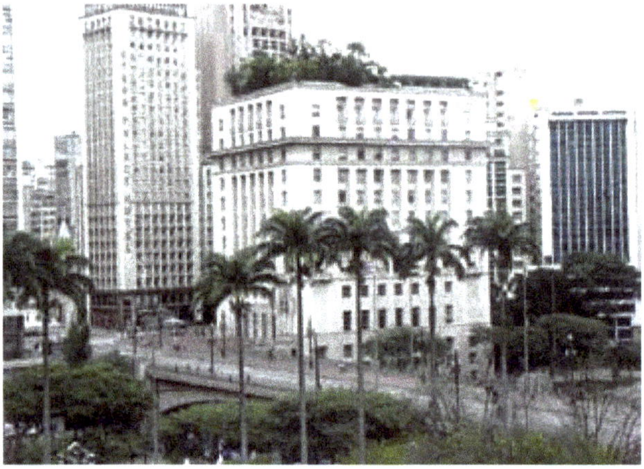

SÃO PAULO S/A takes place between 1959 and 1960, the moment when foreign automobile industries settled in São Paulo and when the country experienced what is known as its 'desenvolvimentista' (translated as 'developmental') period. Large and small businesses experienced great enthusiam, as did young people discovering the opportunities that came with the country's wave of growth. Amongst these young people is Carlos, an office worker hired by Volkswagen's quality control department. Here he helps Arturo, an Italian who creates his factory's spare parts. After many love affairs, Carlos marries Luciana, more due to loneliness than love. Luciana is ambitious and sees Arturo as an example that Carlos should look up to. Carlos becomes the manager of Arturo's company but ends up living a life that he has not chosen. The film's richness lies in the ambiguity of Carlos's character and his relationship to the city. Carlos represents the dilemma faced by the cinema-going middle class in the city of São Paulo, which imposes itself as the main character of the film. Many sequences show the character's conflictual and ambiguous relationship with the city, most famously in the final sequence when Carlos breaks up with Luciana. After a violent fight in the apartment with a view of the city from the window, Carlos tries to leave Luciana, his job and the city, but returns. In an *aerea* above the city centre and the crowd, Carlos thinks of beginning anew. An eternal new beginning.
Maria Ignês Carlos Magno

Directed by Sérgio Person
Scene description: Carlos leaves the city, only to return.
Timecode for scene: 1:31:27 – 1:46:58

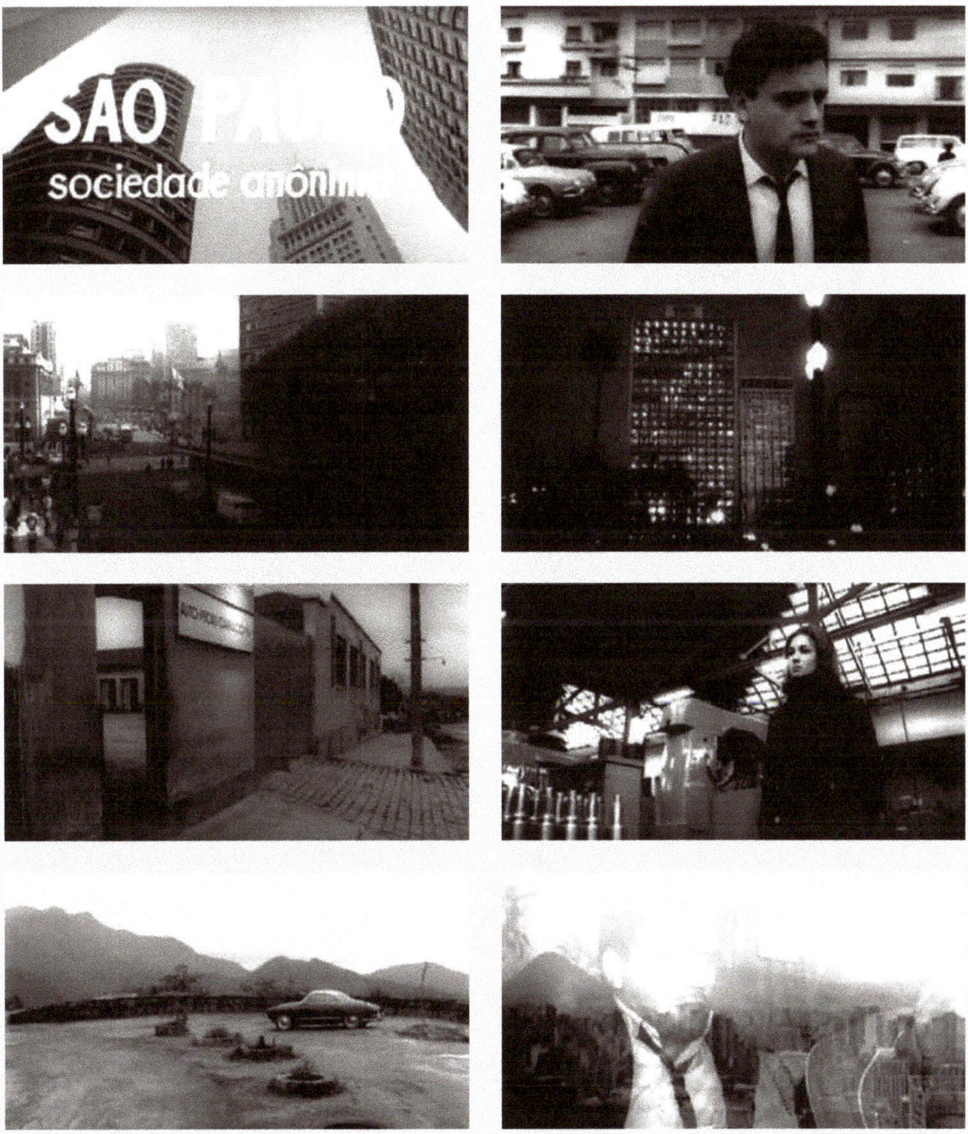

Images © 1965 Socine Produções Cinematográficas

MAZZAROPI: THE PURITAN OF AUGUSTA STREET/ MAZZAROPI: O PURITANO DA RUA AUGUSTA (1965)

LOCATION *Rua Augusta*

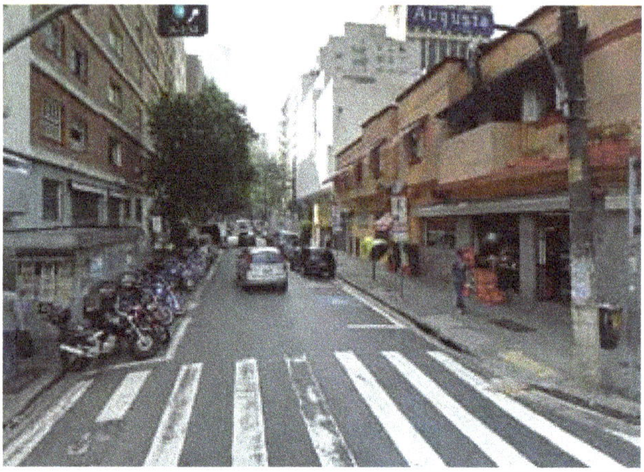

IN THIS PORTRAYAL OF urban life Pundoroso (Amácio Mazzaropi), a conservative man from the interior, arrives in the capital city São Paulo to find that his family (particularly his two sons and daughter) have acquired the behaviour of the contemporary urban bourgeoisie: partying, drinking, dressing in ways he totally condemns, amongst other 'sins'. His attitudes and attempts to enforce his conservative moral values on his family drive them, as well as himself, crazy. But he is not alone on his moral crusade as he is joined by other people who form the 'League', a group that has created the comic 'Book of Sins', in which they write down every sin committed in the city and go around São Paulo trying to impose the moral values they preach. They invade bars, interrupt a rock concert and confront people on the streets in an attempt to put them right. From the very beginning of this film the city is presented as a congested metropolis teeming with cars and people – all shown from Pundoroso's point of view in his car. His conservative values and criticism of the city-dwellers' 'decadent' behaviour, as opposed to that of people in the interior, is comically illustrated by his arrival when he desperately looks for a dress in his mother-in-law's bag to cover a naked statue in the garden. Nevertheless, his attitudes change after some time when he has a heart attack ... and starts behaving as if he were a young man.
Antônio M. da Silva

Photo © Google maps

Directed by Amácio Mazzaropi
Scene description: Pundoroso's arrival in São Paulo
Timecode for scene: 0:00:01 – 0:06:12

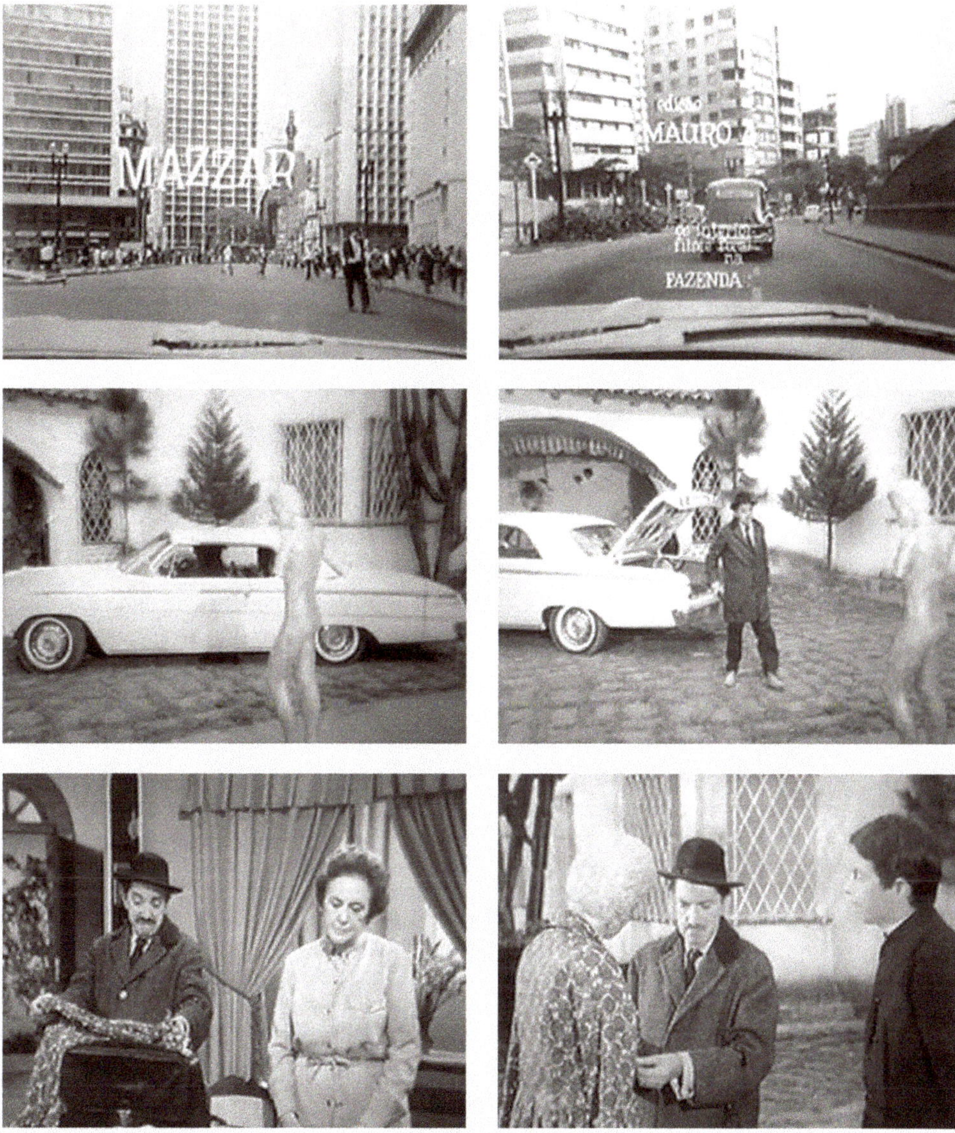

Images © 1965 PAM Filmes

BARE BEHIND BARS/A PRISÃO (1980)

LOCATION *The outskirts of São Paulo*

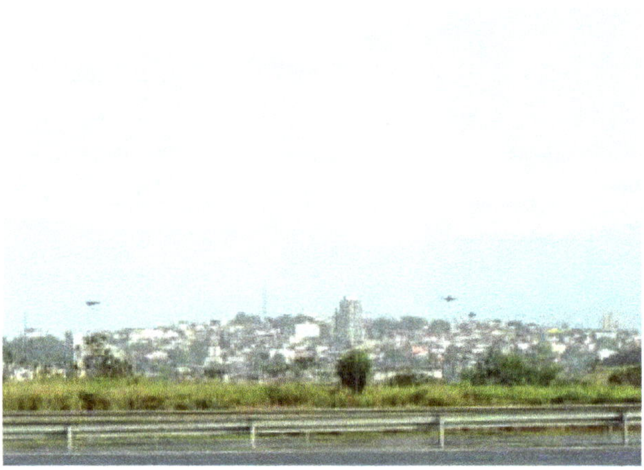

A PRISÃO ('THE PRISON'), which received the saucy title *Bare Behind Bars* in English, is one of the Women in Prison (WIP) films produced in Brazil that is best known among WIP film fans outside the country. Like hundreds of other Brazilian sexploitation films – *pornochanchadas* – this film is set in São Paulo, but unlike the others, not in its red light district. Most of the film takes place in a prison where many features of the genre are exploited: catfights, a lot of lesbian sex, violence and power relations, to cite a few examples. Although intended to titillate – and it does – the film touches on important social issues but because of its exploitation of sex and lack of a consistent plot it has been overlooked. In this case, the film shows the destination and fate of three prisoners who manage to escape – another key feature of the WIP genre – during carnival: they get involved in crime and go to hide on the outskirts of the city. The film explores the location in detail, showing its inhabitants and their living conditions – unpaved streets, poor houses, alcoholism and violence. The sexual and gender aspects that are salient features in the film are well illustrated in a sequence set on the edge of the city. One of the girls is killed by a drunkard, with whom she had moved in, because he catches her having sex with another man. Such an ending suggests that female criminals do not have much future ahead of them and that, if they survive, they are likely to remain in a marginalized place in a society in which patriarchal rule prevails. ➻ ***Antônio M. da Silva***

Photo © Carl Guderian

Directed by Oswaldo de Oliveira
Scene description: Saliem's fate after escaping from prison
Timecode for scene: 1:27:31 – 1:32:05

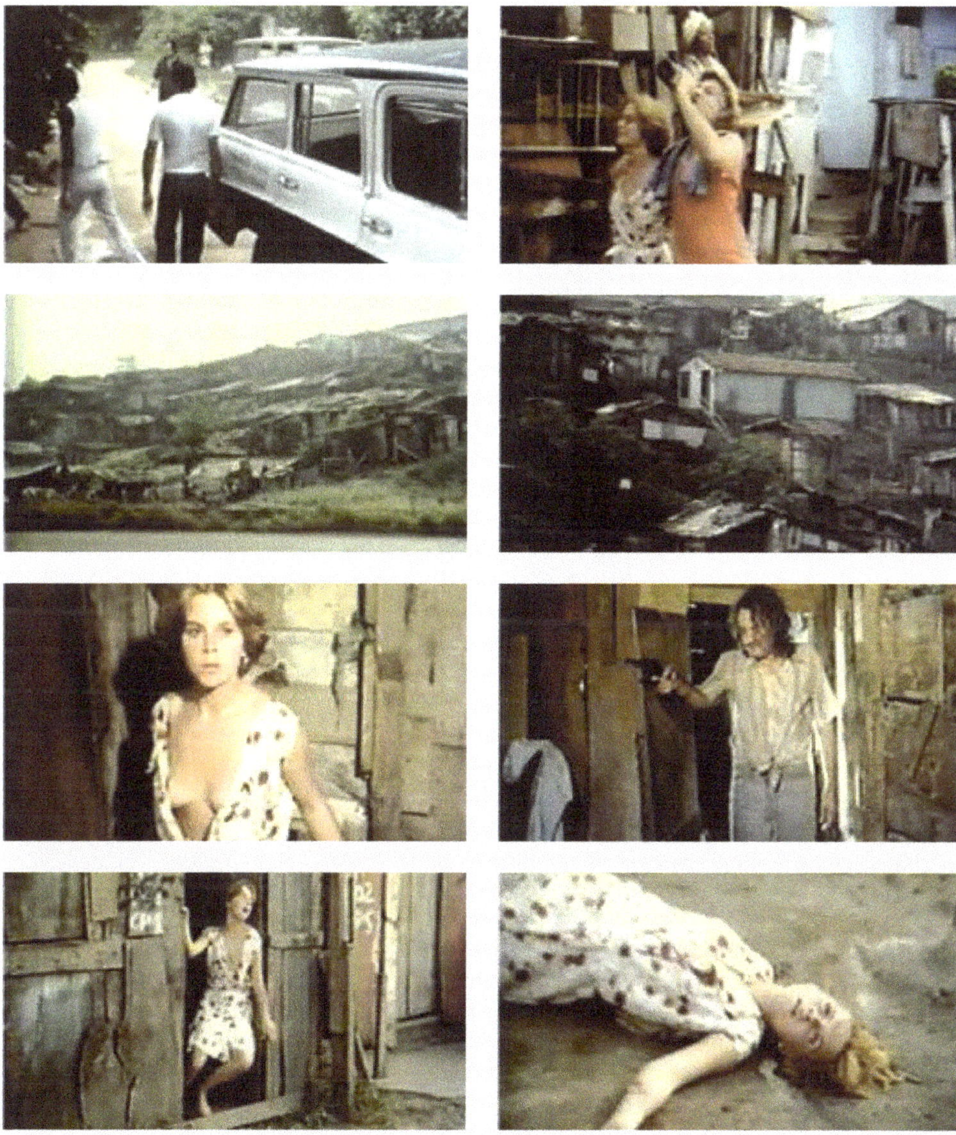

Images © 1980 Ao Lixao Comercio de Moveis Ltda., Galante Filmes

PIXOTE: SURVIVAL OF THE WEAKEST/ PIXOTE: A LEI DO MAIS FRACO (1980)

LOCATION *Praça Ramos de Azevedo*

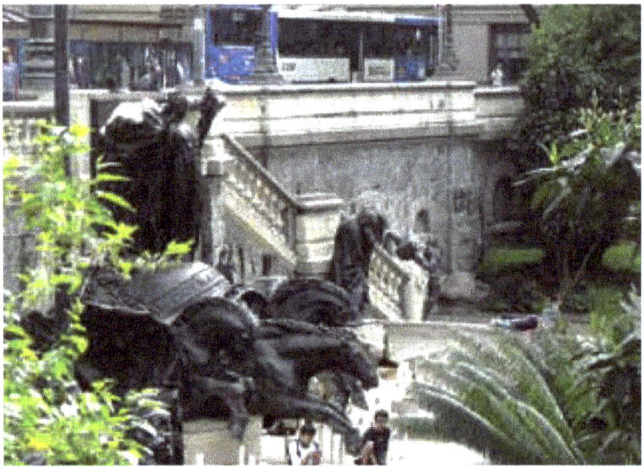

IN A BOLD DOCUMENTARY-INFLECTED STYLE, *Pixote: Survival of the Weakest* immerses us into the world of delinquent children on and off the mean streets of São Paulo and Rio de Janeiro at the turn of the 1980s. Although most of the film's use of space traps the viewer and the children within either the dark and confined world of the juvenile detention centre in São Paulo or some seedy apartments in Rio, daylight strikes midway through the film to ephemerally invoke a sense of freedom once the boys escape the organized corruption and physical and sexual abuse of the centre. Once the gang resorts to what they know best (pickpocketing and petty thievery throughout Central São Paulo), we are soon yanked back into another side of this underworld that operates freely throughout society within the confines of sexual exploitation and armed robbery. Since the film precedes the real-life statistic of the more than 1,000 children slain per year during 1989–91 at the hands of the police or death squads, it may be of no coincidence that Fernando Ramos da Silva, the actor who played the role of Pixote, was killed by the police in an attempted robbery in 1988 when he was 18 years of age. Although the scene shown here provides a nod to their newfound freedom, we are left knowing that the shackles of crime, hunger, and the lack of true reformatory resources will ultimately be the impetus of their demise. ➾ ***Kyle Black***

Photo © Paulo Silvestrini and Carol Bandeira de Mello

Directed by Hector Babenco
Scene description: Pixote and his friends have recently escaped the juvenile detention centre and are back on the streets of São Paulo trying to survive
Timecode for scene: 1:05:14 – 1:07:26

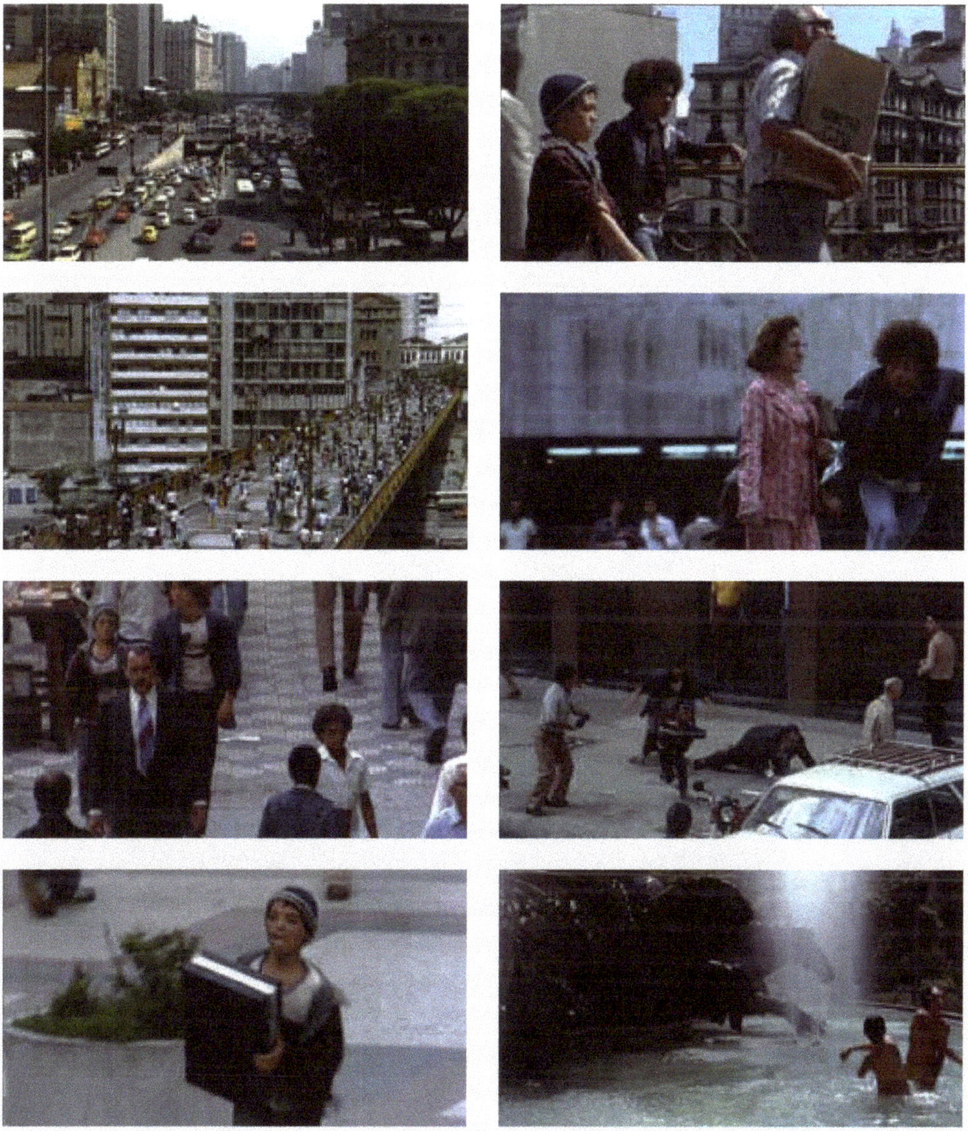

THE MAN WHO TURNED INTO JUICE/ O HOMEM QUE VIROU SUCO (1981)

LOCATION *Jabaquara Metro Station*

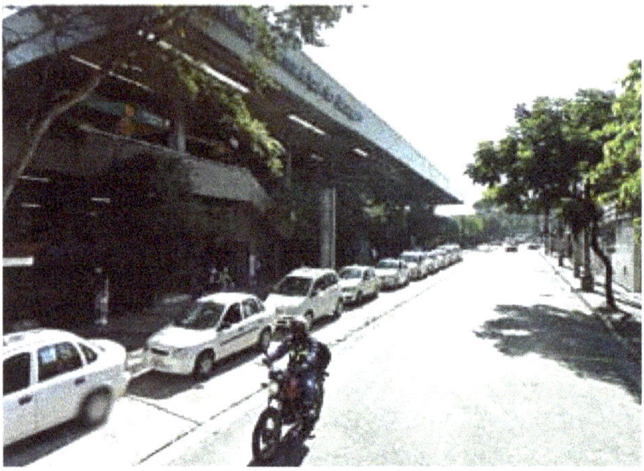

THE FILM PORTRAYS the north-eastern migrant poet Deraldo (José Dumont) in his odyssey in São Paulo. The film is an amalgam of images of the industrialization of São Paulo and shows how the north-eastern migrants are engulfed by the urban space, depicts their role in the construction of the city and the various kinds of marginalization and discrimination they suffer. The iconography of the city illustrates its progress and expansion. The film touches on many social problems that pervaded the city in the 1970s and 1980s and that are still an issue in this bustling Brazilian metropolis, especially class relations. The metro is a good example of the city's development and attempt to cope with the number of people who live in it as well as its many new arrivals. The film also shows that the city's poor areas were growing at the same speed as its industrialized areas. From beginning to end the film insists on portraying the city in extreme long-shots and bird's-eye perspectives which show the social tensions faced by people in both urban spaces. It shows not only the migrants' disconnection from the city but also the city dwellers' refusal to accept cultural differences and the latter's rampant xenophobia towards the migrants, which is evident not only in the language the characters use but also visually. An instance is when Deraldo goes to find a job in the metro construction after having tried to work in other places. The 'educative' film which the recruiter shows to the newcomers leaves Deraldo offended, as he understands what the city does to a migrant like him.
Antônio M. da Silva

Directed by João Batista de Andrade
Scene description: Deraldo looks for work in the metro construction
Timecode for scene: 0:46:42 – 0:54:00

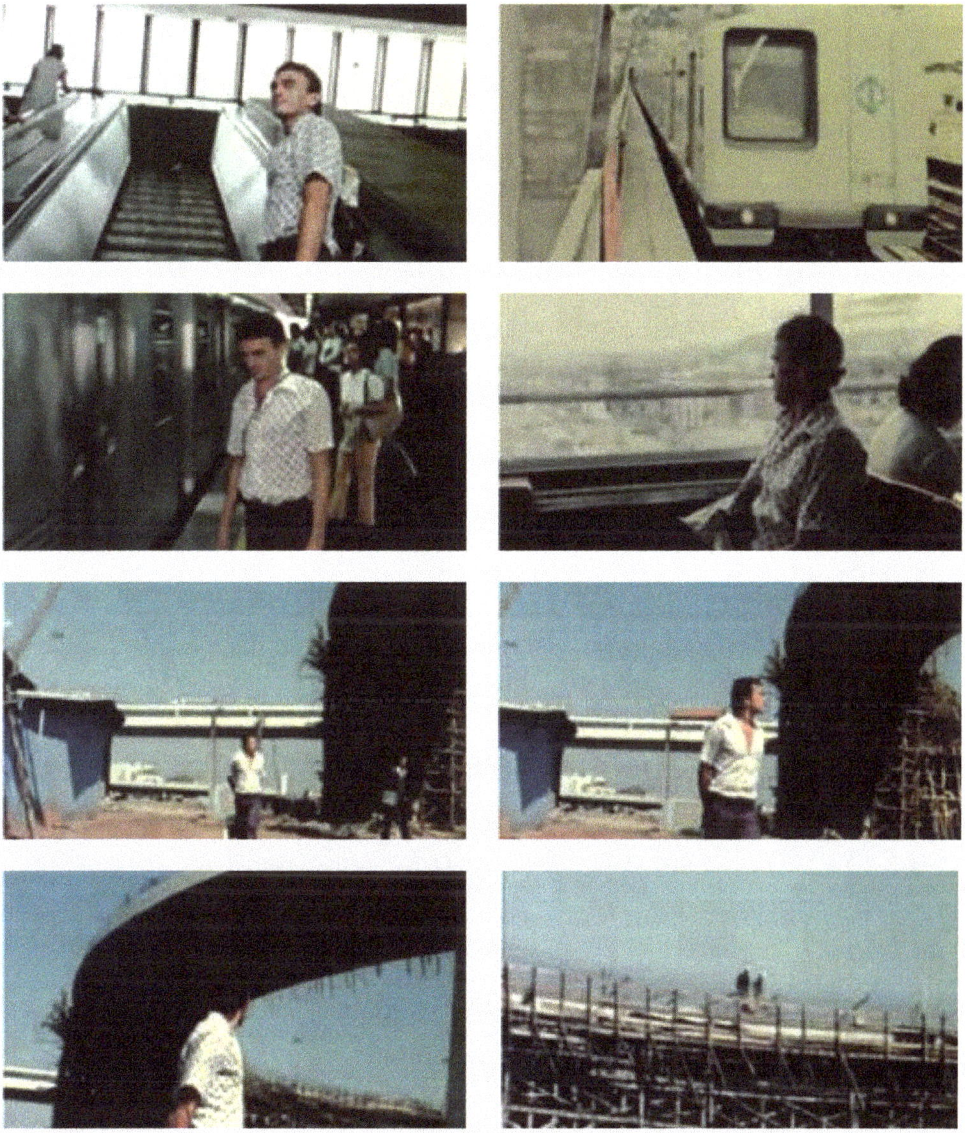

SPOTLIGHT

PAULISTA FILM INDUSTRY

An Overview

Text by FÁBIO UCHÔA

THROUGHOUT ITS HISTORY, Paulista film production has developed in cycles demarcated by the presence or absence of the State as an organ of mediation and development for cinema. The 1920s in São Paulo saw the consolidation of the incipient film industry on the back of an economy that had been geared towards imports. Film-making was artisanal, performed by immigrants with technical knowledge but inadequate equipment. The exhibition sector was a further obstacle in the way of the release of films in São Paulo. In a market dominated by foreign exhibition companies, national cinema was considered lacking in quality and profitability. The biggest problem in confronting this lack of interest was the search for investment, which was obtained from entrepreneurs, students of the first film schools, and, only very occasionally, from the state. Funded by José Medina and Gilberto Rossi, the Rossi Films company managed to continue film production in this period. The funding given by the Government of the State of São Paulo to the founding of a cinejournal named *Rossi Actualidades* kept their production alive, including the making of fiction films such as *Exemplo Regenerador* (José Medina, 1919) and *Fragmentos da Vida* (José Medina, 1929). At the end of the decade, Kenemy and Lusting created Rex Film, which made the documentary *São Paulo, Sinfonia da Metrópole/ São Paulo, A Metropolitan Symphony* (Adalberto Kemeny and Rodolfo Rex Lustig, 1929).

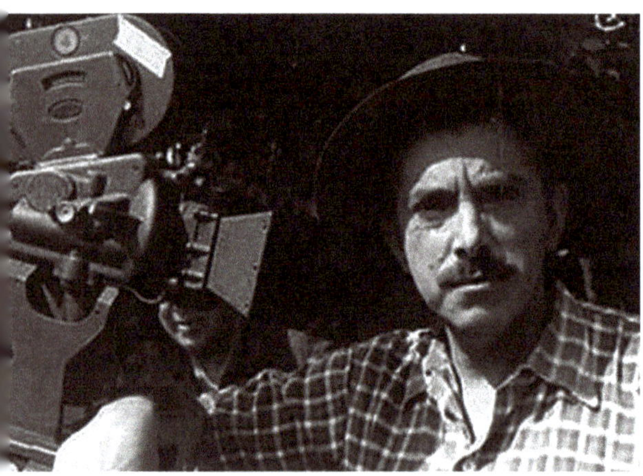

If in the 1920s there was scarce Paulista cinematic production, the picture changes with the onset of the 1950s and the solidification of attempts to industrialize Paulista cinema, inspired by the Hollywood Studio system. In the context of a vibrant cultural moment and the industrialisation of São Paulo city, the Companhia Cinematográfica Vera Cruz (1949-54) was created under the power of the industrial entrepreneur Franco Zampari. It was a moment in which the Paulista elite decided to develop the artistic production of the city into a patronage model without official cultural support. The company's general producer was the internationally famous Brazilian film-maker Alberto Cavalcanti, who brought famous foreign technicians into the Brazilian industry. The company produced eighteen fiction feature films, gaining international awards. Big investments in film promotion and hiring of actors with exclusivity clauses paved the way to an increase in costs, and shooting ceased in 1953. Following the studio's model, although unsuccessfully, other companies that attempted to maintain quality with a low budget appeared in the 1950s, including Brasil Filmes, which was a sort of continuation of Vera Cruz, Maristela, Kino Filmes and Multifilme. During the same period, firstly in Vera Cruz films and then Pam Filmes, Paulistas witnessed the emergence of the actor-producer Amácio Mazzaropi. Merging theatrical traditions with the clichés of Paulista rural culture, the comedian brought the figure of the 'Jeca' into the

Opposite Amácio Mazzaropi
Below *O Signo da Cidade/The Sign of the City* (2007)

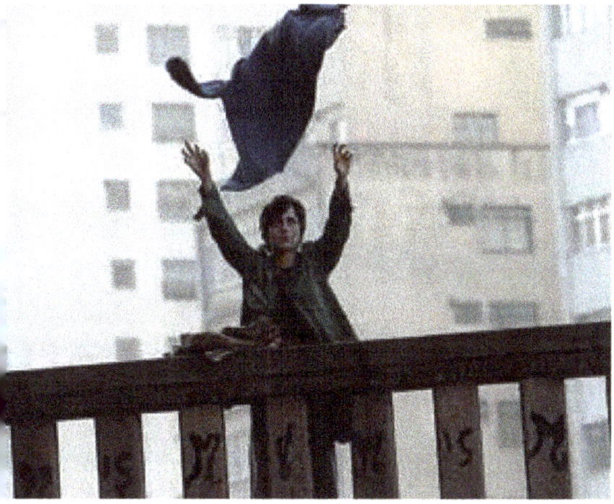

Above © 2007 Pulsar Cinema, Coração da Selva, Globo Filmes

cinema, a stereotype of the country dweller of São Paulo state, who is naïve and lazy.

During the Military Dictatorship (1964-84), the Brazilian government's modernization project included direct intervention into the film market. The creation of federal agencies such as the Instituto Nacional de Cinema (INC) (1966-75) and Embrafilme (Empresa Brasileira de Filmes S.A.) (1969-91), contributed to the State presence in film production, distribution, promotion and maintenance of national cinema's share in its domestic market. Along with the increase in film production, these measures also affected the exhibitors with the strengthening of the obligation to exhibit national films. Within this context, Cinema da Boca do Lixo emerged in the surroundings of the Luz neighbourhood in São Paulo, which was to last throughout the 1970s. These films were cheap, quickly produced, and explored eroticism and vernacular language, funded by private investments and in direct contact with the exhibitors. Amongst the main companies in this region were Servicine, Cinedistri, Dacar and Maspe Films. The quantity and variety of their films is extensive, including erotic comedies starring David Cardoso and Ody Fraga, José Mojica Marins' horror films, as well as the humorous and aggressive tendency of films by Rogério Sganzerla, José Agrippino de Paula, João Batista de Andrade and Carlos Reichenbach.

The 1990s were marked by the so-called Cinema da Retomada, which took place within a globalized cultural market.

At the beginning of the 1980s, a group of young Paulista film-makers who were students at the Escola de Comunicações e Artes da USP invested in the production of feature films, often funded by Embrafilme. Inspiration from advertising, artificiality, as well as generic and stylistic mixtures, associated them with pos-modern cinema, later to be known as 'Cinema da Vila Madalena'. This group includes film-makers such as Chico Botelho, Sérgio Bianchi, Wilson Barros, André Klotzel and Alain Fresnot.

The 1990s were marked by the so-called Cinema da Retomada, which took place within a globalised cultural market. In 1991, the extinction of Embrafilme plunged cinema into another crisis that started to be overcome only in 1995 through a law of fiscal incentives by the Government that lad to a considerable increase in the production of Brazilian films. In this way, Brazilian film production generated independent producer companies that financed their films along with private agents and public companies, whose investments in cinema are written off the tax owed to the State.

Through this scheme emerged a heterogeneous production that questions Brazilian identity and unfolds in the representation of a country marked by social conflicts, violence and poverty. Paulista film-makers include newer and established names from national production such as Ugo Giorgetti, Beto Brant, Suzana Amaral, André Klotzel and Sérgio Bianchi. The period is also marked by the creation of Globo Filmes, a branch of TV Globo Organization, the largest Brazilian television network in the market of national film production. Since 1998, Globo Filmes has co-produced a number of films with independent producers through the particular scheme of offering a slot in its TV schedule to launch the films. The funding, on the other hand, is raised by its associate producers through the laws that write off taxes. Through these co-productions that count on the technicians and actors of the Globo television network, Globo Filmes creates hybrid products that explore the boundaries between cinematic and televisual language. Although the station is situated in Rio de Janeiro, its co-productions include films set in São Paulo and it is associated with Paulista productions such as *Carandiru* (Hector Babenco, 2003), *Não Por acaso* (Philippe Barcinski, 2007) and *O Signo da Cidade/The Sign of the City* (Carlos Alberto Riccelli, 2007). ⁜

LOCATIONS MAP

SÃO PAULO

maps are only to be taken as approximates

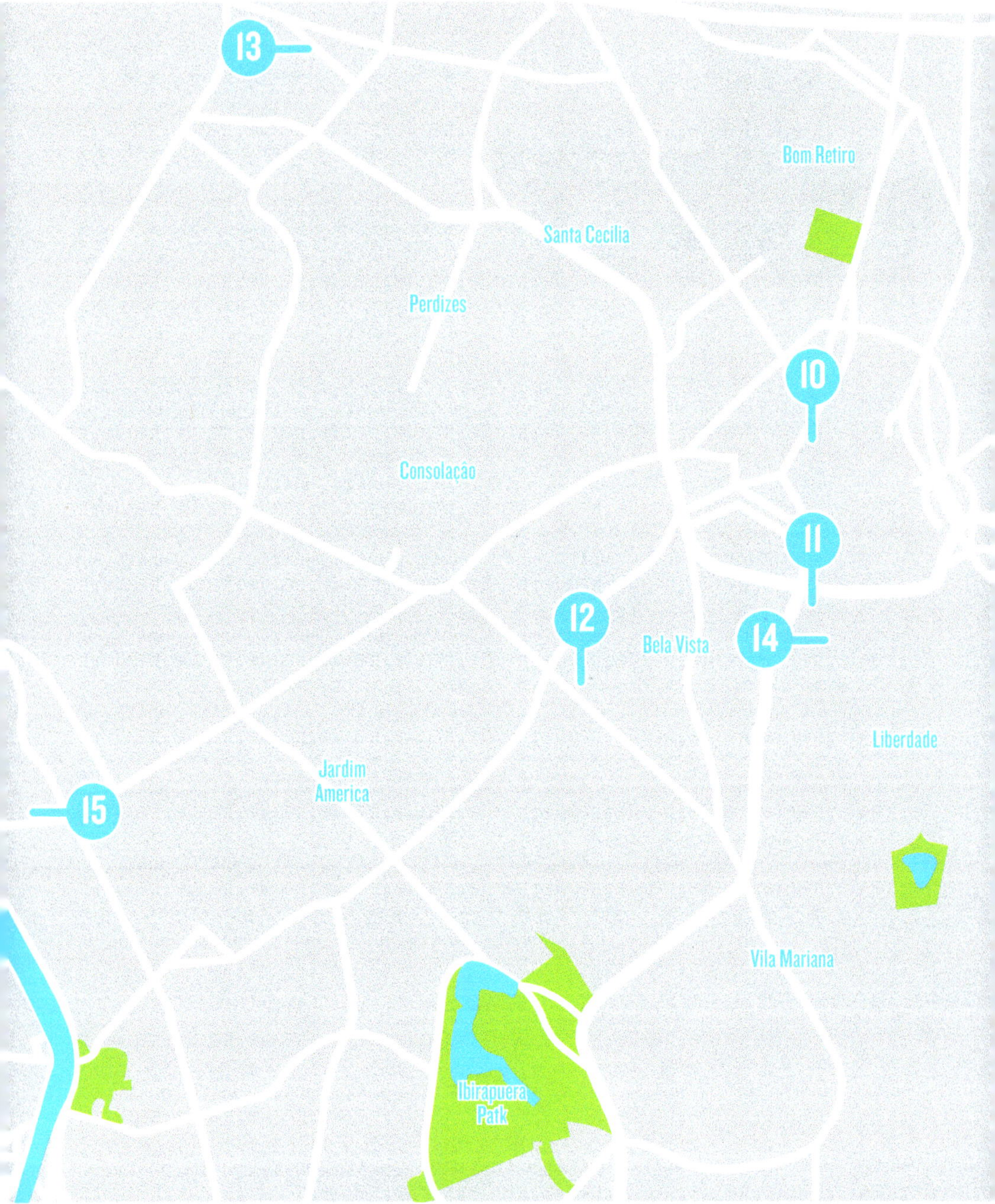

SÃO PAULO LOCATIONS
SCENES 9-15

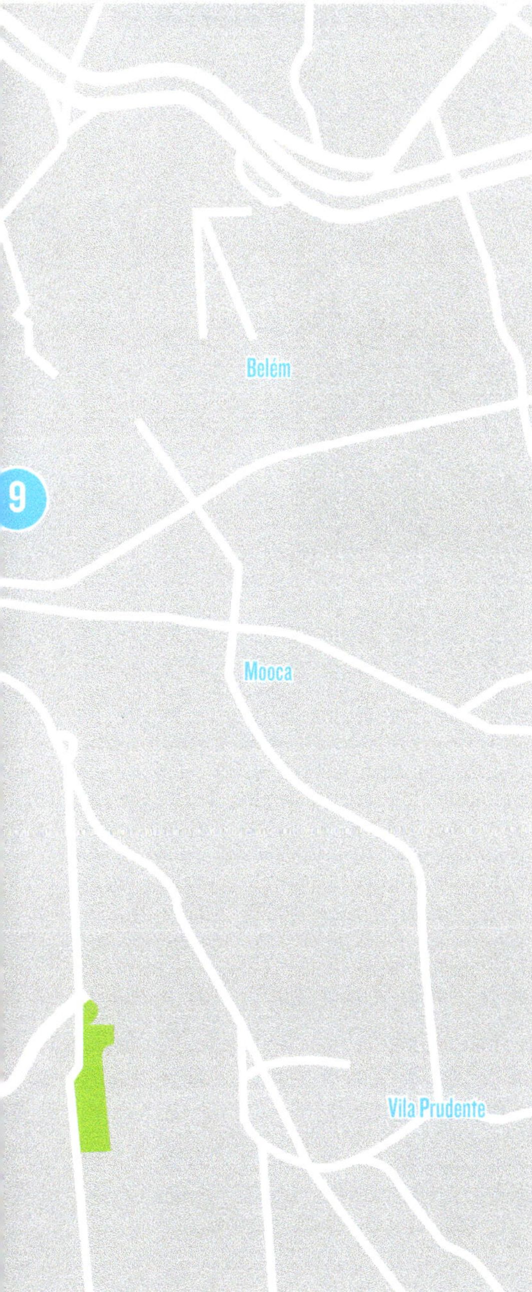

THEY DON'T WEAR BLACK-TIE/ ELES NÃO USAM BLACK-TIE (1981)

LOCATION

Central Única de Trabalhadores (currently in Rua Caetano Pinto, Brás)

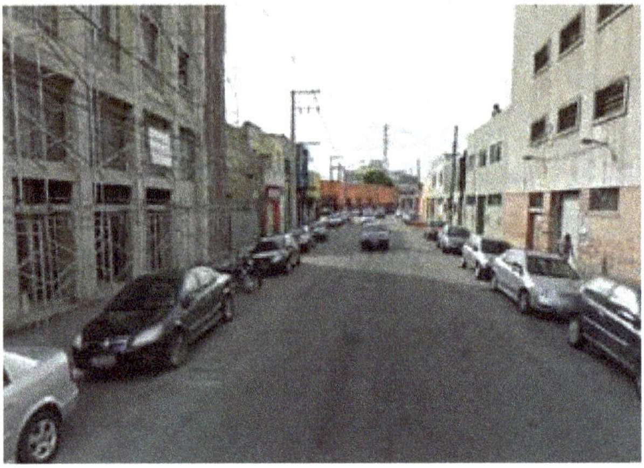

THE FILM IS SET in the industrial ABC Region that belongs to Greater São Paulo, cradle of the union CUT (Central Única de Trabalhadores) and the political Workers' Party (Partido dos Trabalhadores) through which Luiz Ignácio Lula da Silva became president between 2003 and 2010. *They Don't Wear Black-tie* adapts the homonymous play by Gianfrancesco Guarnieri, a milestone of Brazilian modern drama from 1958. It is transposed to the political reality of the late 1970s, when the metalworkers of the automobile industry initiated a number of strikes that were actually forbidden under the military regime. The movement was to have a deep sociopolitical impact and finally lead to the public's demand of free elections. Inspired by the political climate, the film is a realistic portrait of the conflicts and contradictions faced by a working-class family that is involved in the strike. It argues that the class struggle is more important than family ties. While the father, played by the playwright Guarnieri, is an old unionist and key figure in the strike, his son Tião becomes a strike-breaker, since he is more concerned with his immediate future as a father to be. Even before the strike turns into a violent confrontation between the workers and the police and a co-worker gets killed, his family and fiancée expel him from his home because of his lack of class-consciousness. Neither the factory nor the poor neighbourhood are specified. The problem is quite obviously a general issue of the working class in Brazil and elsewhere, even though the radical point that the film makes seems today out-dated. At the time, it won Fernanda Montenegro, who plays Tião's mother, her first international best actress award and the film the Special Jury Prize at the 1981 Cannes Film Festival. ⊷ ***Carolin Overhoff Ferreira***

Directed by Leon Hirszman

Scene description: Tião is expelled from home and a worker dies

Timecode for scene: 1:41:23 – 1:57:47

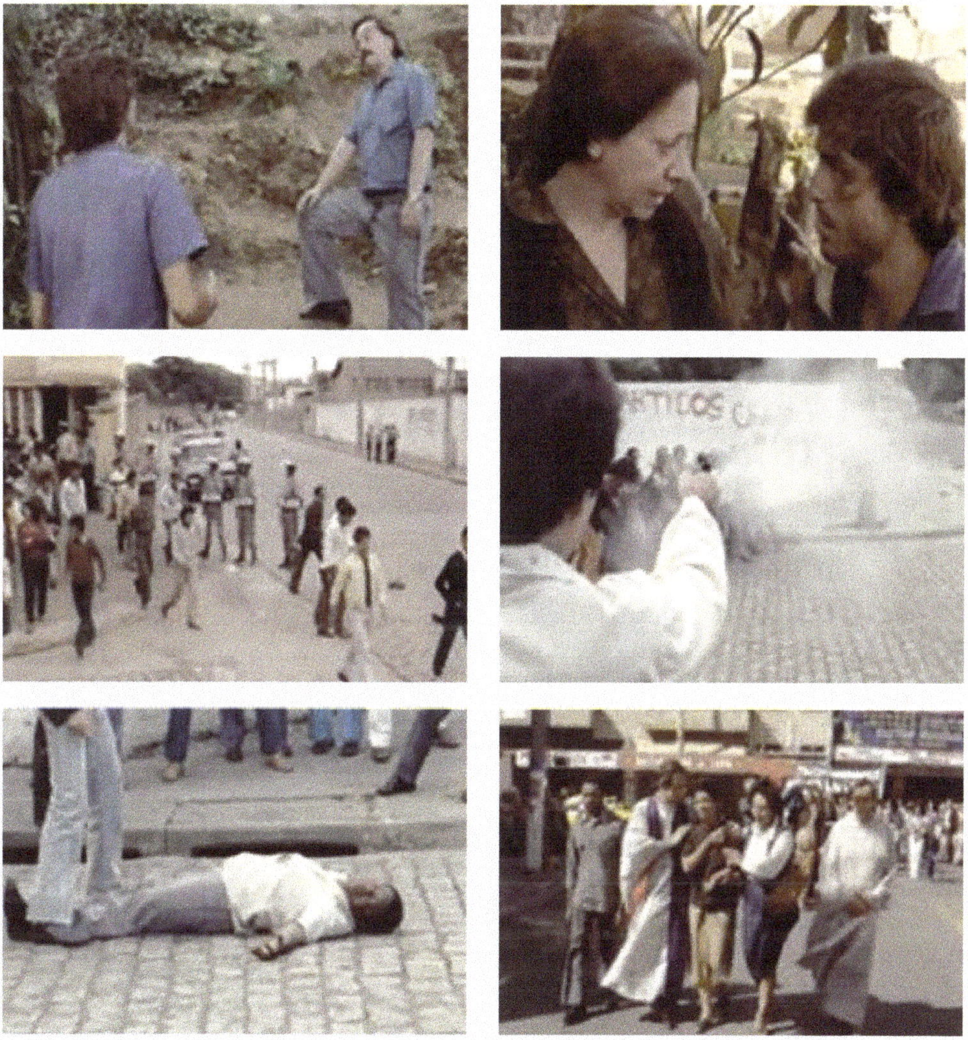

HIDDEN CITY/CIDADE OCULTA (1986)

LOCATION *Bairro da Liberdade*

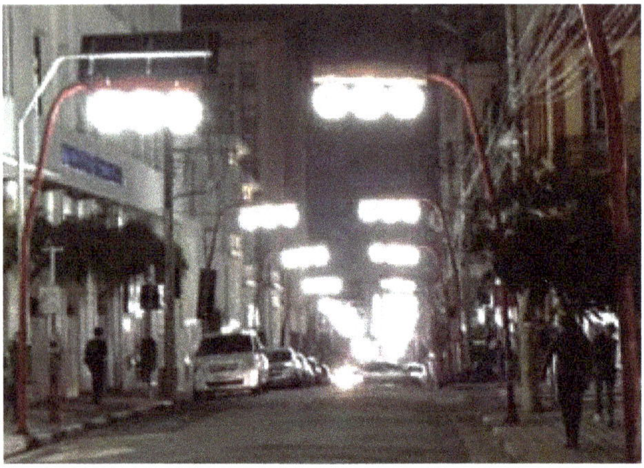

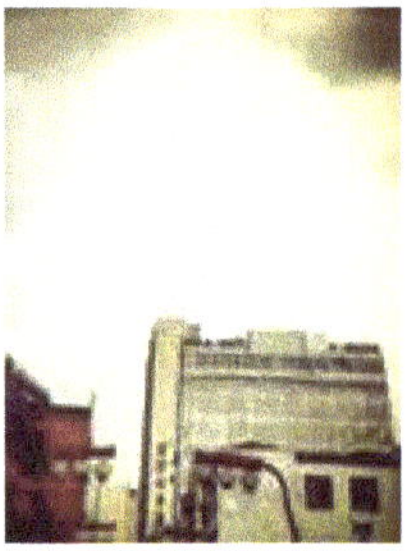

A DIVE INTO THE UNDERWORLD of the city of São Paulo, which has little in common with the image of the 'capital of progress and work' promoted by the media during the military dictatorship that ended in the previous year. Anjo is a reformed ex-prisoner convicted for drug trafficking who decides to reform and now works in a dredger in the Pinheiros River, equivalent to working in a sewer. He is approached by other criminals who believe that Anjo has hidden a fortune worth of drugs before going to jail. He is persecuted by police chief Ratão who is also addicted to drugs and who has taken the drugs brought by Anjo. During this persecution, Anjo and Japa, a man of Asian descent and member of a gang, become friends and search the city for a hideout, arriving in the Japanese neighbourhood in São Paulo, Liberdade. They pass through a Japanese party in Avenida Liberdade, go amidst a group of drummers and dancers in kimonos, and walk onto streets flanked by neon signs and shop windows showing products from Japan. They arrive in a karaoke bar where a final conflict with the police takes place, surrounded by the typical Japanese lamps and gates which decorate Liberdade. *Hidden City* is a typical example of 'neon-realism', a postmodern variant of Brazilian cinema. Like an artificial sun, the neon light illuminates the city nights, its crimes and characters appearing to have been taken out of a noir film or comic strip.
→ *Renato Luiz Pucci Jr*

Photos © Gustavo Nagib

Directed by Francisco Botelho

Scene description: Two men search the city for a hideout

Timecode for scene: 1:00:08 – 1:06:07

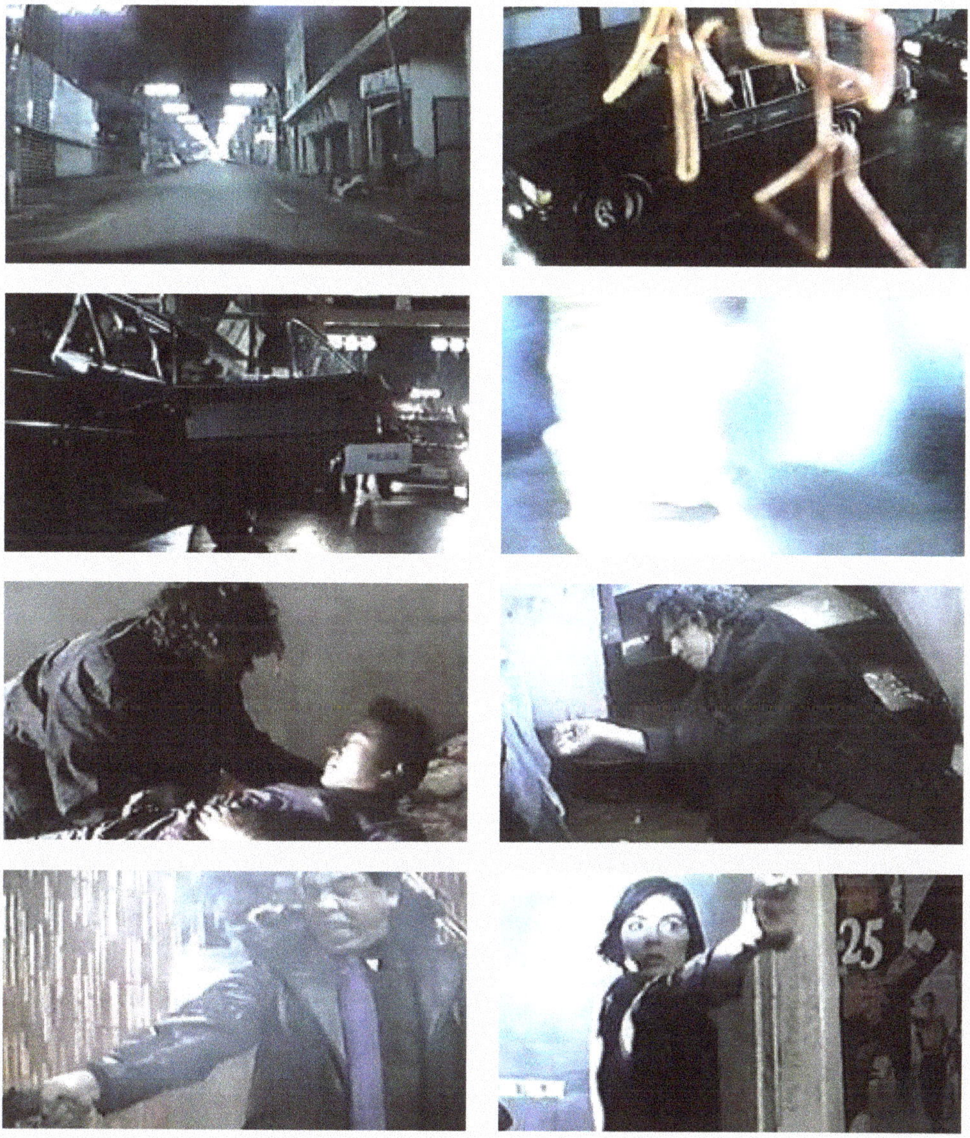

NIGHT ANGELS/ANJOS DA NOITE (1987)

LOCATION *Avenida Paulista*

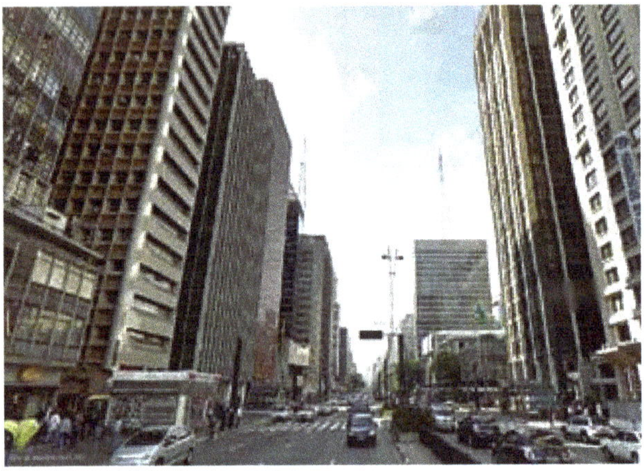

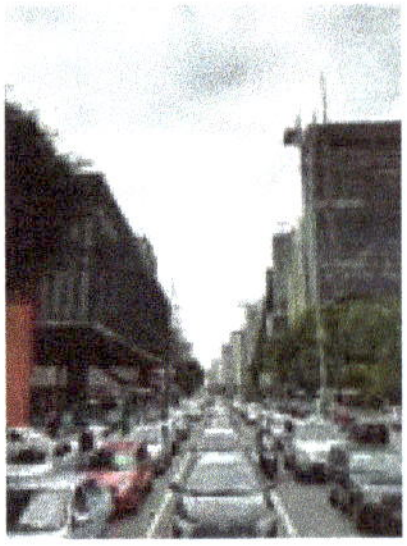

A PORTRAIT OF SÃO PAULO at night showing numerous characters crossing each other´s paths. There is no realism because the city and its dwellers are constructed in a postmodern fashion within artificial environments and a parodic and playful tone, employing highly aestheticized and explicit intertextuality. In one sequence former lovers Guto and Teddy are in a car with Marta, a decadent actress, who with stereotypical diva-like gestures, remembers her glory days. The streetlights reflect on the car windshield and on Guto's face. Their cold, white reflections suggest his dissatisfaction during the conversation as Marta tries seducing the young man on the back seat. The reflection of a golden tower passes over the windshield and across Marta's face in a magical moment that bathes the character in artificial light. It was already possible to know their location: within the tower, which was at that point the only one of its kind in the city. More precisely, they are on the Avenida Paulista, formerly the site of the coffee barons' mansions that was subsequently transformed into the financial centre full of skyscrapers which has ever since been the main postcard image of São Paulo. Guto loses his temper and throws them out of the car. An opening shot of a night scene begins with images of the real avenue, one of the most important sites of São Paulo. Those images replace the previous shots that were obviously taken in a studio. In a lively way the film centres on characters who wander through the night, immersed in memories and fantasies. **➻*Renato Luiz Pucci Jr***

Photo © Google maps

Directed by Wilson Barros
Scene description: Fake tower and lights on the Avenida Paulista
Timecode for scene: 1:05:32 – 1:08:50

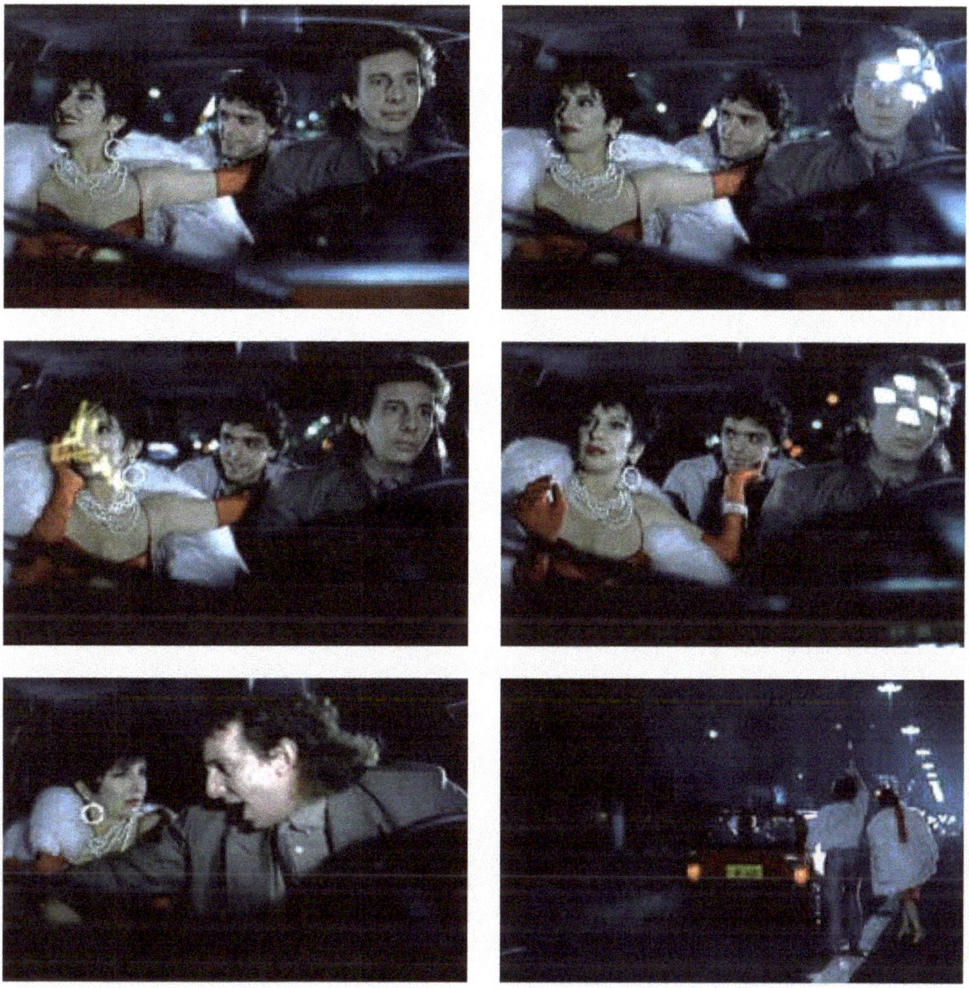

THE LADY FROM SHANGHAI CINEMA/ A DAMA DO CINE SHANGHAI (1988)

LOCATION *Teatro São Pedro (Rua Barra Funda) and Cine Oasis (Avenida São João)*

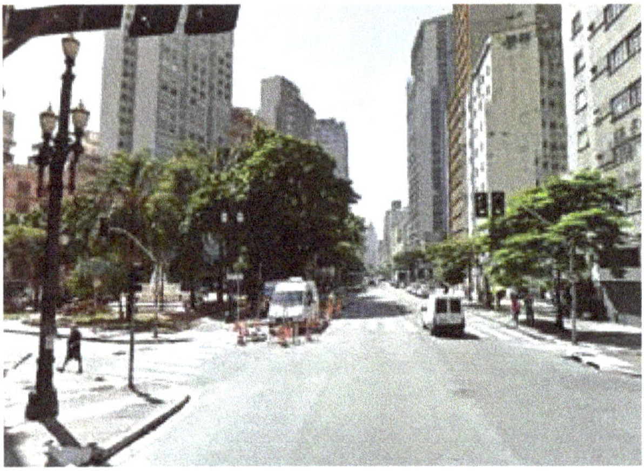

DURING THE 1980S, the cinema of São Paulo went through what can be described as a paradigmatic postmodernist phase, ironically known as 'neon-realism'. *The Lady from Shanghai Cinema* is emblematic of this trend in its nostalgic pastiche of noir films, and features excellent performances, exciting action sequences shot on location in Brás Train Station, and a perfectly woven web of both overt and hidden references, topped by a great soundtrack and lots of neon lights. The film opens with one of the most memorable sequences in recent Brazilian cinema, in which real estate agent and former boxer Lucas decides to go to the cinema to escape from the heat, only to find out that the air conditioning is broken. In there he will see the mysterious Lady of Cine Shanghai for the first time. She looks just like the actress on the screen, the protagonist of a noir thriller who convinces her lover to kill her husband, with the promise of running away with him in the end. Real life and cinema will soon prove to be less distinguishable than Lucas would have hoped for. The first sequence inside the fictional Cine Shanghai was filmed in the Teatro São Pedro, located on Rua Barra Funda near the city centre. But the film's self-reflexive coda, which sees Lucas leaving the cinema, was actually shot outside Cine Oasis on Avenida São João, now one of the many defunct cinemas of a bygone era, one to which Almeida Prado pays a beautiful homage.
→ ***Cecília Mello***

Photo © Google maps

Directed by Guilherme de Almeida Prado

Scene description: Lucas meets the mysterious Lady of Cine Shanghai

Timecode for scene: 0:02:10 – 0:14:35

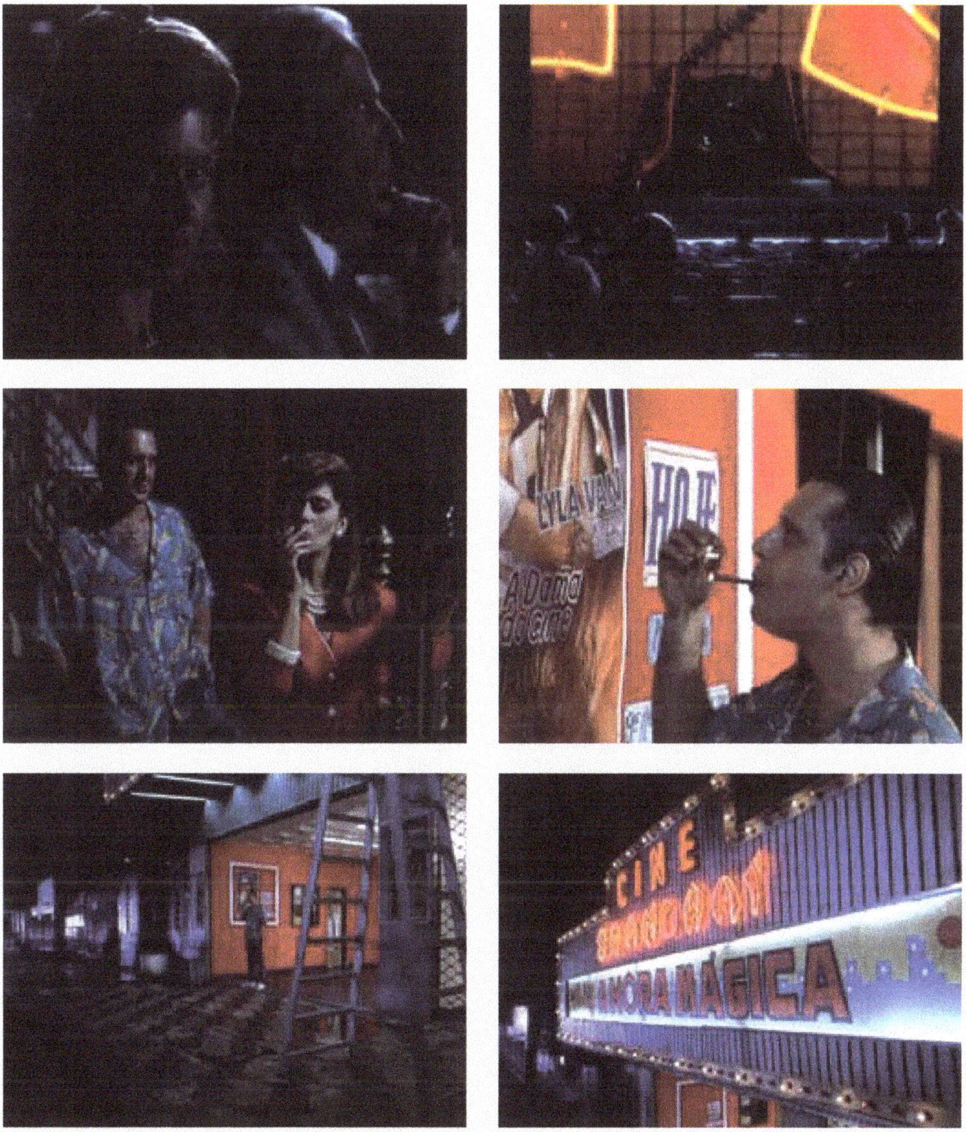

SCENT OF GARDENIA/ PERFUME DE GARDÊNIA (1992)

LOCATION *Rua José Ferreira Rocha, Liberdade*

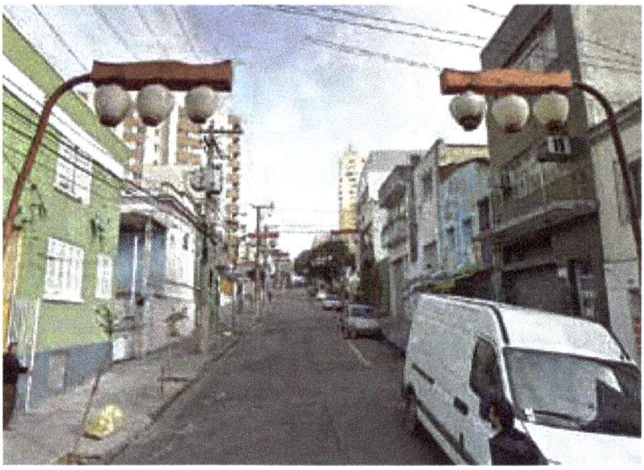

THIS STYLIZED NEO-NOIR FILM explores São Paulo's day and night-time iconography with its numerous colourful and neon signs. The city is shown through the taxi driver Daniel's (José Mayer), and later on his son's, various trips around the city. However, instead of concentrating only on the busy areas of the city, the film also focuses on a quiet suburb within this metropolis, where Daniel, a male chauvinist, lives with his wife Adalgisa (Christiane Torloni) and their son Joaquim (Walter Quiroz). The turning point of the film comes when a film crew is shooting on location in their street and Adalgisa ends up playing a small role in the film, replacing an actress who had had an accident. But she did this without her controlling patriarchal husband's permission as he was away working. Because of their financial struggles, Adalgisa decides to embrace the career opportunity offered to her. But this leads Daniel to leave her and take Joaquim with him – a boy who would only see his mother again when he had become a young adult. Hence, in *Scent of Gardenia* São Paulo is not just the location of the film but becomes a cinematic space where film-making takes place within the actual film (this reference to film-making is typical of the director's other films). The film portrays a city in which criminality is high and takes a myriad of forms. Moreover, life in it is rather gloomy, as seen in the artists' decadent lifestyle – their drug and alcohol abuse, sexual relations and criminality. ➾ ***Antônio M. da Silva***

Directed by Guilherme de Almeida
Scene description: Adalgisa's first step into stardom
Timecode for scene: 0:11:59 – 0:15:15

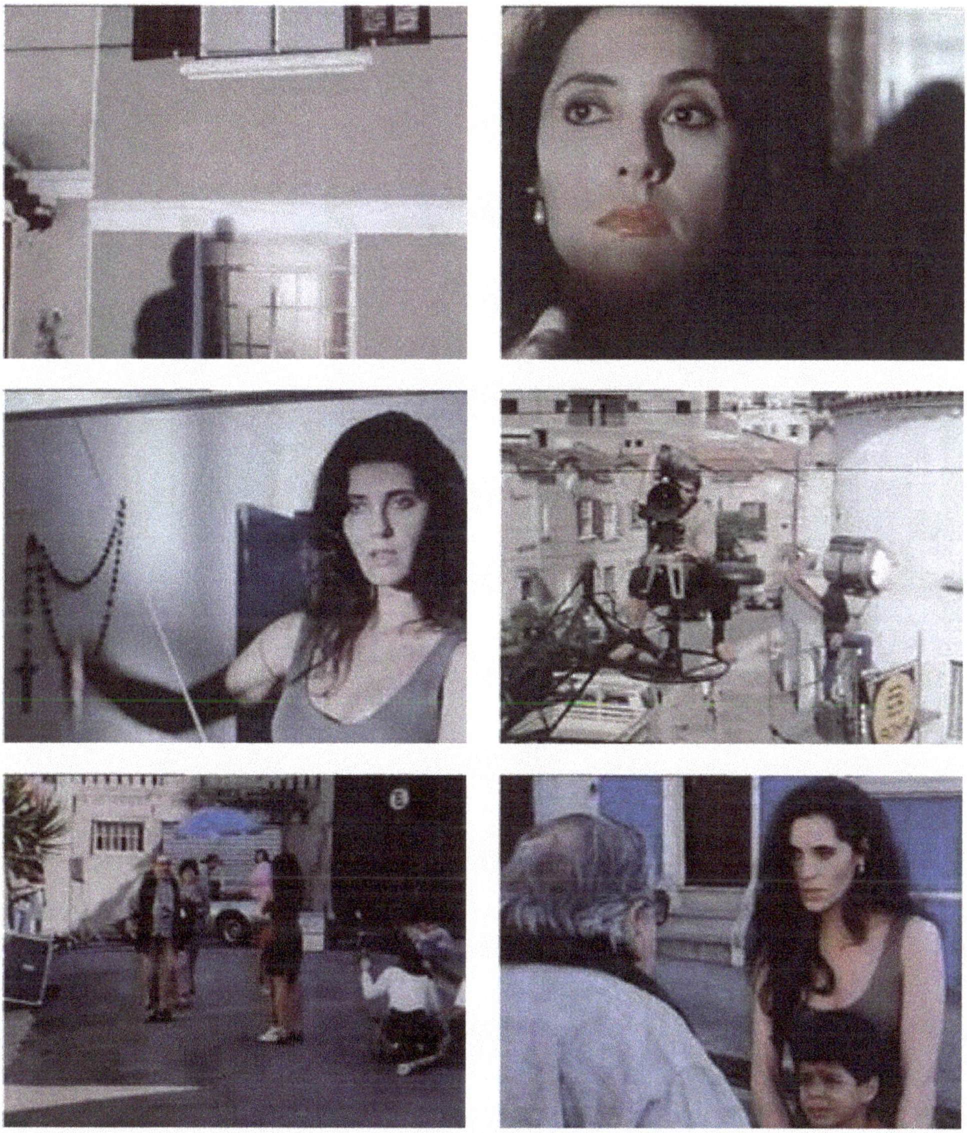

SÃO PAULO, SYMPHONY AND CACOPHONY/ SÃO PAULO, SINFONIA E CACOFONIA (1995)

LOCATION *City centre streets*

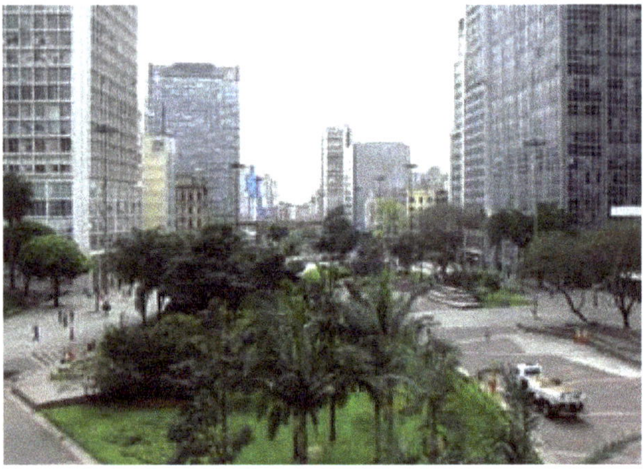

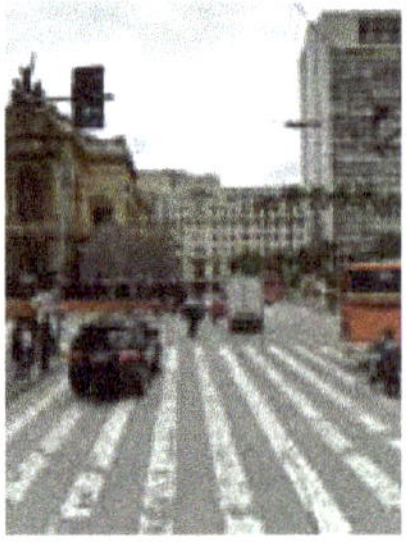

PART OF A SCIENTIFIC RESEARCH project, Jean-Claude Bernadet's film is quite different from other city films that were made during the historical avant-garde, such as *São Paulo Sinfonia da Metrópole/São Paulo, a Metropolitan Symphony* (Adalberto Kemeny and Rodolfo Rex Lustig, 1929), which it quotes. An archive film, it edits footage from more than 100 films (out of 350 films that were watched during the project), documentaries and features made between 1960 and 1980 by giving the prefabricated images new meaning. As the title indicates, the idea of a harmonious orchestration is extended towards a contemporary view of the city as disorderly, chaotic, harsh and discordant. Accordingly, there is no interest in constructing the city's history or its filmic portraits in a chronological fashion. The film's montage is, on the contrary, based on associations that can be visual or thematic, but always lead to a new meaning that supersedes the images' meanings in the context from which they are taken. Central are the people who live in the city. Shots of characters wandering the streets open the film and are followed by sequences in which they enter buildings or inhabit them and their surroundings. The tone gets more sombre and weird while the film proceeds, and the characters' activities ever more uncanny. São Paulo is portrayed as multi-centred and polyphonic, and multiple visual links between past and present make us experience continuities and ruptures. The idea of symphony and cacophony translates into a complex picture that denies generalizations or globalizations, as well as any coherent idea about São Paulo or the film history it inspired.
Carolin Overhoff Ferreira

Photo © Paulo Silvestrini and Carol Bandeira de Mello / Google maps

Directed by Jean-Claude Bernadet
Scene description: People walking the streets of São Paulo
Timecode for scene: 0:02:00 – 0:05:30

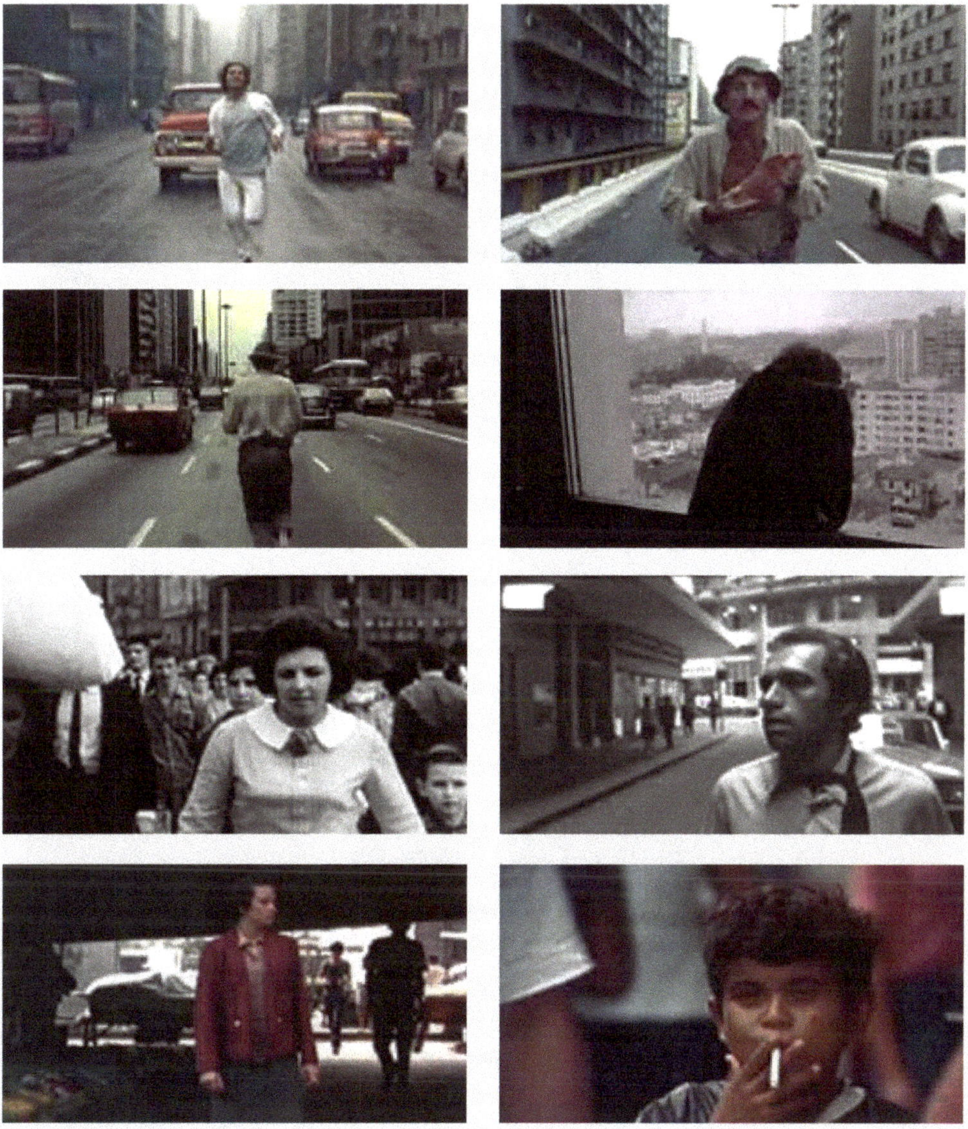

THE TRESPASSER/O INVASOR (2002)

LOCATION *Ponte Eusébio Matoso*

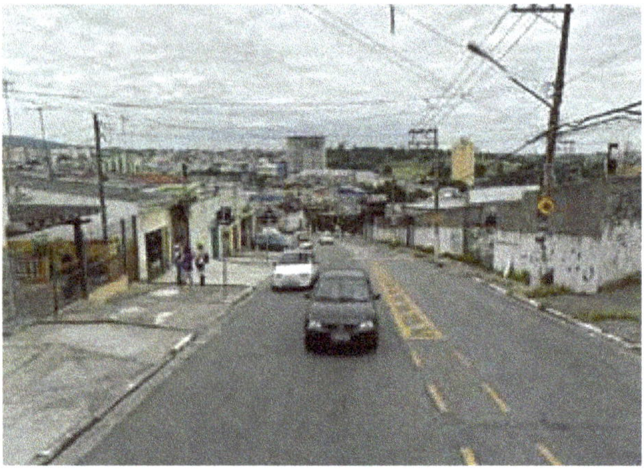

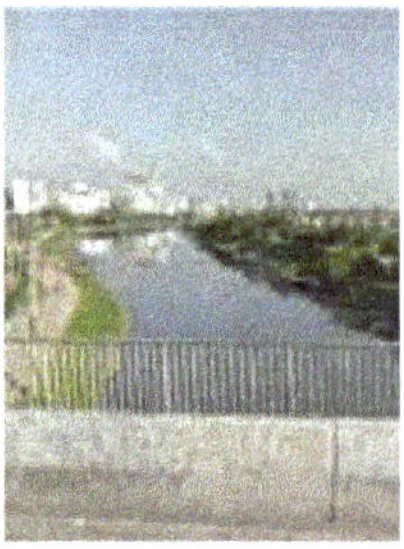

TWO BUSINESSMEN hire a killer to do away with a third associate; the murderer reappears, blackmails them to fund a friend's rap recordings, and insinuates himself into the affections of the dead man's daughter. In this scene he takes her from her privileged surroundings to multiracial, often derelict streets in the 'Zona Sul', the name of the rap which forms the soundtrack to their automotive wanderings. The rap is by Sabotage, whose cameo appearance gives an extra level of reality to a film generally understood as a portrait of modern Brazil. The murder of a Brazilian businessman and his wife by their daughter's boyfriend gave the film further newsworthiness after its release, as would the gang shooting of Sabotage himself, victim to one of the many obstacles to the fantasy escape that the film allows his character and the hit man-'trespasser' Anísio (see Nagib 2007). The local flavour of the fragmented snapshots of street life occur with the cool of a music-video aesthetic that is easily assimilable by international audiences, and pays no respect to realistic geographic coherence. The couple cross the Pinheiros River over the Eusébio Matoso Bridge. Then they cross Ponte Engenheiro Ari Torres, but are suddenly travelling north instead of south. Director Beto Brant filmed in the Vila Brasilândia, which is more photogenic than the southern slums that recently ranked amongst the world's most dangerous places. In this sequence, the invader is not Anísio, nor even his privileged invitee, but the film's implied spectator, voyaging in the picturesque exotica of *favela* tourism. **Louis Bayman**

Directed by Beto Brant

Scene description: A hit man and the daughter of the man he killed take a ride through the favelas

Timecode for scene: 0:42:12 – 0:44:23

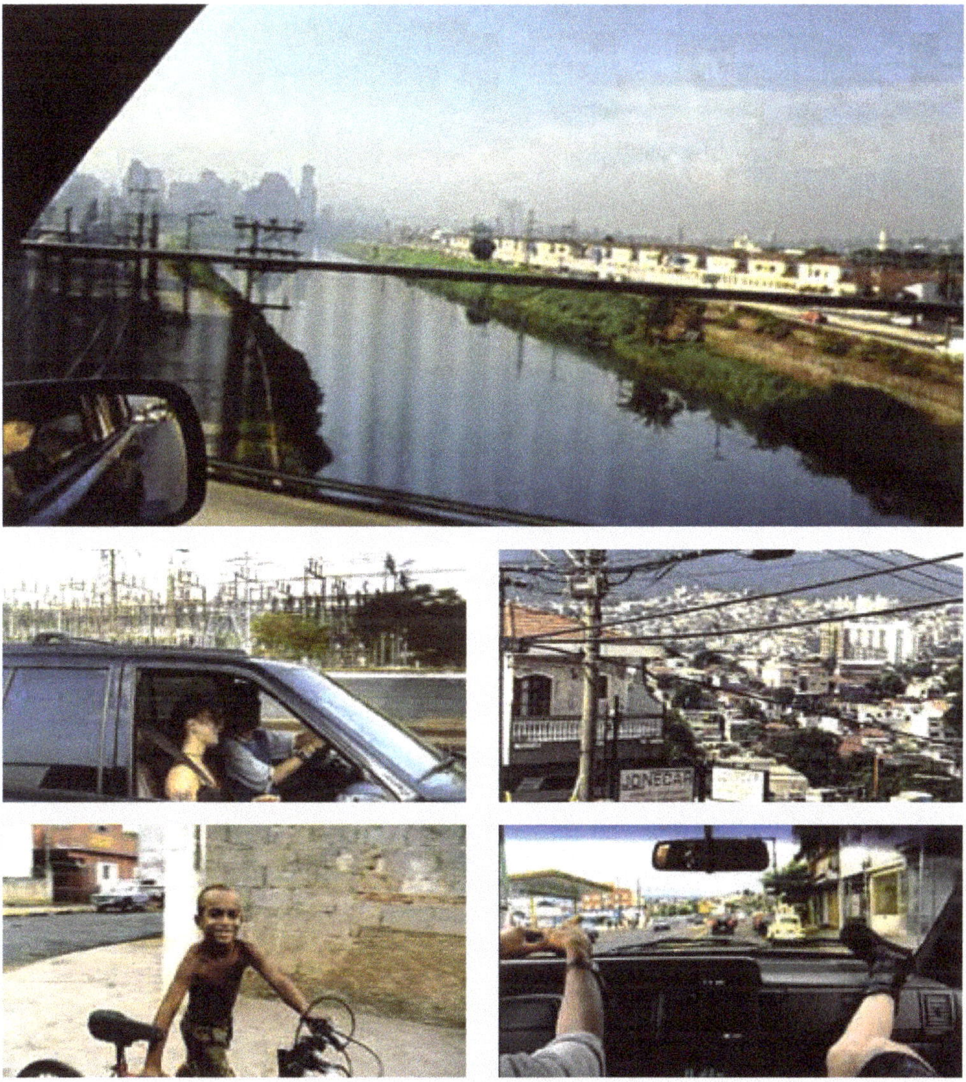

SPOTLIGHT

CINEMA MARGINAL

Text by DANIEL SERRAVALLE DE SÁ

This degraded subworld, traversed by grotesque processions, condemned to the absurd, mutilated by crime, sex, and exploitation, hopeless and fallacious, is, however, animated and redeemed by its inarticulate wrath.
Paulo Emílio Salles Gomes on 'Cinema Marginal' (quoted in Johnson and Stam 1995: 248)

SÃO PAULO CITY, a gigantic concrete stretch built on the highlands of Serra do Mar, is different from much of the rest of Brazil and yet, in its complex distinctiveness, fittingly encompasses and characterizes a perennial national drama: the dilemma of a country that produces large amounts of wealth but is unable to distribute it evenly among its citizens. In the late 1960s, during the years of Brazilian military dictatorship, the issue of poverty and its impact on those who live on the fringes of urban society entered cinema via a generation of young rebels who started producing independent low-budget films of wrenching intensity. Their anarchic creations employed randomly found locations, non-professional actor, and improvised dialogue, featuring a fictional world of disjunctive representations which occasionally tend to incoherence but which also express distress over the aspects of Brazilian life where social contradictions appear most severely.

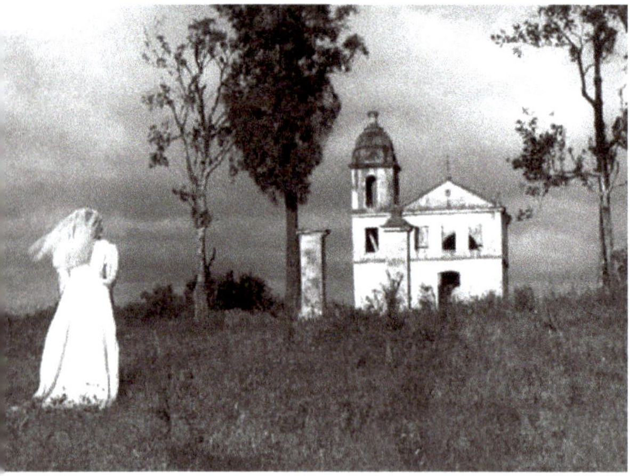

This new film culture emerged with such quirky defiance that, in hindsight, even its participants diverged over what to call it. Critic and film-maker Jairo Ferreira refers to the movement as a cinema of *invention*, due to its formally innovative and politically nonconformist narratives. Carlos Reichenbach deems it *subterranean*, in reference to underworld types that are the protagonists of this group of films. José Mojica Marins calls it *damned* cinema, since part of its production emerges in association with an impoverished area in São Paulo's city centre called Boca do Lixo or garbage mouth Cinema Novo's Glauber Rocha named it *udigrudi*, a snide spin on the English word 'underground', in retaliation to what he considered the 'filial' treachery of this new generation of film-makers. The upstarts neither rejected nor accepted this tag and rebutted the provocation from the leading figure of the film establishment of the time, labelling the opposing group Cinema Novo Rico or *nouveau riche* cinema

In the end, the adjective *marginal* prevailed over the other definitions and given the word's different usage and several undertones in Brazilian Portuguese there is no better way to describe proudly this foul-mouthed, upfront and incredibly daring production cycle that took place approximately between 1967 and 1973.

Ozualdo Candeias's *A Margem/In the Margins* (1967), filmed on the banks of Tietê River, which is contoured by a motorway known as Marginal Tietê, is a breakthrough in use of the subjective camera. His strange tale of love among characters that exist on the fringes of society can be thought of as an early example of Cinema Marginal.

Rogério Sganzerla's *O Bandido da Luz Vermelha/The Red Light Bandit* (1968) is a watershed feature based on the real-life story of an infamous criminal of the period, whose reign of terror over São Paulo city provided the ideal subject matter for a violent and politically charged film. Feared by the authorities, desired by housemaids, mystifying the press who reported on him, the suave assassin broke into mansions and made chit-chat with their rich victims in the dimness of a trademark red flashlight before

Opposite *A Margem/In the Margins* (1967)
Below *Bangue Bangue/Bang Bang* (1971)

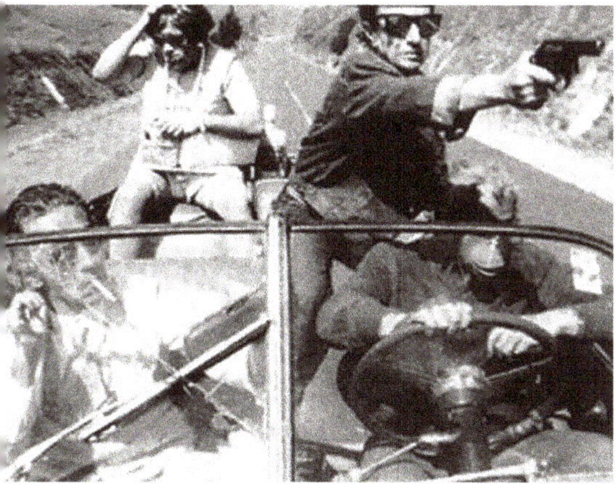

raping and murdering them. The film employs the structure of a sensationalist radio broadcast of crime journalism, combining avant-garde and pop-art references within a framework of startling editing choices. Ruthless and enjoyably crude, *The Red Light Bandit* locates crime and stardom in the streets of the bustling metropolis, and is to this day a classic of Brazilian cinema.

In *A Mulher de Todos/The Woman of Everyone* (1969) Sganzerla showcases freewheeler Flesh and Bones Ângela, performed by Helena Ignez, muse of both Cinema Novo and Cinema Marginal. Ângela is a memorable female character of Brazilian cinema whose abnormal sexual desires and audacious behaviour attracts an assorted range of lovers. Her erotic drive reflects both the anxious, obsessive side of the modern woman and the liberal attitude that does not tolerate vain masculinity. 'I am free, and the others? There is no individual freedom without collective freedom,' she says – perhaps an allusion to the curtailment of freedom imposed by the military regime.

Júlio Bressane's *Matou a Família e foi ao Cinema/Killed the Family and Went to the Movies* (1969) depicts a lower-middle-class man who murders his parents and heads to the cinema to watch a film called 'Perdidas de Amor' about two women engaging in a lesbian relationship. A wealthy and unsatisfied woman travels to her country house where she receives a visit from an old girlfriend. Interspersed with scenes in which they dance, talk about men and caress, are stand-alone scenes of violence in deprived families. In *O Anjo Nasceu/The Angel is Born* (1969) Bressane again uses this meta-linguistic style to tell the story of the thugs Santamaria and Urtiga who speak of salvation through the coming of an angel whilst engaging in a chaotic journey of crime and violence.

It is often claimed that Cinema Marginal is a rupture with Cinema Novo when, in fact, it should be seen as the culmination of some of its ideals.

Bressane, Ignez and Sganzerla founded the production company Belair, which is responsible for making some of the most representative films of Cinema Marginal. Their pioneering adventure resulted in seven full-length films which experimented with the radicalisation of film language and syntax before they were silenced by the dictatorial clampdown and forced to seek exile; some of their works never received a public release.

Other influential film-makers and films from this period that proclaimed their marginal identity by searching out the dark corners of Brazilian life are André Luiz de Oliveira's *Meteorango Kid, o heroi intergaláctico/Meteorango Kid, Intergalactic Hero* (1969); João Trevisan's *Orgia, ou o Homem que deu Cria/Orgy, or the Man who Gave Birth* (1970); Luiz Rosemberg Filho's *América do Sexo/America of Sex* (1970); and Neville Duarte d'Almeida's *Jardim de Guerra/Garden of War* (1970); Elyseu Visconti's *Os Monstros de Babaloo/The Monsters of Babaloo* (1970) and Andrea Tonacci's *Bangue Bangue/Bang Bang* (1971). After 1972 some of these film-makers started returning from exile and, although many would carry on proclaiming their marginal identity, the creative spur reached its exhaustion.

It is often claimed that Cinema Marginal is a rupture with Cinema Novo when, in fact, it should be seen as the culmination of some of its ideals. Behind their different approaches and strategies lies the essential issue of representing the national; however, Cinema Marginal substitutes the social didacticism and epic allegories of Cinema Novo for a more disillusioned and testimonial form of expression that focuses on the lives of subaltern subjects. If Cinema Marginal chooses to deride rather than to celebrate the achievements of their predecessors (who cannot be said to be starchy) such an attitude can perhaps be understood as the act of wilful, non-conforming upstarts barely in their twenties. In the face of a bleak social reality, Cinema Marginal chose to scorn absolutely everything, even itself, assuming an ideologically nihilistic attitude full of twisted, self-deprecating humour in a universe of visual shocks, angst and chilling violence. Rivalry here was created upon mutual resentment rather than ideological differences. The history of Cinema Marginal is all the more intriguing because some of its protagonists have disappeared from the map of world cinema, and many of their groundbreaking films have been reassembled with difficulty, while others are officially listed as missing. ⁜

LOCATIONS MAP

SÃO PAULO

maps are only to be taken as approximates

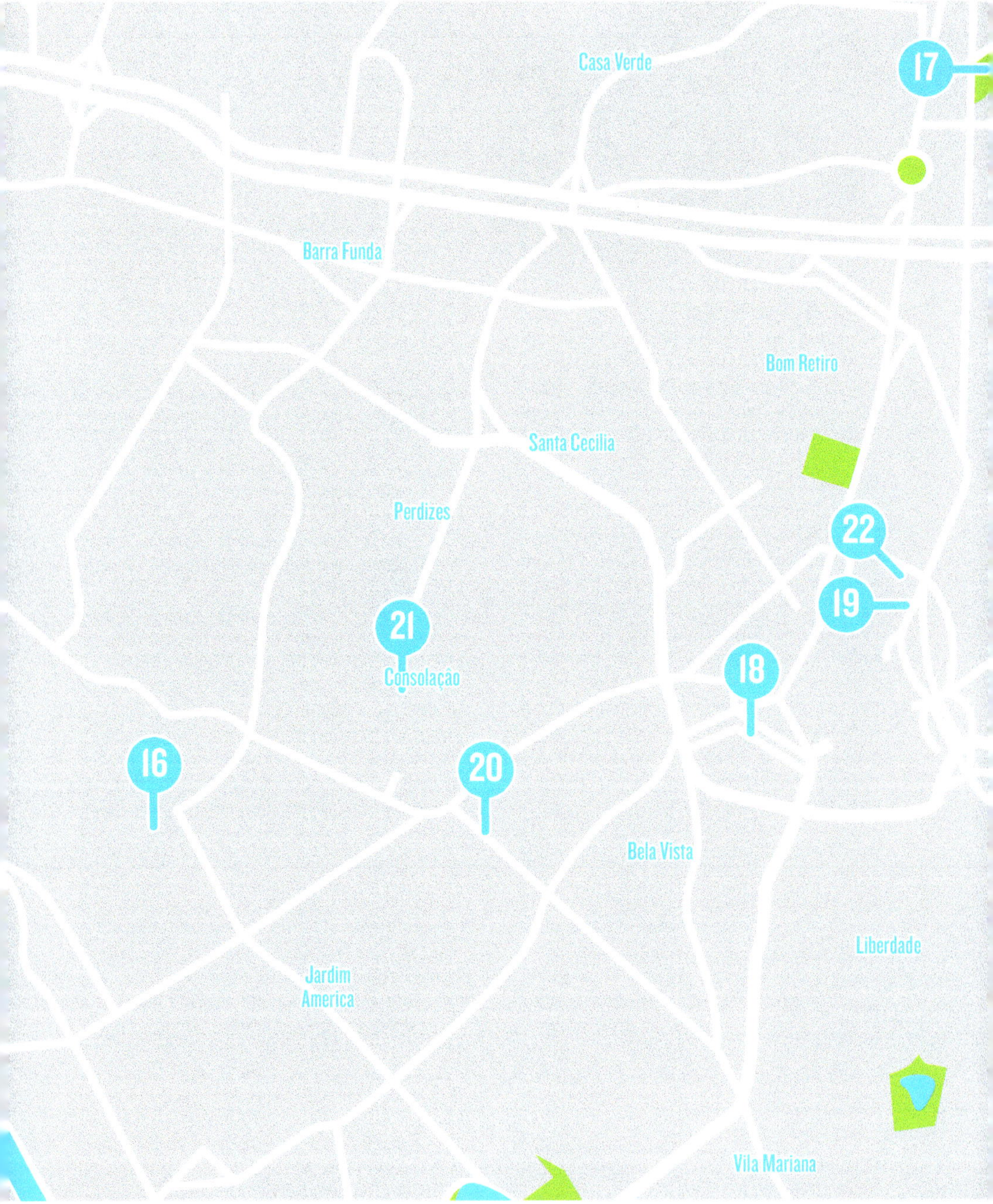

SÃO PAULO LOCATIONS
SCENES 16-22

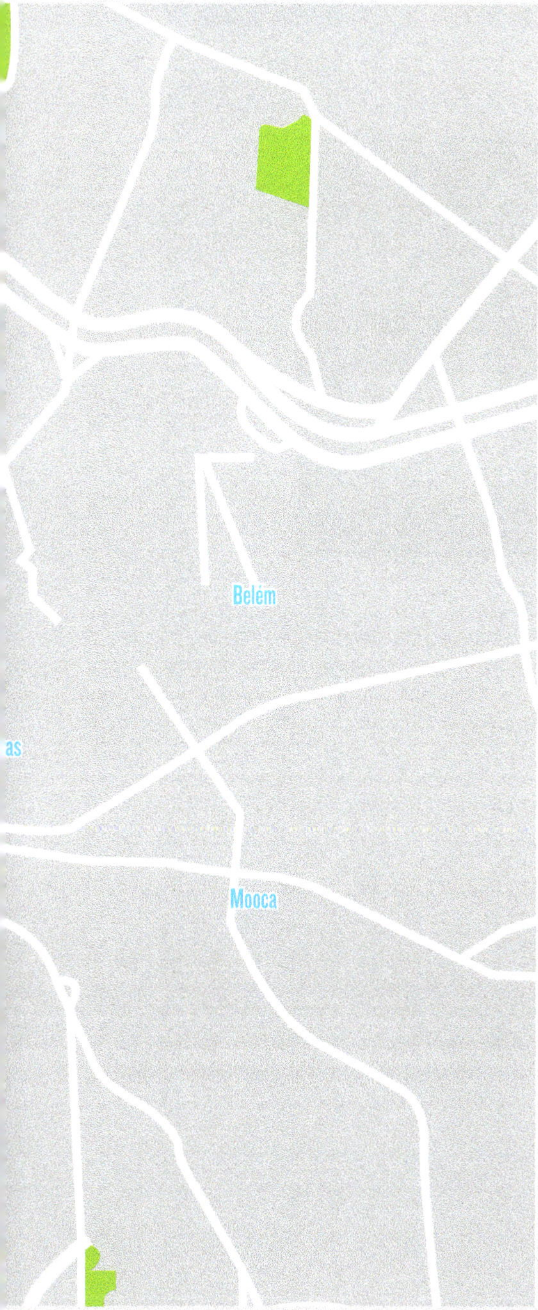

16.
DURVAL DISCOS (2002)
Rua Teodoro Sampaio
page 50

17.
CARANDIRU (2003)
Carandiru Prison
page 52

18.
NINA (2004)
Viaduto Jacareí, República
page 54

19.
WELCOME TO SÃO PAULO/
BEM VINDO A SÃO PAULO (2004)
Avenida do Estado, 3170, Baixada do Glicério
page 56

20.
UNDERGROUND GAME/
JOGO SUBTERRÂNEO (2005)
Consolação underground station
page 58

21.
ROMEO AND JULIET... GET MARRIED/
O CASAMENTO DE ROMEU E JULIETA
(2005)
Estadio Municipal Paulo Machado de
Carvalho
page 60

22.
ALL THE INVISIBLE CHILDREN (2005)
Municipal Market of São Paulo
page 62

DURVAL DISCOS (2002)

LOCATION *Rua Teodoro Sampaio*

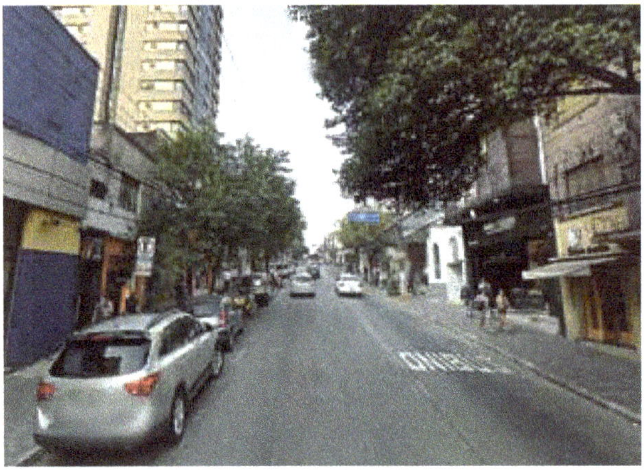

THE FILM NARRATES THE STORY of Durval, a 40-year-old with a record shop in Rua Teodoro Sampaio, in the busy Pinheiros neighbourhood. The shop is in an old two-storey house where Durval lives with his mother Carmita. It is in decline due to competition from CDs, 1995 being the last year that the Brazilian music industry released discs on vinyl. Durval is passionate about the format and will not sell CDs. Durval decides to hire a housekeeper, Célia, who has a 5-year-old daughter, Kiki. Célia leaves, asking them to take care of her daughter until she comes back. Kiki radically changes Durval and Carmita's lives. As Durval was used to reminding his costumers, vinyl was better than CDs because it had an A and a B side. The arrival of Kiki in their lives will make them experience the 'B' side of life. Amongst many memorable scenes is a chariot ride through Pinheiros featuring the song 'Besta é Tú' by Novos Baianos (1972), and the opening sequence, a four-and-a-half-minute take following the moves of skateboarders to music by Mestre Jonas. The camera leads us past cars, street signs, stickers, T-shirts, banners, bar menus, amusement arcades and musical instrument shops, and the posters that display the credits until we see the last credit on a street sign which, instead of the street name, reads 'a film by Anna Muylaert'.
→ *Maria Ignês Carlos Magno*

Directed by Anna Muylaert
Scene description: The film credits appear written on different places of the street
Timecode for scene: 0:00:10 – 0:04:50

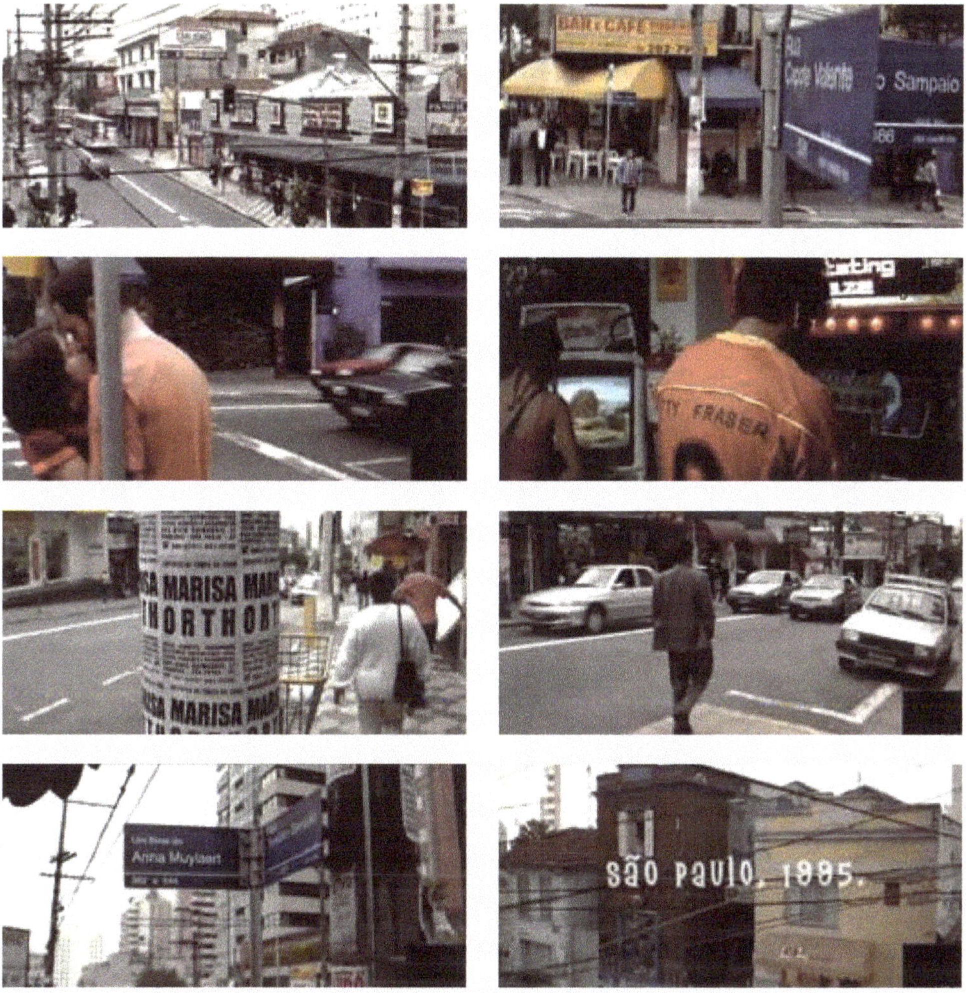

CARANDIRU (2003)

LOCATION *Carandiru Prison*

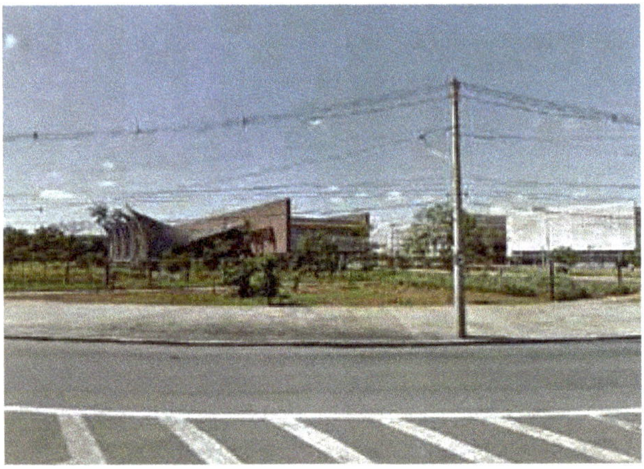

CRITICS OFTEN NOTE THAT, when it is used well enough, a filming location can function as a supporting character. But, in some films, a filming location is so central to the story it goes beyond even that and becomes the film's protagonist, making human characters seem secondary. Such is the case in *Carandiru*, which was filmed almost entirely inside the eponymous prison. While it stood, Carandiru was the largest, and possibly the most infamous, penitentiary in Latin America: built to hold 4,000 inmates, it was used to hold twice as many. They established their own systems of government, and codes of conduct and commerce, and were victim to horrendously high rates of AIDS. When a riot erupted on Friday 2 October 1992, it was brutally put down by police using horses, attack dogs and automatic weapons. The result was the death of over 100 prisoners; there were no police casualties. A recreation of this notorious episode provides the climax of Hector Babenco's film. In an extended sequence of astonishing savagery, the prisoners are persuaded to give up their weapons and then slaughtered regardless. When the chaos subsides, the survivors are ordered to strip naked and sit on the prison's muddy football pitch, creating the most unforgettable image in a film full of unforgettable images. The Carandiru massacre turned public opinion against the prison, which eventually closed in 2002. Its last act was to be used as the setting for this film: the final shots are actual footage of Carandiru's demolition. ***Scott Jordan Harris***

Photo © Google maps

Directed by Hector Babenco
Scene description: The Carandiru massacre
Timecode for scene: 1:53:25 – 2:11:52

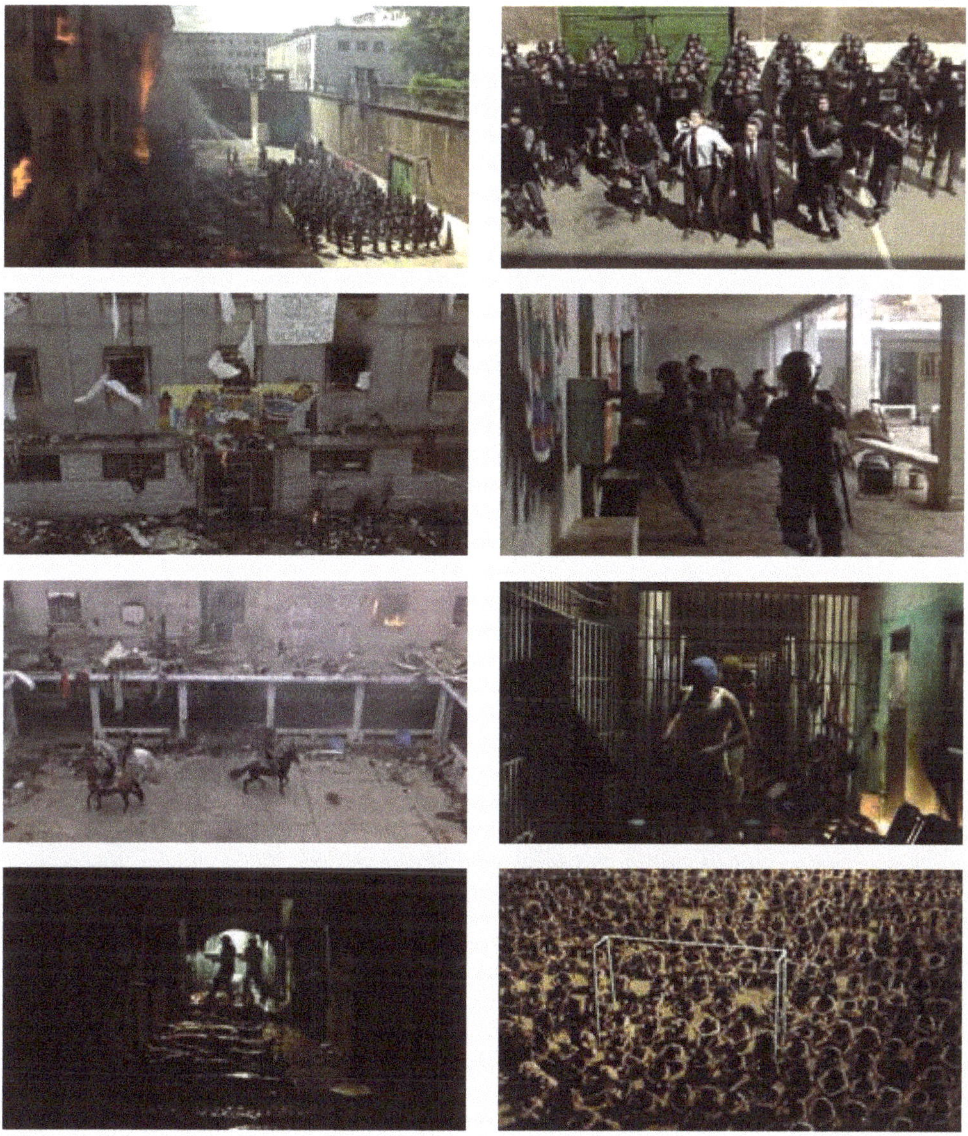

NINA (2004)

LOCATION *Viaduto Jacareí, República*

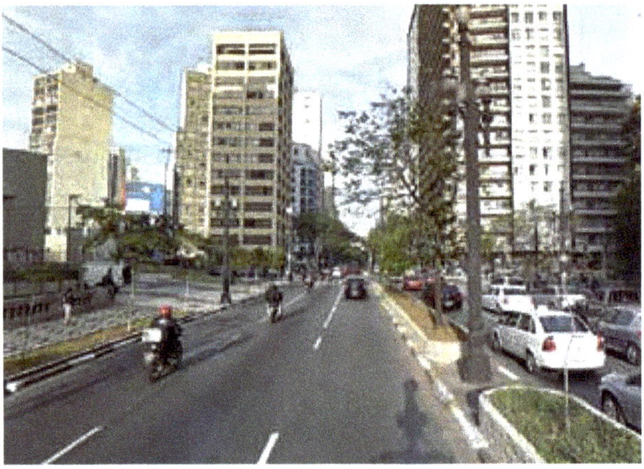

THE DRAMA BASED on *Crime and Punishment* by Dostoiévski (1866) narrates the story of Nina, a fragile young girl who tries to survive in the São Paulo metropolis, and her landlady Eulália, who owns an apartment where Nina rents one of the rooms. Eulália is aware of Nina's fragility and takes advantage to exploit and humiliate her tenant. Nina attempts to get a job in order to pay her debts with Eulália. Amidst struggles to get a permanent job and her experiences in the Paulista night-time, Nina starts to draw everything she sees. Drawings that cover whole walls of her room and illustrate the notes in her diary, exposing the spectator to the psychological drama lived by Nina until she gets involved with Eulália's death. The sequence shows Nina's despair when she finds out she will not have a place to stay as she wanders around São Paulo´s old city centre showing Praça Roosevelt, Maria Paula, Santo Antonio, Bela Vista and Avenida São Luis. In the stairs of the Viaduto Jacareí, Nina talks to a friend and asks for shelter. Her friend says she cannot provide her with accommodation but offers her money. Nina reacts violently because she does not want money, but a place to stay. Desperate, Nina crosses the streets and viaducts without direction. Hallucinations and visions start, delirium takes over her body and she wakes up by Praça Roosevelt.
→ ***Maria Ignês Carlos Magno***

Photo © Google maps

Directed by Heitor Dhalia
Scene description: Nina's Eviction
Timecode for scene: 0:46:17 – 0:47:27

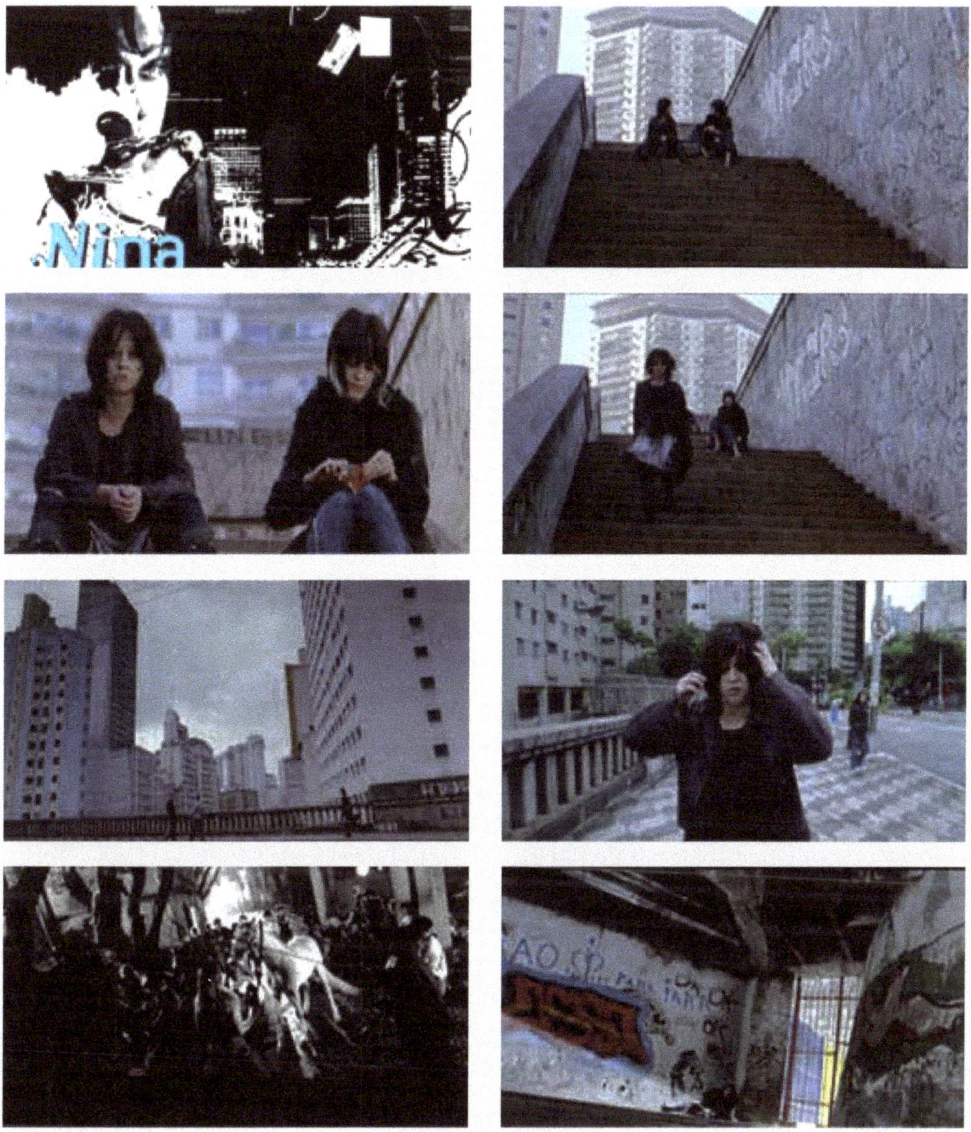

WELCOME TO SÃO PAULO/ BEM VINDO A SÃO PAULO (2004)

LOCATION *Avenida do Estado, 3170, Baixada do Glicério*

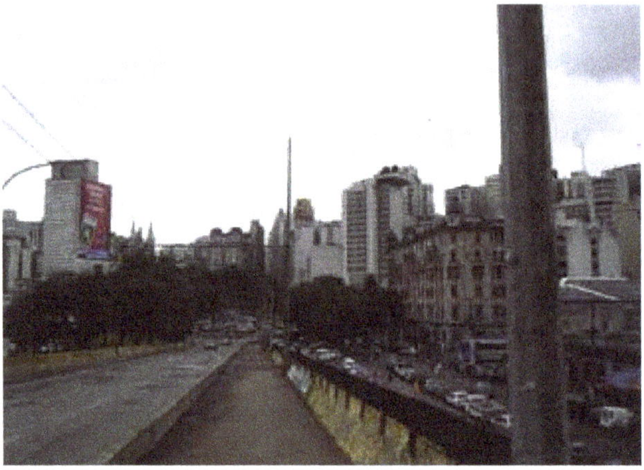

SÃO PAULO IS MOST interestingly pictured in the short film 'Aquário', by Tsai Ming-Liang, which is part of the film *Welcome to São Paulo* (2004), the upshot of a São Paulo International Film Festival project that brought together several international film-makers with the purpose of conveying different views of the fourth largest city in the world, interwoven with narratives written by festival director Leon Cakoff. Ming-Liang focuses his gaze on the architecture of lonely life inside a slum tenement, filming the windows of a condemned building. Through these windows, one can see locked up people looking out at the street, smoking or simply placing a small flower pot on a dirty and grey windowsill. Drum-beating, rain, and thunderclaps make up the hubbub of the Brazilian metropolis. The director thus notes one of the biggest problems in São Paulo, which is property speculation, and how the precariousness of living conditions fails to shelter the inhabitants of the city, putting them in the same situation as small fish sold in plastic bags. The building in the city centre was demolished in 2011, but the images highlighted here still remain a concrete picture of life in São Paulo.
→ ***Márcia Carvalho***

Photo © Fabio Burgos (www.saojudasnu.blogger.com.br)

Directed by Tsai Ming-Liang
Scene description: Windows of a condemned building with people inside like fish in plastic bags
Timecode for scene: 0:50:00 – 0:52:43

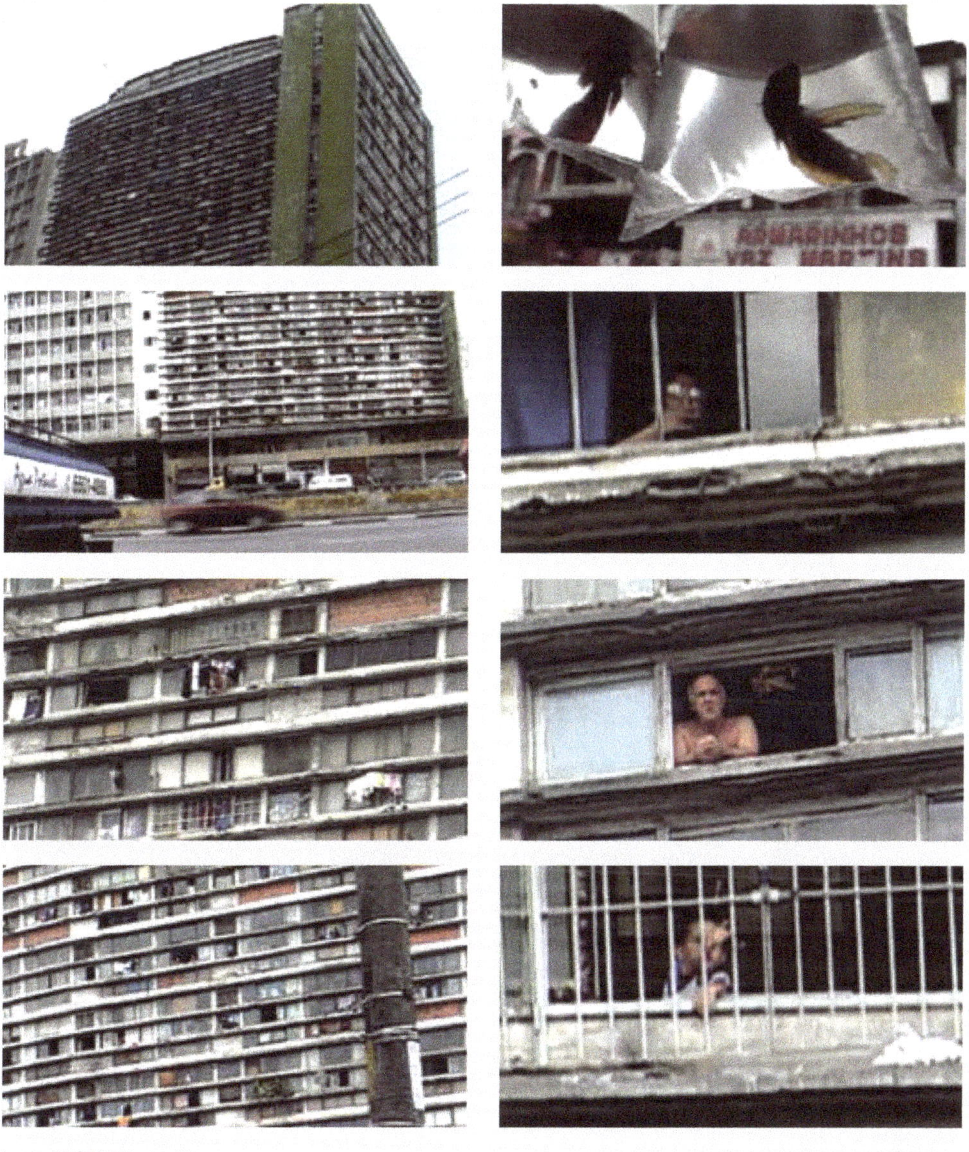

UNDERGROUND GAME/ JOGO SUBTERRÂNEO (2005)

LOCATION *Consolação underground station*

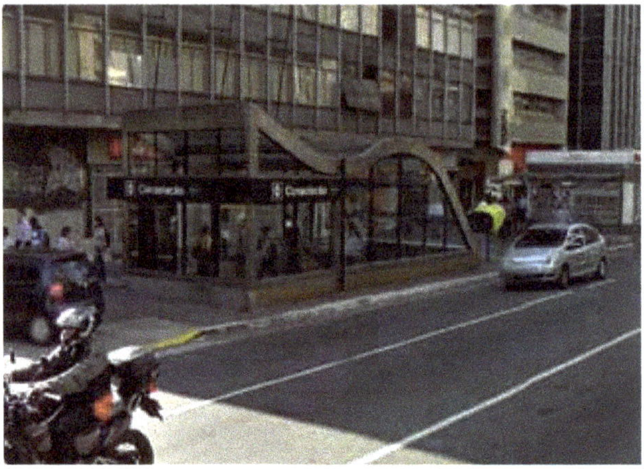

BASED ON JULIO CORTÁZAR'S short story 'Manuscript Found in a Pocket' (Manuscrito hallado en un bolsillo), 1974, *Underground Game* narrates the story of Martin, a piano player who makes up a game to play on the underground: he chooses a woman and waits to see whether she is going to take the same route. If she does, he approaches her. In his hopeful and obsessive game, some women cross his path, but none of them brings him happiness until he meets Ana, whose route he has not charted. Their first encounter takes place above ground, on the stairs to the Consolação underground station in the Avenida Paulista. The game restarts in a sequence that is as fraught as the movements of the trains and the tension between Ana and Martin. However, it is not the game previously played by Martin, because it has become unpredictable. After they exchange their first glances in the carriage, Ana fears that Martin is an enemy and makes the Consolação, Clínicas, República, Anhangabaú and São Bento Stations part of an escape route to the Viaduto Santa Efigênia, in the central region and the old financial centre of the city. The underground city is the chosen setting for the fiction, and the encounters happen above ground during the daylight in São Paulo, which in turn is often represented as a grey city. ⇝***Maria Ignês Carlos Magno***

Photo © Google maps

Directed by Roberto Gervitz

Scene description: The meeting between Martin and Ana
Timecode for scene: 0:22:23 – 0:30:40

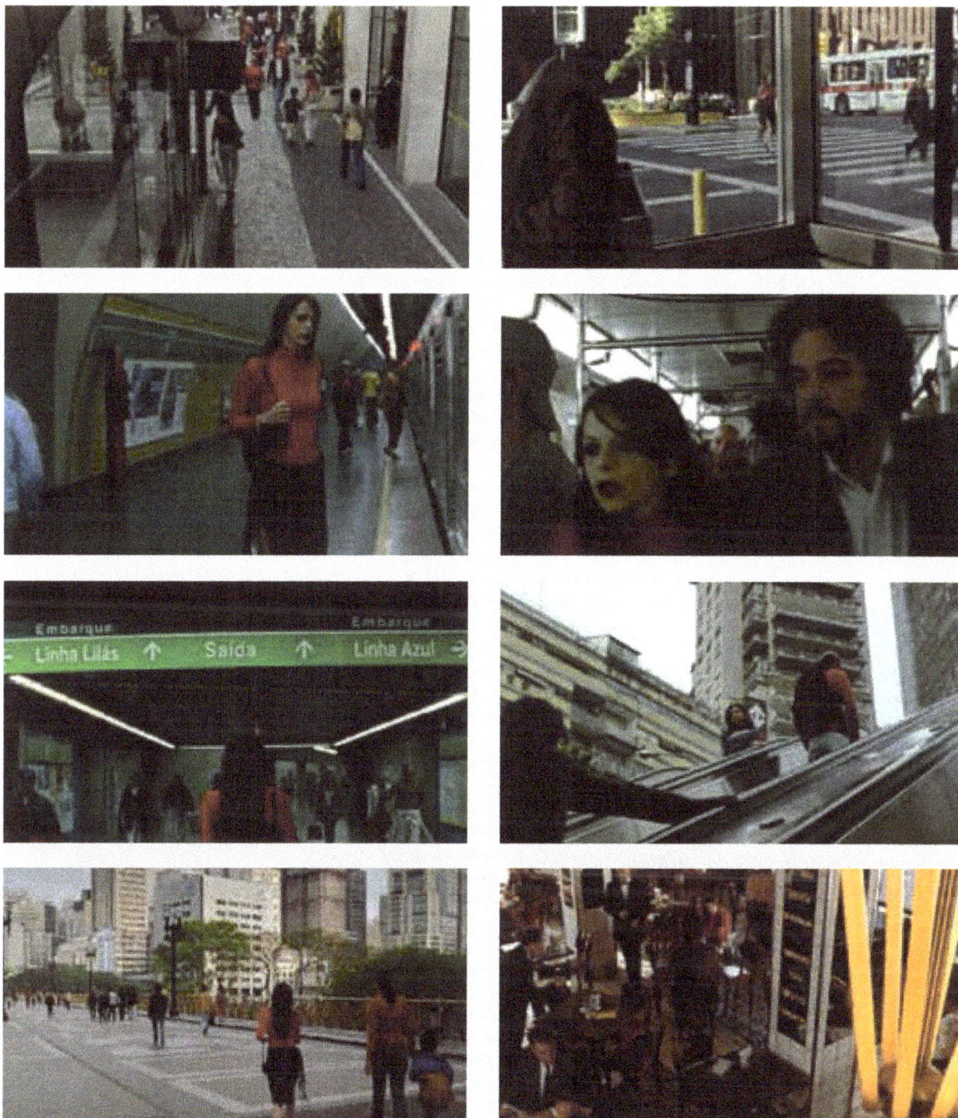

ROMEO AND JULIET... GET MARRIED/ O CASAMENTO DE ROMEU E JULIETA (2005)

LOCATION *Estadio Municipal Paulo Machado de Carvalho*

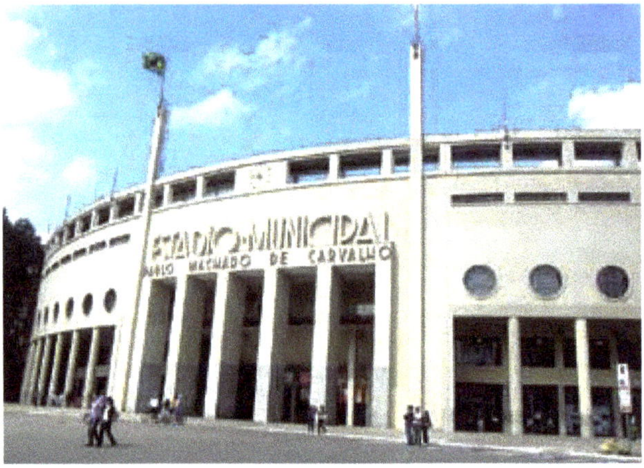

IT WOULD SEEM ONLY NATURAL that a contemporary Brazilian interpretation of Shakespeare's *Romeo and Juliet* would base its intra-family conflict around the two most important football-team rivalries of São Paulo: Corinthian F.C. and S.E. Palmeiras. In this loose take on a classic work, we are introduced to the two sides of fanaticism within the very first moments at a match in the Municipal Stadium Paulo Machado de Carvalho, home of Corinthians and where both sides of the pitch conclude in a peaceful draw. Julieta (Luana Piovani) is the daughter of Alfredo Baragatti (Luis Gustavo), chairman of the board of directors of the opposing Palmeiras club. Once Julieta's eyes find Romeu (Marco Ricca) through her binoculars, we are to expect the plot of love triumphing over tradition and passion that originates, in this case, with the family. Although the juxtaposition of actual game footage with the choreographed scenes of Julieta and her family in the stands of the stadium is almost too noticeable, we can appreciate the culminating moment at the end of the scene where both sets of actors exit the stadium among the real fans of this rivalry. To introduce the extremes of this athletic passion, Romeu ends up carrying his great-grandmother and avid Corinthians fan Nenzica (Berta Nemel) on his back to avoid her being trampled by the younger, yet no less passionate followers. For the remainder of the story, insert a classic tale of pursuing love at the cost of innocently betraying (and later recuperating) one's lifelong loyalty. ➺ ***Kyle Black***

Photo © Wally Gobetz

Directed by Bruno Barreto

Scene description: Part presentation, part foreshadowing of the general thematic of the film, in the home stadium of the football team Sport Club Corinthians Paulista

Timecode for scene: 0:05:06 – 0:10:30

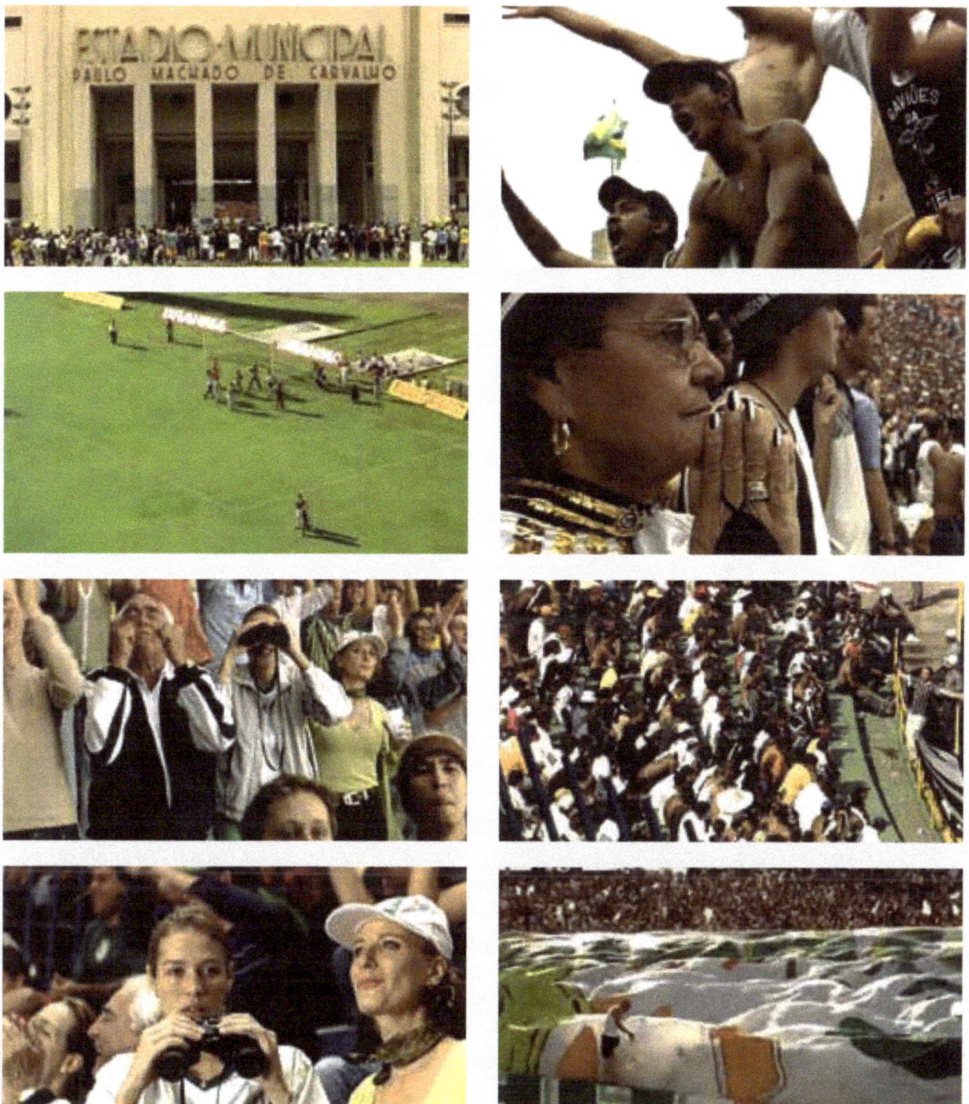

ALL THE INVISIBLE CHILDREN (2005)

LOCATION *Municipal Market of São Paulo*

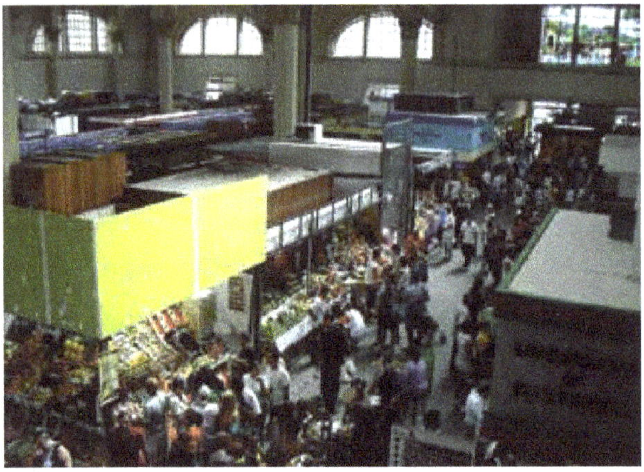

THE MOVIE *ALL THE INVISIBLE CHILDREN* is a collection of several short fiction films featuring socially excluded children who have suffered from the disorder of their social environment. 'Bilu and João', a short film directed by Katia Lund, presents the life of two children who work as collectors of recyclable materials. The story's stage is the city of São Paulo, Brazil, which is compared to a car racing game as the protagonists wander through its wide avenues. The visual metaphor explored by the director represents not only these children's imagination but also has the purpose of displaying the grandeur of the metropolis, where people live their lives in the fast lane. The race also represents people's battles for position and struggles for survival, leading them, including the children, to live in subhuman conditions. The chosen scene presents the fair, a typical and culturally rich Brazilian setting where child labour is sometimes legitimated. Multiculturalism, creativity and craftiness depict Bilu and João, boys who face their routine with a sense of humour by exploring new spaces as well as interacting with people such as the north-east citizens who've helped build the city, and also other characters who keep their symbolic traditions within this multicultural environment. By alternating medium- and close-up shots, the director seeks to uncover situations and immerse the viewer in the character's subjectivity. Both the tambourine played by the musical salesmen at the fair, and the hand-crafted toys, symbolize the creativity and culture of São Paulo.
→ *Murilo Gabriel Berardo Bueno, Rafael Mendonça Lisita Pinto and Maria Luiza Martins de Mendonça*

Photo © Raphael Gallego

Directed by Katia Lund, et al.
Scene description: Bilu and João walk through the fair and create and play a game
Timecode for scene: 1:00:39 – 1:01:47

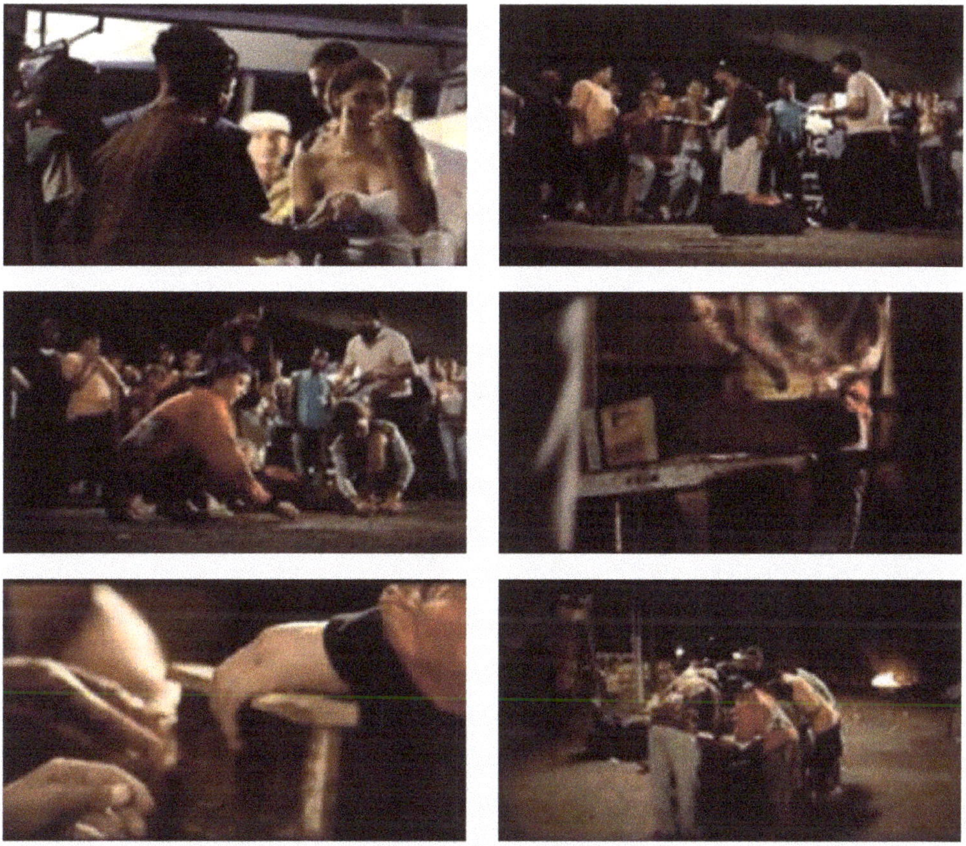

SPOTLIGHT

TATA AMARAL

Text by MARCIA CARVALHO

The City of São Paulo as Depicted in Tata Amaral's Movies

TATA AMARAL STARTED HER CAREER in the movies during the 1980s, joining a generation of film-makers from the Brazilian state of São Paulo who carried out a renewal of short-film productions. This generation of Paulistas has addressed the ongoing crisis of film-making in Brazil with movies that are noticeable by their cinephilia, humour, urban theme, and several forms of intertextual allusions.

Amaral's first short productions already displayed her strong attachment to urban life as a locus of tensions and conflicts, with characters and circumstances drawn from social experiences, bringing the city of São Paulo into the spotlight. These are features which are of great importance both to her documentary films and to her fictional ones.

Amaral's first two short movies, co-directed with Francisco César Filho, were made in 1986: *Poema-Cidade*, which picks up on the inspiration of Augusto de Campos's concrete poetry on São Paulo's urban landscape, handing out poems around the city; and *Queremos as Ondas do Ar!*, an activist film about freedom in Brazilian telecommunications, arguing for the need of community and pirate radio TV stations. Amaral and César Filho also made a documentary video called *Vintedez* (2001), about teenagers and hip hop culture in Santo André, a nearby town.

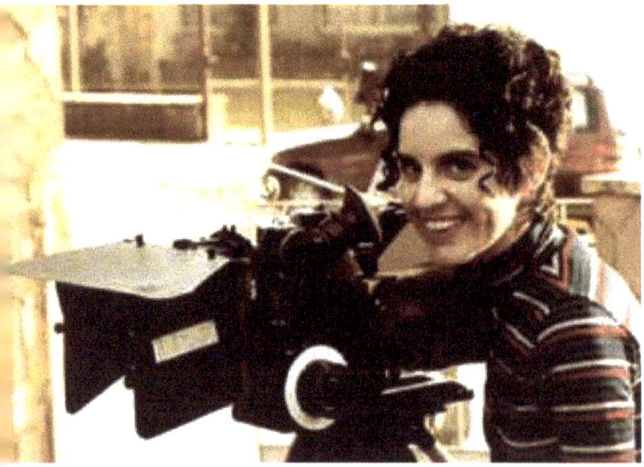

In 1988, Amaral kicked off a career in fictional cinema with the one-reeler *História Familiar*, in which a couple tries to keep a love meeting going on while they are watching TV, answering the phone, and eating pizza. But her most successful short film has been *Viver a Vida* (1991), about the daily life of an office-boy whose job consists of running tiresome errands, the performing of which shows him standing in lines, waiting for long stretches of time, and getting himself involved in trickery.

Amaral's first feature film, *Um Céu de Estrelas* (1996), tells the story of a hairdresser called Dalva who pins her hopes of changing her life on a trip to Miami. Only her fiancé wants her to give their relationship a second chance. Confined to a small house, in the course of a single day, these two characters live a drama combining violence and eroticism. It is a movie that presents a remarkable cohesion in the composition of space, in the manifold aspects of its relation with the bodies, and in the setting functions built by the way the camera moves in order to show the couple clashing within the privileged space of intimacy. These characters' mysteries are conjured up not so much as to be explained but so as to create a mirror onto which their individual loneliness and dead ends could be projected. Notwithstanding, a way of incorporating some traces of the contemporary social experience is plainly visible in Amaral's portrayal of the house, the conflict and the characters, bringing up the subjects of family breakdown and social decadence in a compelling comment on the socialization process in a huge city like São Paulo, and especially in a broken-

Opposite Tata Amaral / Below *Antônia* (2006)

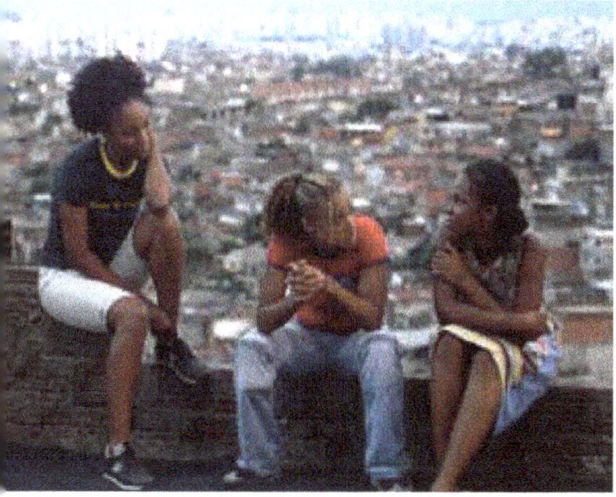

Above © 2006 Coração da Selva, Globo Filmes

down area like Mooca, a neighbourhood in the impoverished Eastern part of São Paulo.

Tata Amaral's second full-length film, *Através da Janela* (2000), focuses on the messy love bond between a mother and her son. Its main traits are the use of the mother as narrator and the reliance on the drama quality of trivial daily actions performed by alienated middle-class characters.

Antônia (2006) tells the story of a rap music group made up of four young women. The band's lyrics unveil the movie's subject matter: the female condition in the urban outskirts and in its hip hop scene. *Antônia* was filmed in cramped rooms and the badly-lit streets of Vila Brasilândia, a neighbourhood in the North of São Paulo, and it included appearances by musical exponents like Negra Li, Leilah Moreno, Thaíde, Sandra de S, and Thobias da Vai Vai. The movie also spawned a TV series broadcasted by Rede Globo (2006, 2007), the leading TV network in Brazil. The storyline has representations of lower-class black women searching for redemption through their natural musical talent, and then yielding to the music industry system, as they accept to play shows for the consuming middle classes. In spite of that, their dreams are ludicrously thwarted when they have to face the pervasive male chauvinism and violence of their family and love relationships.

Amaral's first short productions already displayed her strong attachment to urban life as a locus of tensions and conflicts, with characters and circumstances drawn from social experiences, bringing the city of São Paulo into the spotlight.

Tata then went on to direct *O Rei do Carimã* (2009), a first-person documentary in which she tries to solve a family secret about her father. According to the film-maker, at her mother's funeral she was told by an uncle that when her father, Joaquim Piza do Souza Amaral, was a young man, he was charged and found guilty of financial fraud on account of his having issued a non-sufficient-funds cheque. The documentary has Tata acting, for the first time, as a protagonist. She looks for the truth in relatives' accounts, newspaper article, and judicial records. She puts together a thoughtful documentary, allowing the viewer to get a glimpse, mainly through dialogues she has with her adviser Jean-Claude Bernardet (a famous film critic and screenwriter), of her entire research and production process.

Hoje (2012) is a movie that takes place on a day in 1998, inside a São Paulo apartment. An ex-militant called Vera is paid a financial compensation by the Brazilian government for the disappearance of her guerrilla husband 24 years ago, and she uses this money to buy an apartment. But her husband reappears on the day she is moving to the new flat, and then Vera, like most Brazilians, wants to know what happened during that period of military dictatorship. As in her first movies, Amaral focuses on the dialogue between a walled-in couple, as a disruption in their private lives suddenly brings to light all their city's landscape and country's history.

São Paulo presents social and economic inequalities typical of a large city geographically spread out, grey and polluted, crammed with decayed buildings, crippled by cars and buses and helicopters and traffic jams, and abounding in job opportunities and cultural attractions. It is the most populated city in South America, with a shocking number of abandoned children and people wandering the potholed streets, as well as an appalling crime rate and disgusting levels of political corruption. Notwithstanding, in Tata Amaral's movies São Paulo is a claustrophobic city, shutting its inhabitants within walls of solitude and violence. To her, the best way of bringing out this city's landscape and life is through female portraits, including her own, when she produces a first-person documentary. With this, one notes her unique way of filming faces, bodies, small gestures and human relationships, when an individual experience uncovers a mirror to society. ✦

Locations Map

SÃO PAULO

maps are only to be taken as approximates

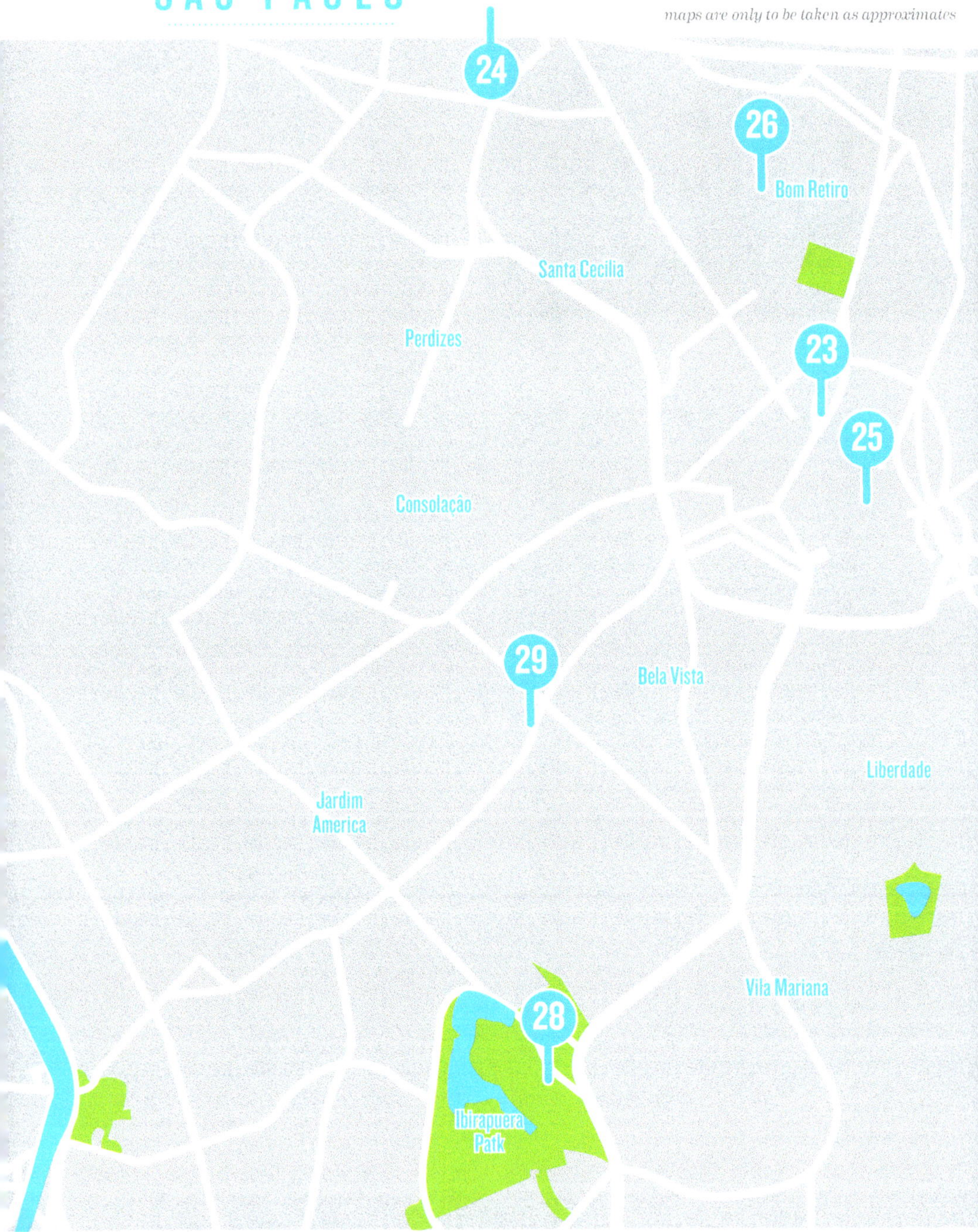

SÃO PAULO LOCATIONS
SCENES 23-29

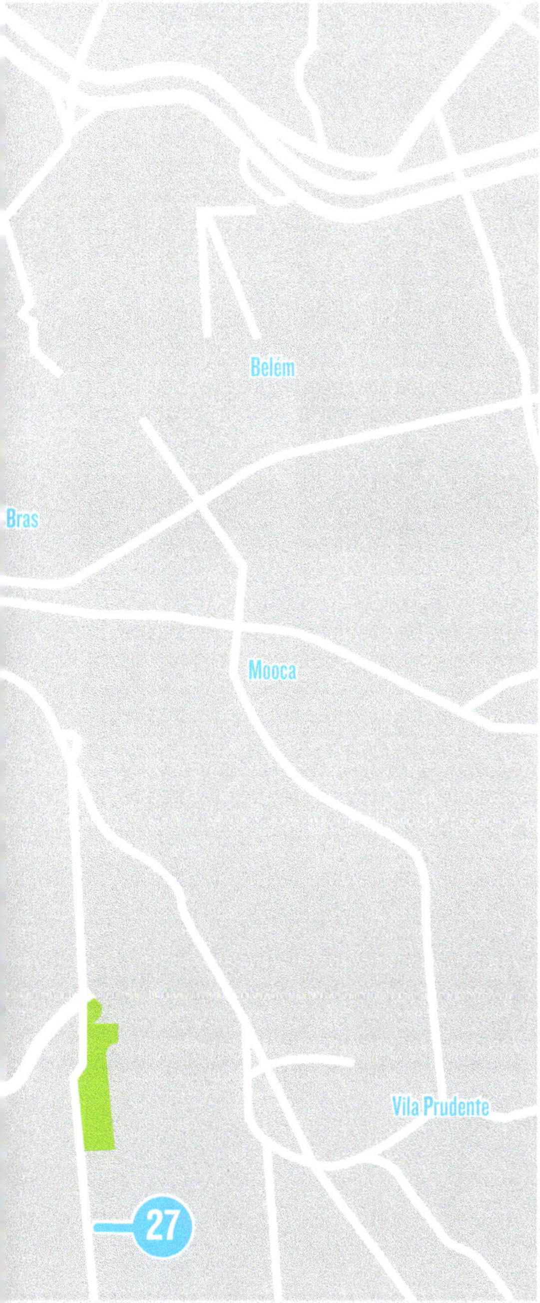

23.
JOURNEY TO THE END OF THE NIGHT/
12 HORAS ATÉ O AMANHECER (2006)
Viaduto Santa Efigênia and Rua do Seminario
page 68

24.
ANTÔNIA (2006)
Vila Brasilândia - Zona Norte
page 70

25.
THE TWELVE LABOURS/
OS 12 TRABALHOS (2006)
Secretaria da Justiça do Estado de São Paulo, Pateo do Collegio
page 72

26.
THE YEAR MY PARENTS WENT ON VACATION/O ANO EM QUE MEUS PAIS SAÍRAM DE FÉRIAS (2006)
Bom Retiro
page 74

27.
DRAINED/O CHEIRO DO RALO (2006)
Generic streets and buildings in Sé and Ipiringa that depersonalize São Paulo
page 76

28.
THE PAST/EL PASADO (2007)
Oca (Pavilhão Lucas Nogueira Garcez), Parque do Ibirapuera, São Paulo
page 78

29.
NOT BY CHANCE/NÃO POR ACASO (2007)
Avenida Nove de Julho
page 80

JOURNEY TO THE END OF THE NIGHT/ 12 HORAS ATÉ O AMANHECER (2006)

LOCATION *Viaduto Santa Efigênia and Rua do Seminario*

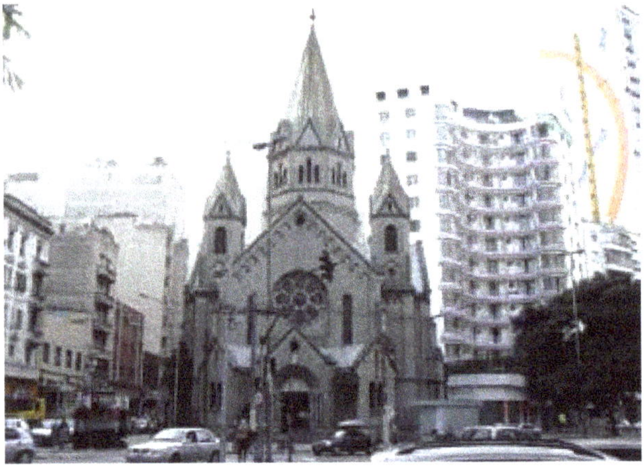

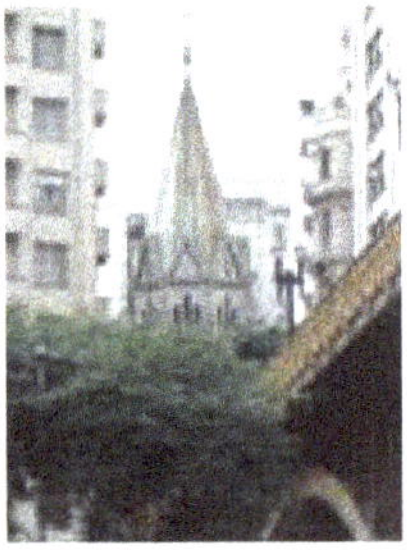

AMERICAN EXPATRIATE, drug dealer and brothel owner Rosso (Scott Glenn) prepares a last drug deal before escaping to a new life with his young wife and child, but his older son Paul (Brendan Fraser) ruins his plans, turning the story into a Third World bloodbath. A dark, chaotic and suffocating São Paulo is suggested throughout, a megacity that, in a way, could be any other city in the era of globalization – New York, Hong Kong or Mexico City. Nevertheless, it still manages to strengthen the stereotype of Latin America as a land of crime. Although much of the film was shot outdoors, we see very little of the city – apart from a series of iconic images during a bike escape through the Liberdade neighbourhood (with its unusual Chinese-lantern-like lamp posts), over the Viaduto Santa Efigênia Bridge, and ending up at the corner of Rua do Seminario, where Wemba (Mos Def), a Nigerian dishwasher drafted into service as a drug mule by Rosso, discovers that his passenger Monique (Alice Braga) has been shot, and walks sullenly down the street as the police arrive. Beyond this fraught and rapid tour across the city, a grainy, dark picture and claustrophobic locations prevail. For those interested in city chase scenes, and those willing to see São Paulo as conveyed via a rather typical American action movie image, the film offers just that.
Santiago Oyarzabal and Michael Pigott

Directed by Eric Eason

Scene description: Wemba and Monique escape on a motorbike

Timecode for scene: 1:08:00 – 1:12:30

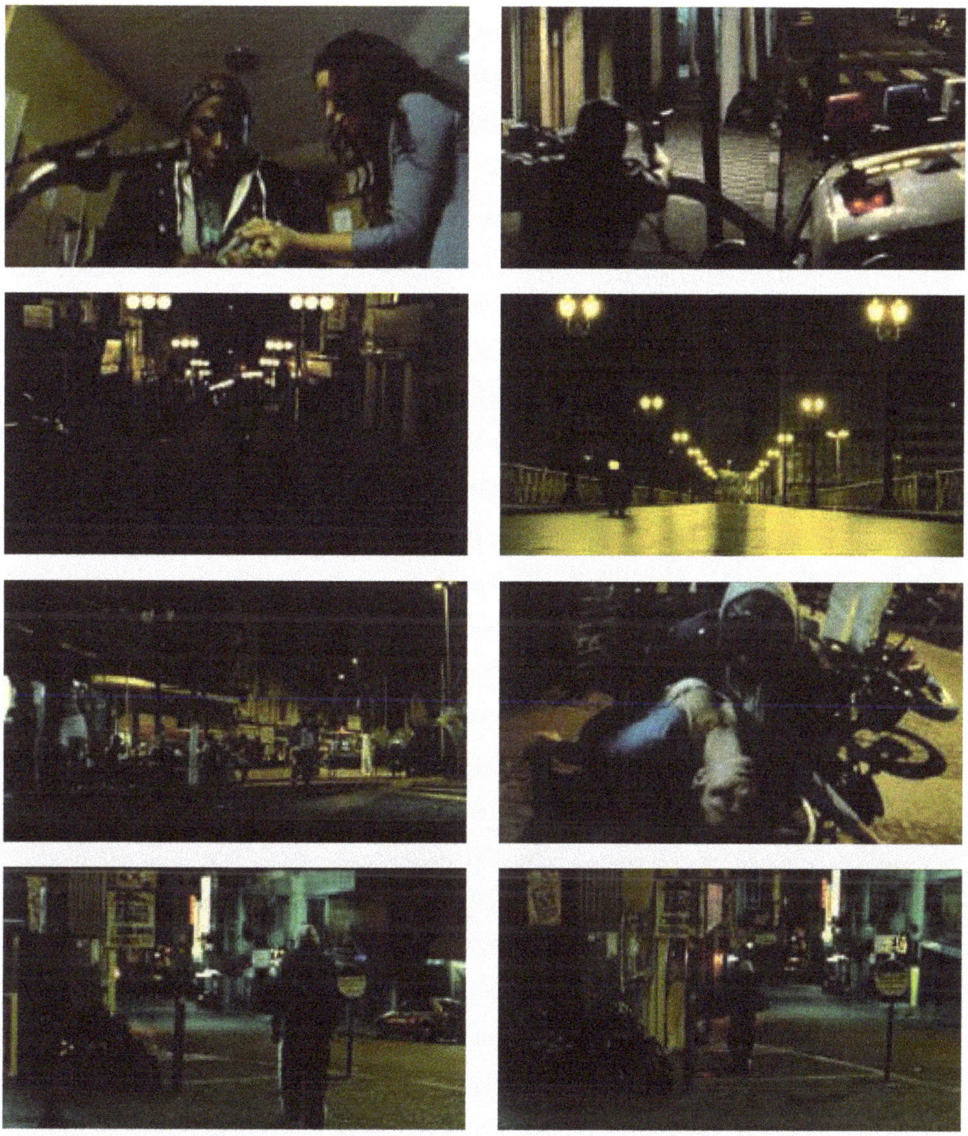

ANTÔNIA (2006)

LOCATION *Vila Brasilândia – Zona Norte*

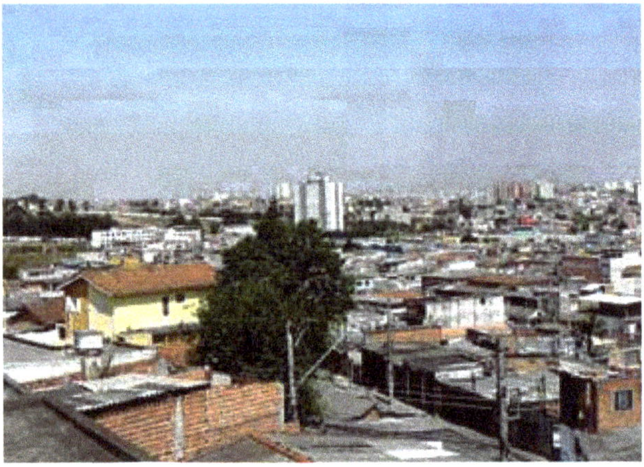

TATA AMARAL'S THIRD FEATURE FILM *Antônia* tells the story of the eponymous music group formed by four female friends who live in Vila Brasilândia, a poor district in the north zone of São Paulo. It belongs to the traditional *favela* genre in Brazilian cinema in its focus on life in the periphery of a big city, reinforcing the much-discussed co-relation between the environment and the characters' lives and state of mind. All characteristics of a revelatory realism are present: non-professional actors, improvised dialogue in the vernacular, and a mobile camera on location in one of São Paulo's roughest areas. The film indeed opens with a shot panning downwards to reveal a sea of houses typical of Vila Brasilândia (and many São Paulo suburbs alike), establishing the location quite firmly before we see the four friends emerging towards the camera from a steep slope. Behind them the informal architecture of the *favela* takes over the background, piles of half-finished houses which sprawl over a hill and leave no empty space. This and various other shots taken from vantage points in Vila Brasilândia run the risk of, on one hand, aestheticizing poverty by making it photogenic to middle-class audiences. But *Antônia* manages to effectively combine the point of view of the outsider (the director who does not belong to the world being portrayed) with that of the insider, by allowing the actors who hail from the suburbs to contribute to the dialogue and to write the rap music of the group Antônia, thus adding new layers of realism to the film. ⊷ ***Cecília Mello***

Directed by Tata Amaral
Scene description: Walking around Vila Brasilândia
Timecode for scene: 0:01:00 – 0:01:48

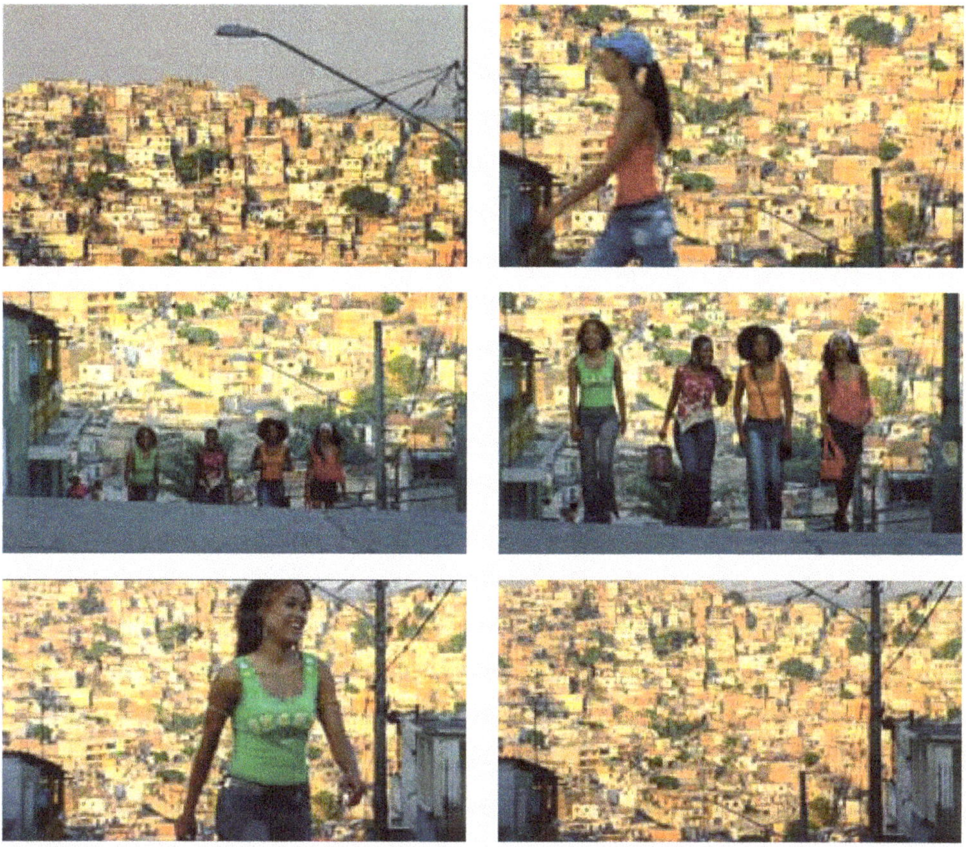

THE TWELVE LABOURS/ OS 12 TRABALHOS (2006)

LOCATION *Secretaria da Justiça do Estado de São Paulo, Pateo do Collegio*

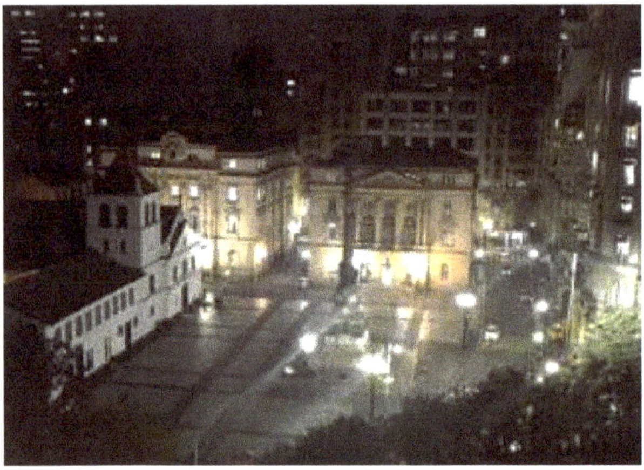

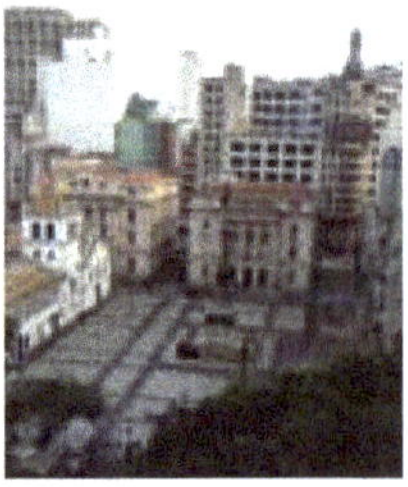

THE TWELVE LABOURS gets on board a motorbike to unveil the city of São Paulo. The film belongs to a new trend of Paulista films which saw an emphatic use of the real city as location after the postmodernist wave of neon-realism. Here, the private hero is Heracles, a young man recently out of a reformatory who gets a job as a delivery boy, having to complete his twelve labours in one day to prove that he is up to the task. The logic of work dominates his trajectories, interspersed here and there by unexpected occurrences which will put him to the test. Heracles travels through lots of easily identifiable streets such as Rua da Consolação, Avenida Sumaré, Viaduto do Chá, Avenida São João and quite prominently, Avenida Paulista, one of São Paulo's most symbolic thoroughfares. The camera is oftentimes mounted on the motorbike, punctuating the film with the subjective shots of Heracles. In one particular sequence he goes to the heart of São Paulo, the Pateo do Collegio (School Yard), where the city was founded in 1554. His destination is the Department of Justice, located in a building projected by architect Ramos de Azevedo in the late nineteenth century. Inside, Heracles faces an uncooperative employee who refuses to stamp a receipt as proof of the delivery of a document. His insistence is of no avail, but as he is about to leave he sees another carrier delivering a document and inconspicuously moving towards an empty desk and stamping his own receipt. Heracles follows suit and leaves in a hurry to complete his next task. ➜ ***Cecília Mello***

Directed by Ricardo Elias
Scene description: Heracles tackles one of 12 labours
Timecode for scene: 0:37:09 – 0:39:56

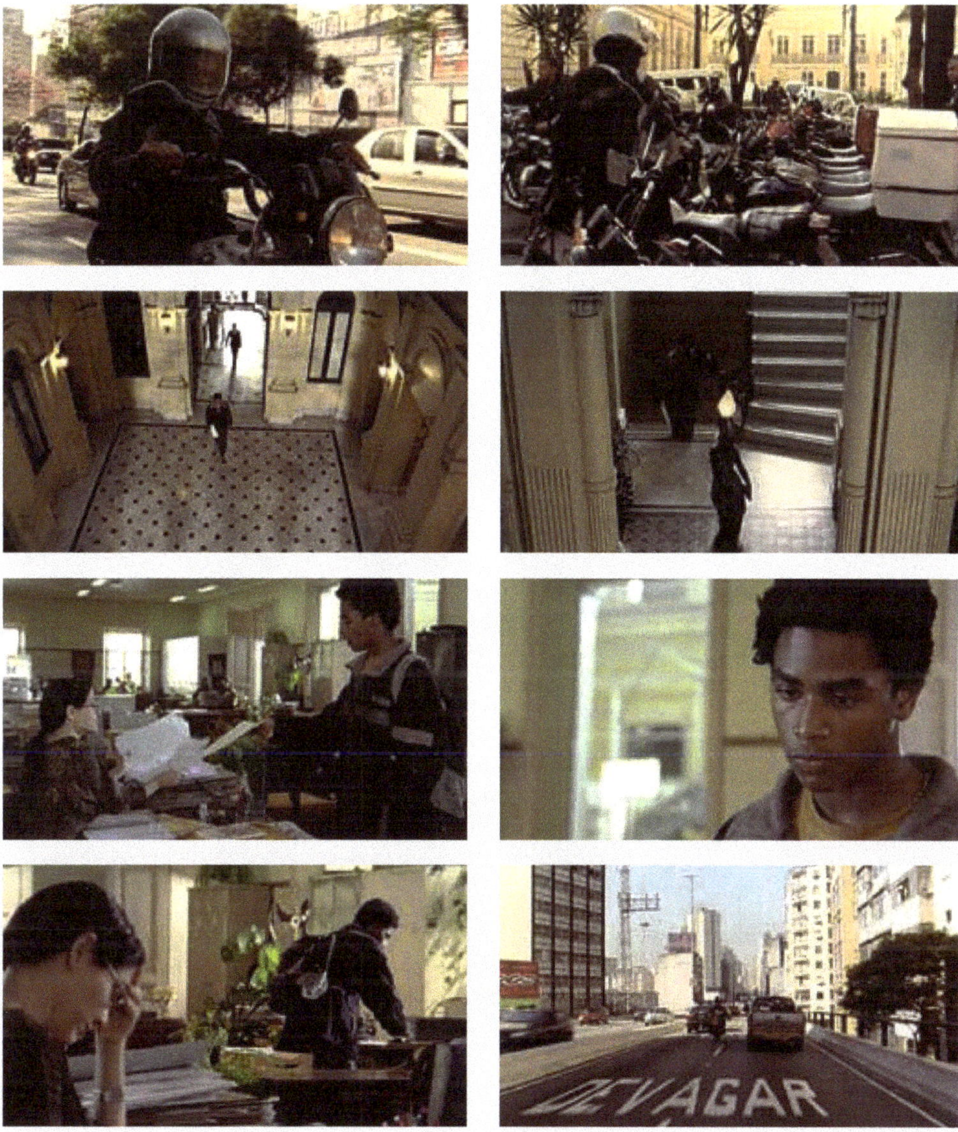

THE YEAR MY PARENTS WENT ON VACATION/ O ANO EM QUE MEUS PAIS SAÍRAM DE FÉRIAS (2006)

LOCATION *Bom Retiro*

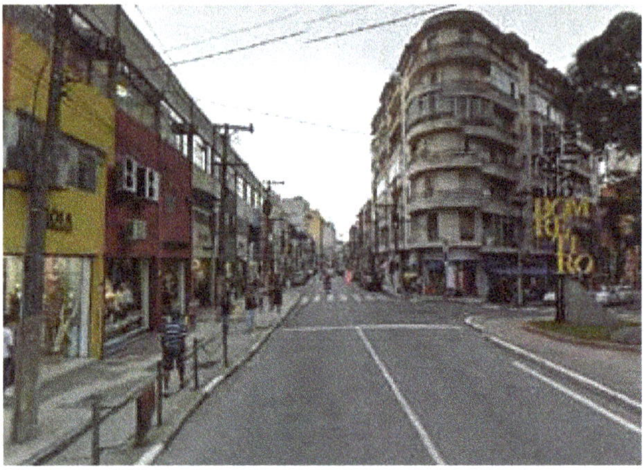

CONSIDERING THE ENORMOUS urban evolutions that Bom Retiro has experienced over the last 40 years, one can appreciate the limitations that director Cao Hamburger was forced to address in attempting to recreate the aesthetics of this neighbourhood as it was in 1970. For the most part, any action taking place outside of this apartment building happens just down the street at the local *Lanchonete* (diner) or behind Hanna's (Daniela Piepszyk) mother's clothing shop, thus providing a narrow yet intimate entrance to the neighbourhood of its time. During the introduction of the film when 12-year-old Mauro's (Michel Joelsas) parents drop him off to stay with his grandfather (Paulo Autran), his father Daniel (Eduardo Moreira) consoles him with the notion that they will return once the World Cup begins. From this day forward, Mauro is seen gazing anxiously through the apartment window, hoping that his parent's blue VW Beetle will come strolling down the street. Eventually, the literal and historical moment of the team's victory over Italy in the final match is juxtaposed with the much-anticipated arrival of his mother after almost a year of 'vacation' (i.e. incarceration and torture). While the neighbourhood and country celebrate its nation's athletic superiority, Mauro's situation, as he strolls alone through the street, is part of a reality that popular events like this championship match keep us distracted from the actions of the government that run opposed to the glory achieved on the soccer pitch.
→ *Kyle Black*

Photo © Google maps

Directed by Cao Hamburger

Scene description: This is the culminating moment of the film when Brazil wins the World Cup and when Mauro's mother (sans father) returns home from their 'vacation'

Timecode for scene: 1:27:01 – 1:31:26

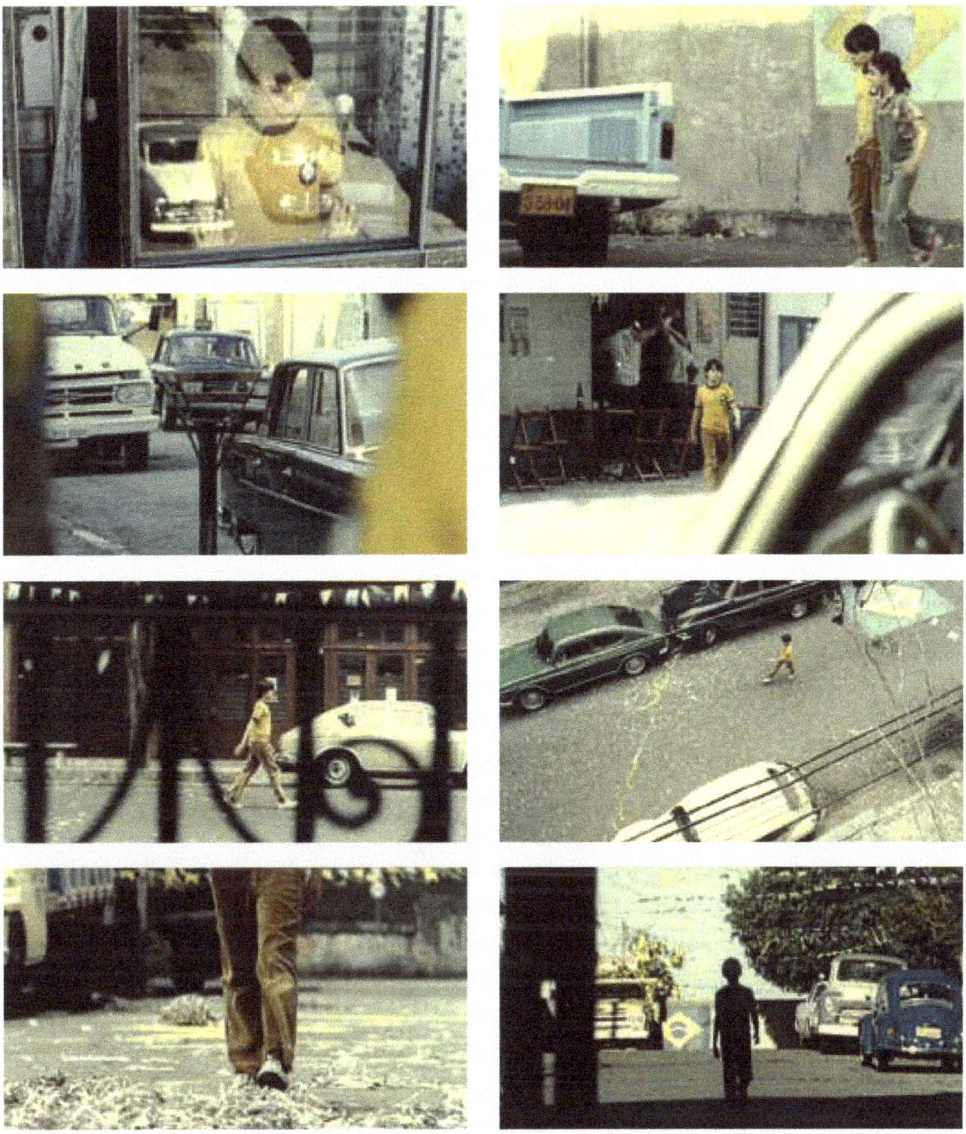

DRAINED/O CHEIRO DO RALO (2006)

LOCATION

Generic streets and buildings in Sé and Ipiringa that depersonalize São Paulo

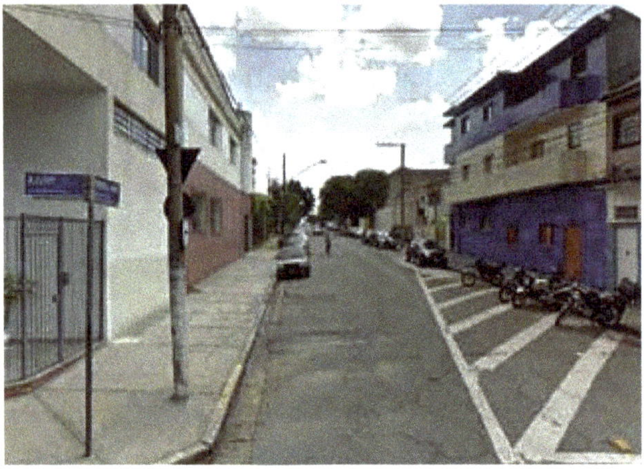

BUYING AND SELLING used goods is more than a business to Lourenço. It is a sadistic game of power played at the expense of other people's desperation. *Drained,* based on comic-book artist Lourenço Mutarelli's first novel (2002), is confined to a few spaces: Lourenço's shop, a dingy diner and a few shots from dirty streets. The film's low budget (around 150,000 dollars) demanded a reduced use of external settings (due, mainly, to city taxes and production restrictions). Therefore, the focus is on Lourenço's Kafkaesque office, presented in shades of grey and brown, stressing his sadistic demeanour towards his clients. A horrible smell comes out from the drain, which, together with his obsession with a waitress's buttocks, causes a disruption in Lourenço's life. The smell from the drain is a metaphor for life in a big city, a hole that engulfs and depersonalizes its inhabitants. As the smell grows stronger, Lourenço's obsessive routine in his monochromatic office gets more and more asphyxiating. The city of São Paulo is, thus, also 'depersonalized' in the few shots from generic streets and buildings. People come and go from the pawn shop and the diner, simply disappearing into the city; in a way they too are drained. ➻ ***Alessandra Soares Brandão***

Photo © Google maps

Directed by Heitor Dhalia
Scene description: The smell from the drain grows stronger
Timecode for scene: 0:38:36 – 0:38:46

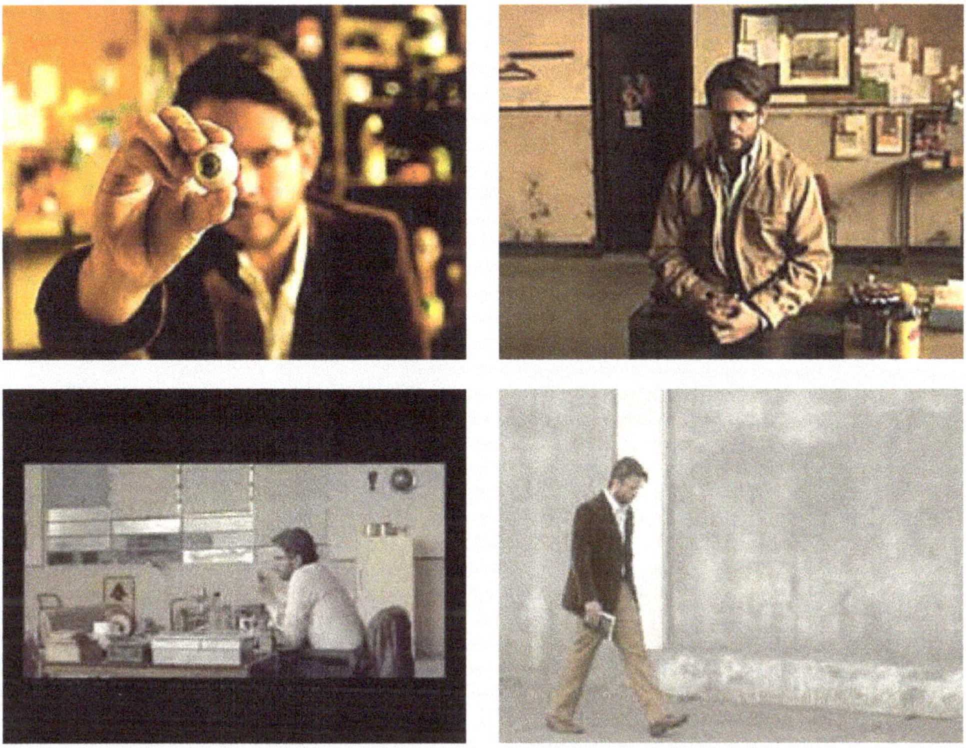

THE PAST/EL PASADO (2007)

LOCATION *Oca (Pavilhão Lucas Nogueira Garcez), Parque do Ibirapuera, São Paulo*

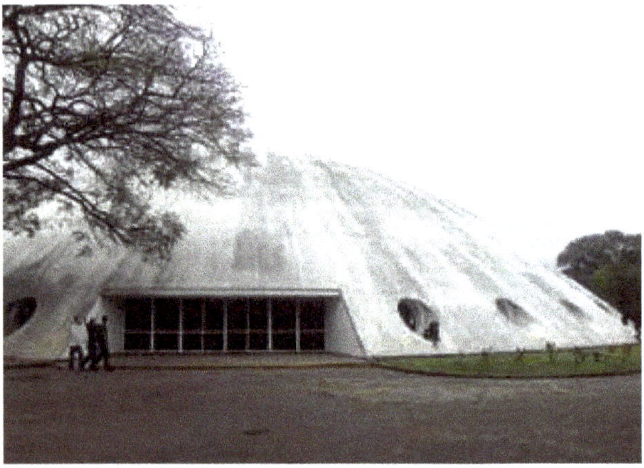

CELEBRATED DIRECTOR HÉCTOR BABENCO was born and raised in Argentina, but after a period in Europe he settled in São Paulo and began a long and successful career in cinema. *The Past,* based on the homonymous novel written in 2003 by renowned contemporary Argentine author Alan Pauls, is a transnational production made with Argentinian and Brazilian funding. It is mostly set in Buenos Aires, but at one point we see the protagonist Rímini (Mexican actor Gael García Bernal) on a short trip to São Paulo. He passes through a busy market, stopping to try on a pair of sunglasses and talk to the vendor. Next we see him in the Pavilhão Lucas Nogueira Garcez exhibition centre, or the 'Oca' as it is known to locals. This unusual building, with its space-age dome and winding interior ramp, was designed by Oscar Niemeyer in 1951, partly to commemorate the city's fourth centenary in 1954. Leaning against the railings of the ramp, Rímini has a view down onto the gallery floor, where he spies his then girlfriend Carmen (Ana Celentano) introducing a large and visually striking artwork to a group of well-dressed people. The piece is 'Nota sobre uma cena acesa ou os dez mil lápis' by José Damasceno, a massive sculpture/mural made out of 10,000 wooden pencils, which is now in the permanent collection of São Paulo's MAM (Museu de Arte Moderna). ➾ ***Santiago Oyarzabal and Michael Pigott***

Photo © Wally Gobetz

Directed by Héctor Babenco
Scene description: A trip to São Paulo
Timecode for scene: 0:51:00 – 0:52:17

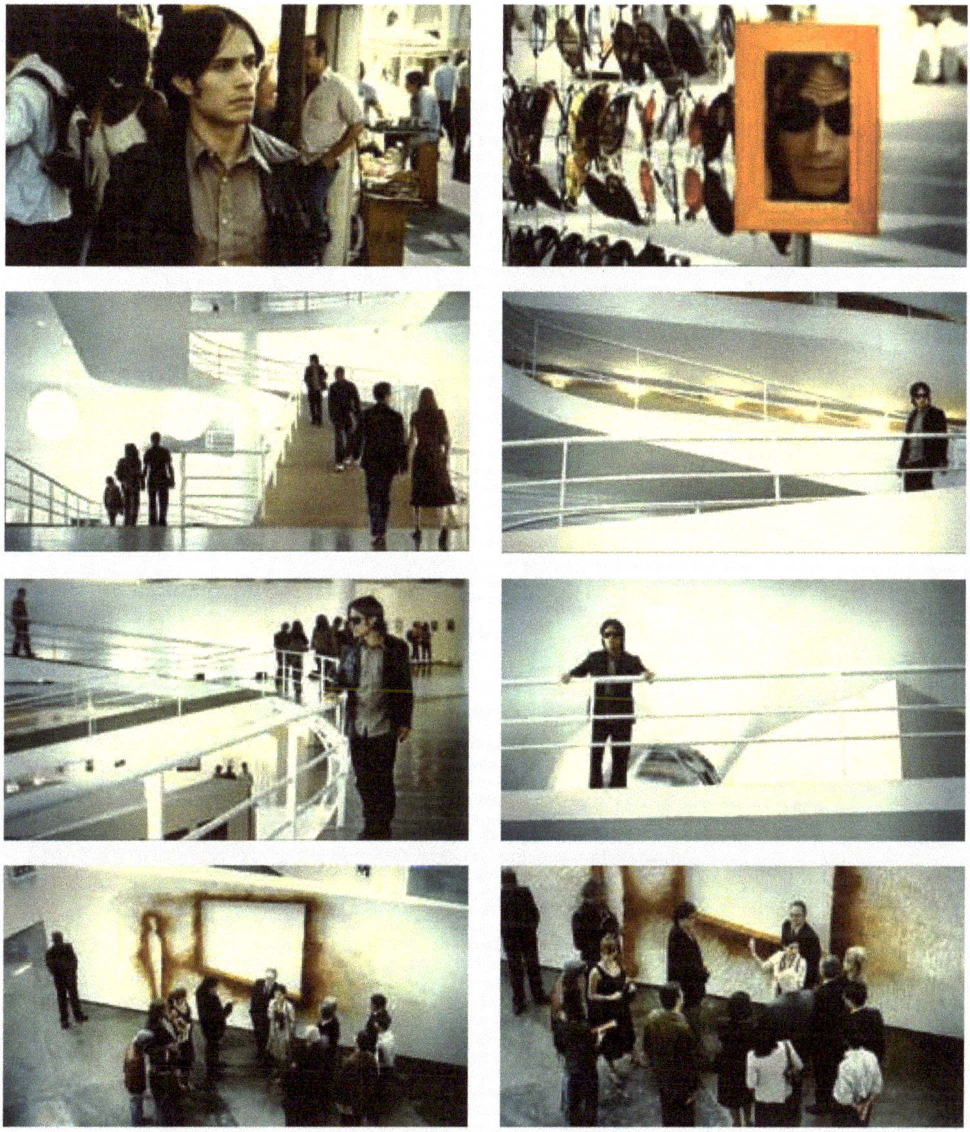

NOT BY CHANCE/NÃO POR ACASO (2007)

LOCATION *Avenida Nove de Julho*

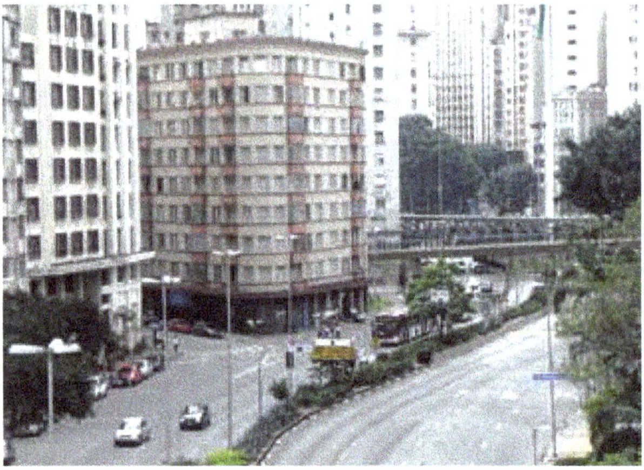

THE SETTING IS THE CITY of São Paulo and the main character is Ênio, a traffic engineer who controls the traffic lights in the city. The establishing shot, a wide-angle bird's-eye view travelling into the city, directs our gaze to the movement of the cars through avenues and highways and takes us to the traffic control office where Ênio works. The initial sounds are of cars and voices stating the names of streets and neighbourhoods and reporting traffic jams and disruption as well as collisions. Sitting in front of his computer, Ênio shows us the city that exists on and outside of his screen. From the camera angle we look at São Paulo from above, and from the monitor screens in the traffic control office we begin to follow a dual narrative: the story of the characters who are constantly dislocated around the city, and that of the city itself, characterized by non-stop movement even when the traffic lights are off or when the daylight darkens to cast its night-time shroud over the people, amidst, as Oswald de Andrade puts it, 'the violet fog that besieges São Paulo'. This idea is well illustrated by Pedro Farkas's photography, which shows the transition from day to night in the lives of the characters and of the city. The city pulses. ⇒ ***Maria Ignês Carlos Magno***

Directed by Philippe Barcinski
Scene description: The traffic in the city can be seen from the protagonist's office
Timecode for scene: 0:01:30 – 0:17:20

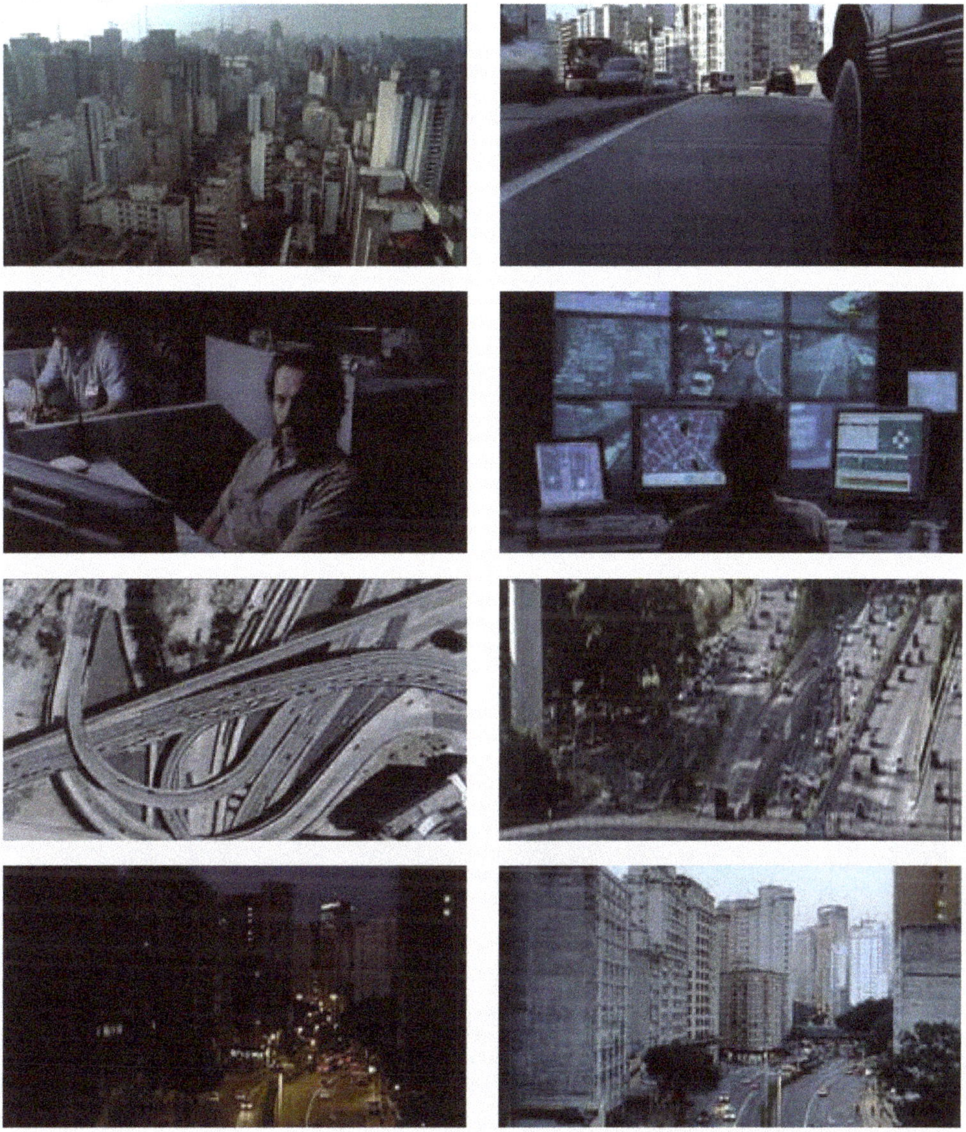

SPOTLIGHT

THE GEOGRAPHY OF SEGREGATION

Text by TIAGO DE LUCA

Violence and Class Division in Contemporary São Paulo Cinema

HOME TO THE VERY RICH and the very poor, Brazil has one of the greatest disparities of wealth distribution in the world, a situation which is particularly visible in its two major cities, São Paulo and Rio de Janeiro. However, unlike Rio's peculiar topography wherein meandering hillsides allowed the poor to live in *favelas* alongside the glamorous quarters of the city, São Paulo has instead followed an urbanization pattern in which the social classes live far apart from each other, with middle and upper classes dwelling in central and vertical neighbourhoods, and the disenfranchised in the precarious and horizontal periphery. Although in recent decades new suburbanization processes have complicated this binary model with the creation of affluent condominiums away from the centre, it is fair to say that the distance between rich and poor in Brazil's wealthiest city conforms to a centre-periphery dynamic. Yet this divisive geography has produced consequences as unwelcome as those of Rio's cheek-by-jowl inequality, with São Paulo witnessing a dramatic rise in crime and violence closely related to urban segregation. Over the last decade, these aspects have been the focus of socially committed fiction films which, averse to victimizing the poor, shed light on this city of contrasts and its processes of marginalization.

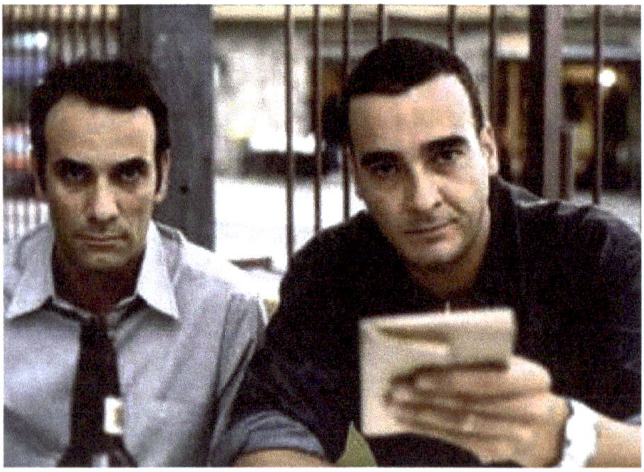

Beto Brant's *O invasor/The Trespasser* (2002), for example, reveals the exclusionist nature of the megalopolis by depicting the unlikely 'invasion' of the bourgeois world by the marginalized. Written by crime novelist Marçal Aquino, the film depicts the story of two white-collar engineers (Alexandre Borges and Marco Ricca) who hire the professional killer Anísio to liquidate the major shareholder of their construction company. After the crime, the hit man manages to trespass and subsequently infiltrate their privileged sphere, and even seduces the victim's daughter, the wealthy and alienated Marina (Mariana Ximenes). Shot entirely on location, *The Trespasser* shows characters relentlessly transiting through São Paulo's recognizable avenues, tunnels and expressways (Dr Arnaldo flyover, Avenida Paulista, Ibirapuera and Anhangabaú tunnels, etc.) in trajectories that link the centre to its enveloping and sordid fringes, as when Anísio takes Marina on a 'tour' from an upmarket part of town through to its impoverished outskirts. Combining documentary techniques and expressionist elements, the film puts forward a nightmarish vision of São Paulo in which the fenced-off world of the rich is gradually enfolded by the violence and crime lurking at its margins.

A more humanist portrayal of the class divide in the city from the perspective of its suburban inhabitants is found in *Linha de Passe/Line of*

Opposite *O Invasor/The Trespasser* (2002)
Below *Linha de Passe/Line of Passage* (2008)

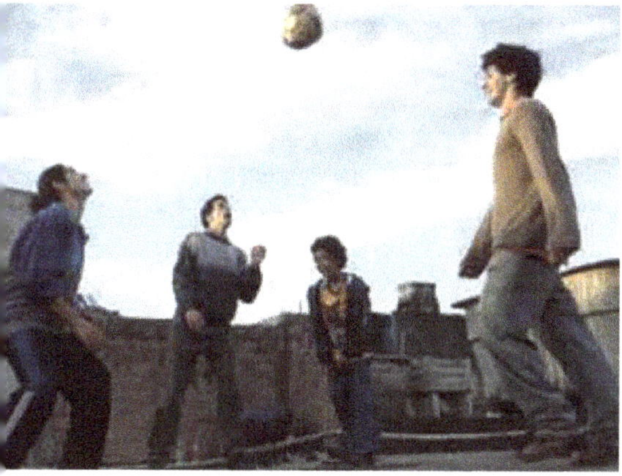

Passage (2008), which saw the return of directors Walter Salles and Daniela Thomas to São Paulo after their *Terra estrangeira/Foreign Land* (1996). Focused on a fatherless interracial family played mostly by non-professional actors, and shot on location in the eastside district of Cidade Líder, the film highlights the physical gap animating the class divide in the city through characters continually shown on its crowded buses. This is the only existing means of transport for the pregnant Cleuza (Sandra Corveloni) to get to the district of Perdizes, where she works as a cleaning maid for a middle-class family - a trajectory which in real life takes nearly two hours. The film implies that the rich and the poor can only co-exist in work-related, hierarchically defined environments, or else violently collide against each other in the city's chaotic traffic as car crashes seem to be witnessed routinely by Cleuza's oldest son Denis. One of the hundreds of thousands of motorcycle couriers zigzagging through the jam-packed roads of the megalopolis, he finds himself participating in smash-and-grab thefts in luxury cars as a means to move up the social ladder. *Line of Passage* also comments on the generalized spread of violence in the city by unfolding during the period in which the organized crime faction PCC (Primeiro Comando da Capital) set fire to hundreds of buses in 2006 as a response to the imprisonment of gang leaders - a horrific incident which also served as the backdrop of two films released in 2009, namely Sérgio Resende's *Salve Geral/Time of Fear* and Sérgio Bianchi's *Os inquilinos/The Tenants*. Drawing on the horror genre, the latter depicts a city paralyzed by fear through the microcosm of a poor family that is confronted overnight with rowdy and violent neighbours. The housewife Iara (Ana Carbatti) contemptuously believes they have moved from a nearby '*favela*' visible from their modest street but which suddenly becomes 'too close', personified by the new tenants living literally next door. The film thus suggests geographical sub-divisions within the periphery itself that add another layer of complexity to the city's centre-margins opposition.

Line of Passage... comments on the generalized spread of violence in the city by unfolding during the period in which the organized crime faction PCC (Primeiro Comando da Capital) set fire to hundreds of buses in 2006 as a response to the imprisonment of gang leaders.

Conversely, *Trabalhar cansa/Hard Labour* (2011), by newcomers Marco Dutra and Juliana Rojas, uses a middle-class family as the stage for São Paulo's contradictions. Predominantly shot in interior locations, the film transfers the city's socio-ethnic tensions to a domestic realm while also dialoguing with the horror genre. Among other narrative threads, it depicts the work relationship of white housewife-turned-small businesswoman Helena (Helena Albergaria) and the *mulata* Paula (Naloana Lima), an unregistered cleaning maid who lives in the house's 'maid room' (*quarto de empregada*). Here, as in many real-life apartments across the megalopolis, São Paulo's class divide is given material form through the kitchen, which literally separates Paula's room from the rest of the house. The direct heir of Brazil's not-so-distant slave past (alluded to in the film through a school play which is tellingly formed by an all-white cast in blackface), Paula's isolated and minuscule *quarto de empregada* is the domestic translation of an urban situation in which the poor are summarily relegated to the fringes of society. The only moment in the film that Paula is given permission to enjoy the house's living room is when Helena allows the maid to watch the carnival parade on television by her side on the sofa. Ironically, the song being played, by samba school Tom Maior, exalts São Paulo's 'progress', 'success' and its glorious history 'at the forefront of the Brazilian economy' - a position which, as the aforementioned films expertly reveal, has been achieved largely at the expense of social equality and urban integration. ✦

LOCATIONS MAP
SÃO PAULO

maps are only to be taken as approximates

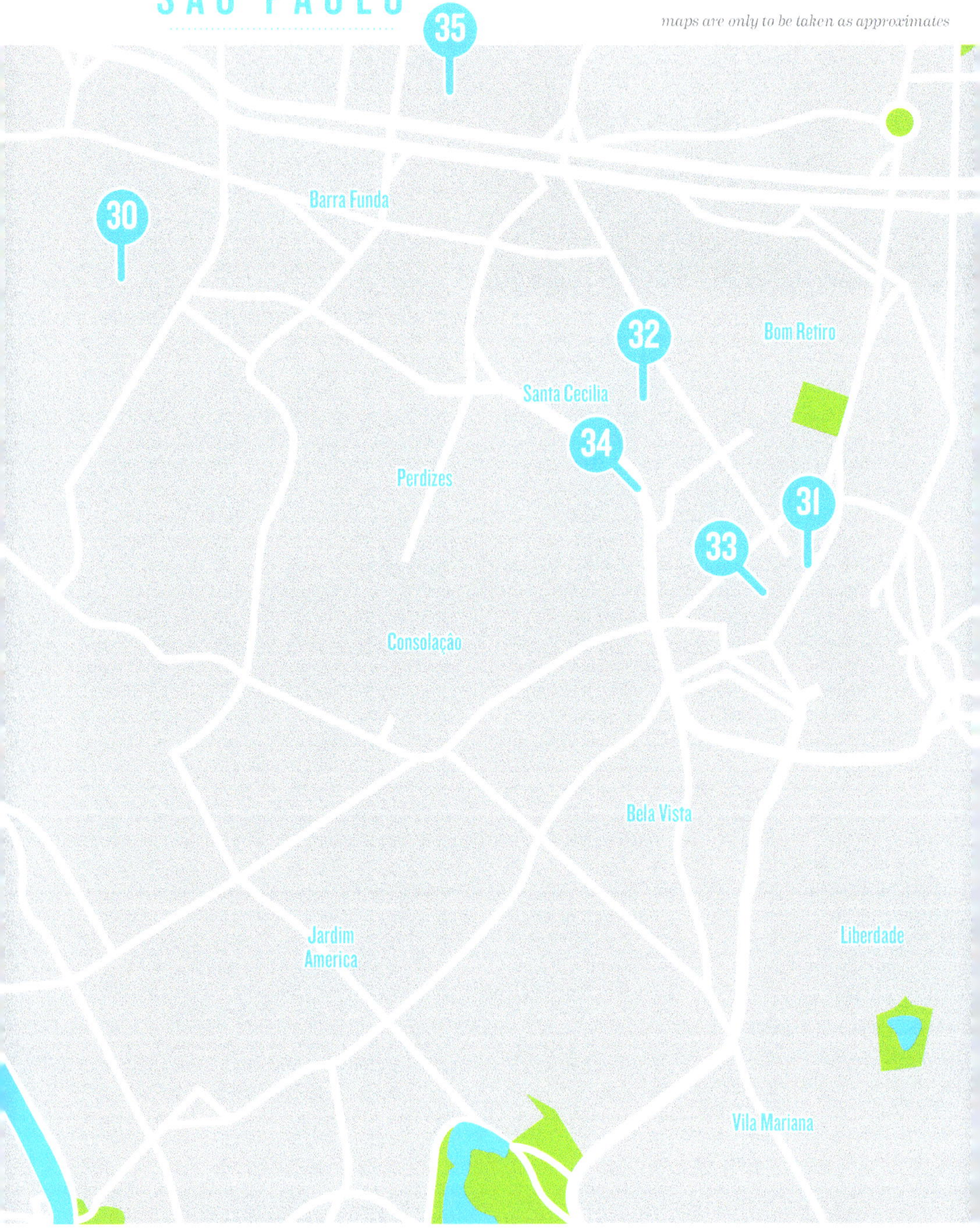

SÃO PAULO LOCATIONS
SCENES 30-36

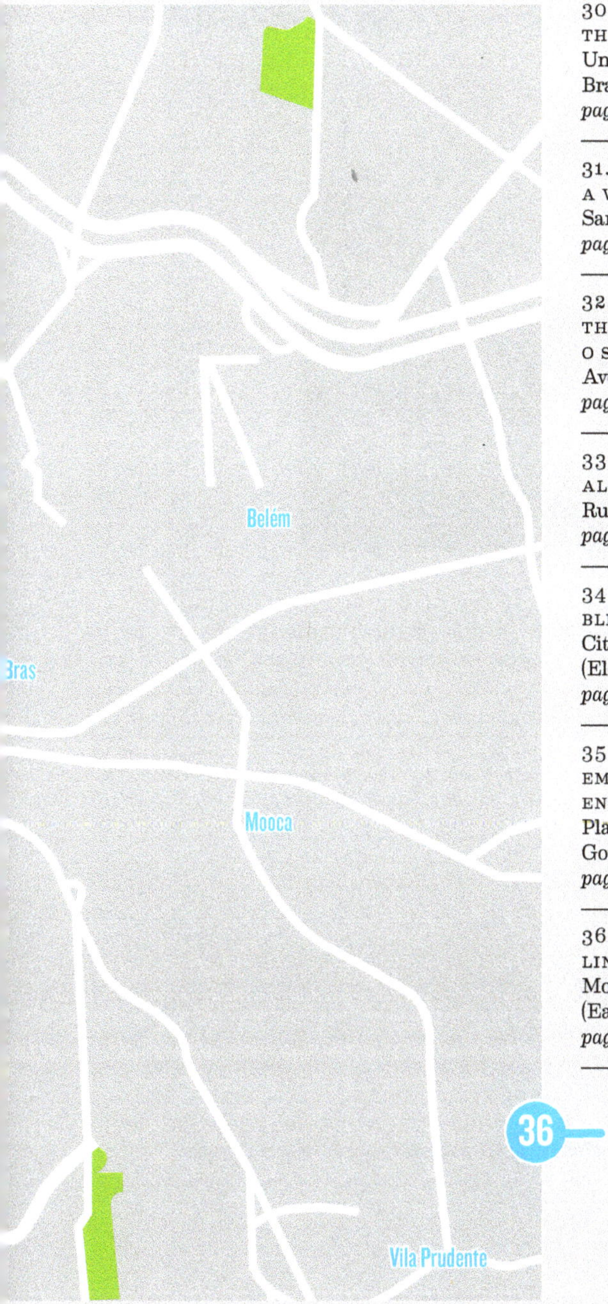

30.
THE BALLROOM/CHEGA DE SAUDADE (2007)
União Fraterna, R. Guaicurus, 27 Água Branca, São Paulo
page 86

31.
A VIA LÁCTEA (2007)
Santa Efigênia Bridge, São Paulo city centre
page 88

32.
THE SIGN OF THE CITY/
O SIGNO DA CIDADE (2007)
Avenida Baràо de Limeira
page 90

33.
ALICE'S HOUSE/A CASA DE ALICE (2007)
Rua Baràо de Itapetininga
page 92

34
BLINDNESS (2008)
City centre, Minhocào
(Elevado Presidente Costa e Silva)
page 94

35.
EMBODIMENT OF EVIL/
ENCARNAÇÃO DO DEMÔNIO (2008)
Playcenter amusement park, Rua José Gomes Falcào, 20 Barra Funda
page 96

36.
LINHA DE PASSE (2008)
Morumbi Stadium, Cidade Líder
(East São Paulo), Rodovia Presidente Dutra
page 98

THE BALLROOM/CHEGA DE SAUDADE (2007)

LOCATION *União Fraterna, R. Guaicurus, 27 Água Branca, São Paulo*

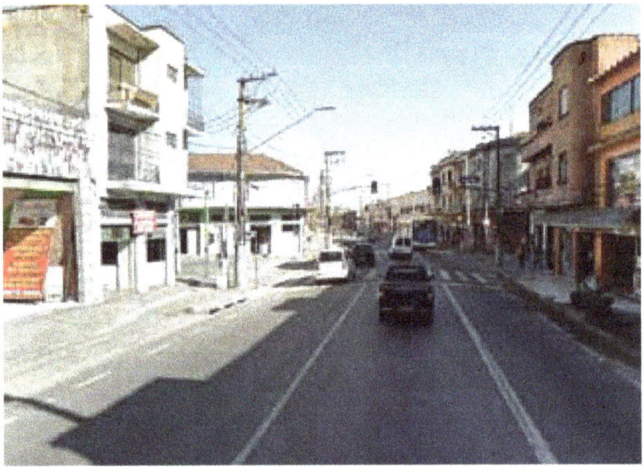

CHEGA DE SAUDADE'S English title – *The Ballroom* – may not do justice to the main theme and sentiment conveyed by the film (as often happens). 'Saudade' is a Portuguese term with no easy translation, often defined as a deep nostalgic longing or yearning. And like Tom Jobin and Vinicius de Moraes's bossa nova song of the same name, Bodanzky's original title means something like 'no more blues'. It is also the name of the local ballroom in which the story is set, taking place over the course of one evening's dancing and entertainment, beginning as the patrons arrive and ending as they spill out onto the street at midnight. The ballroom regulars are aging couples, singles, widows, fake widows and others trying to find clandestine romance or lasting love. Most of them are visibly lonely, hardened or desperate, such as the old dancer Álvaro (Leonardo Villar), bitter at an injury that prevents him from being the great dancer he once was, and the young DJ Marquinhos (Paulo Vilhena), who is filled with anxiety at the sight of his girlfriend enjoying herself on the dance floor. Shot in União Fraterna dance hall – a social club founded in 1925 in the Agua Branca neighbourhood in Lapa, which has historically promoted dance amongst people of retirement age – the ballroom seems in a way the film's main subject, with its checked wooden floor, colourful characters, live music and variety of popular rhythms, from samba to forró and tango. ➾ ***Santiago Oyarzabal and Michael Pigott***

Photo © Google maps

Directed by Laís Bodanzky

Scene description: The night is young in the ballroom

Timecode for scene: 0:09:35 – 0:14:00

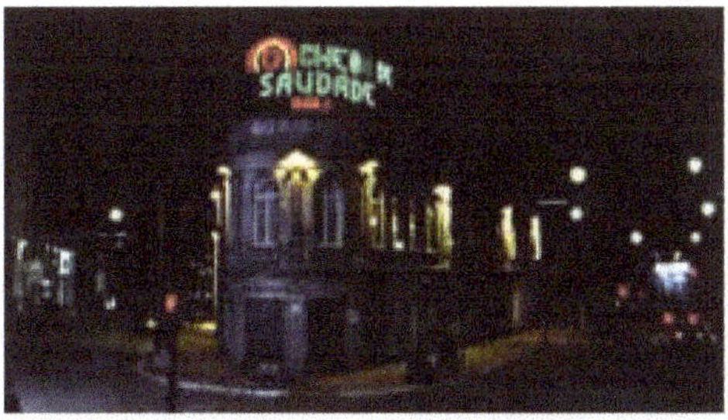
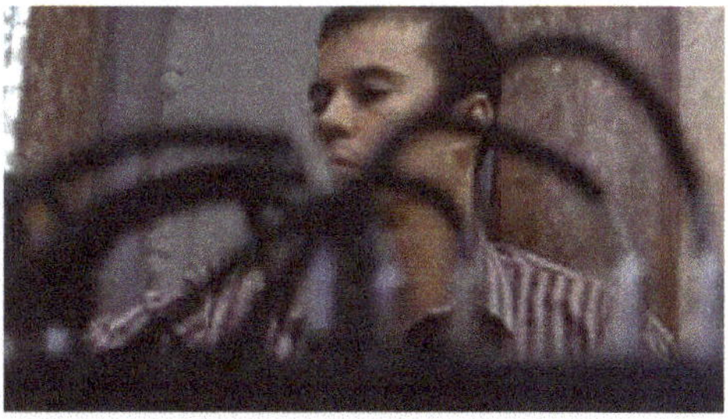
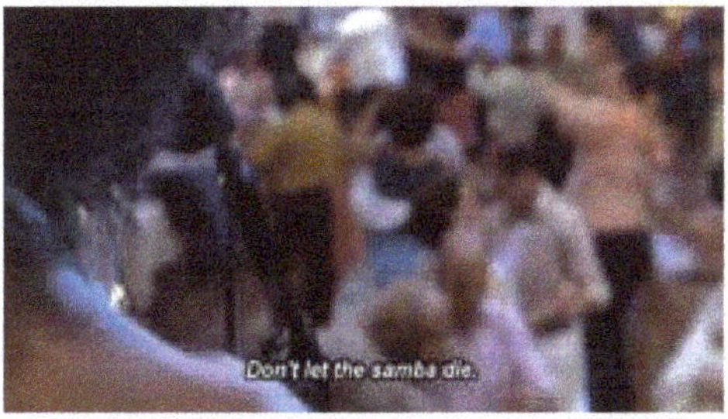

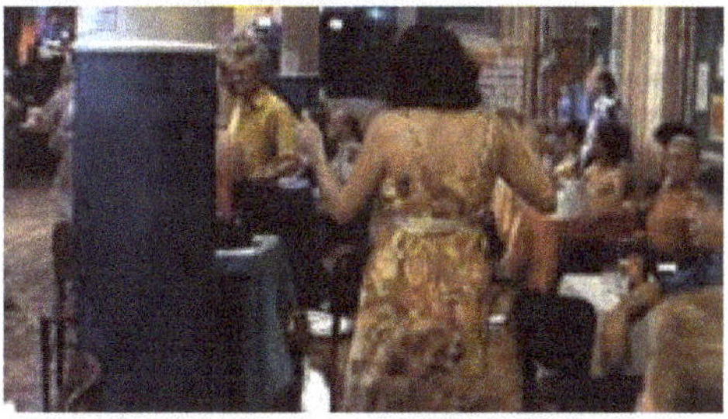
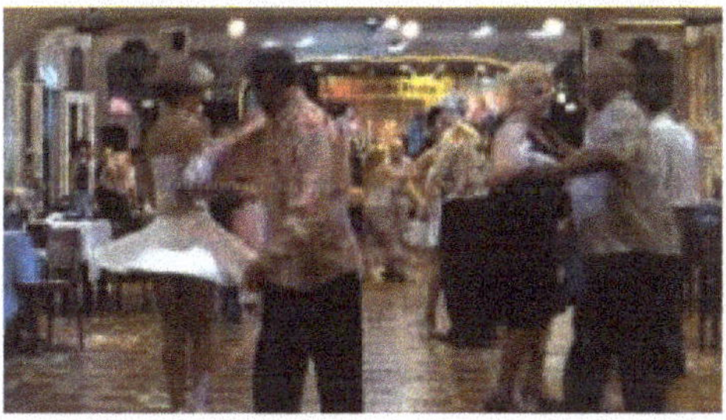
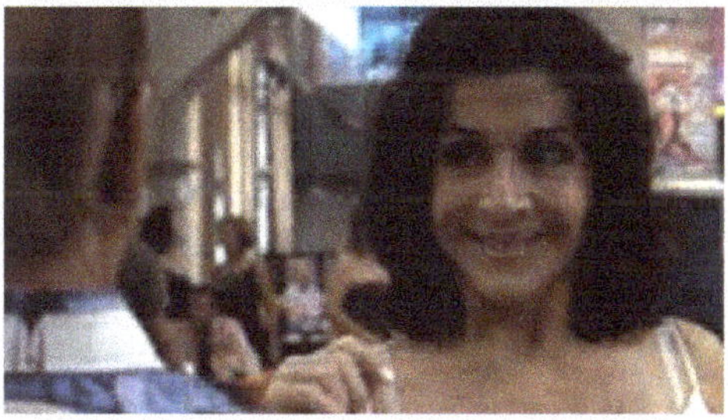

A VIA LÁCTEA (2007)

LOCATION *Santa Efigênia Bridge, São Paulo city centre*

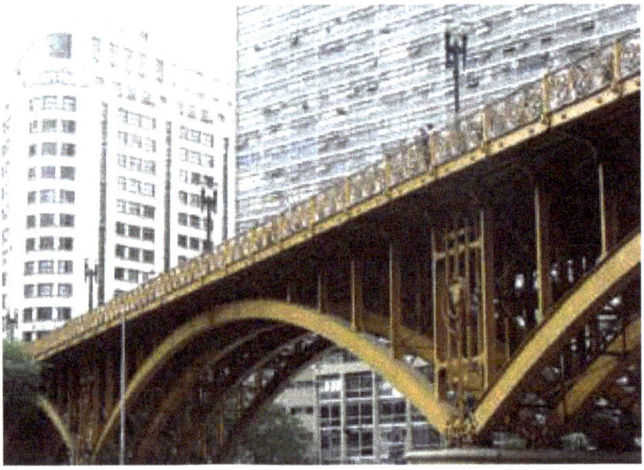

SANTA EFIGÊNIA BRIDGE was built as a showcase for São Paulo's belle époque, when the city's social and economic life was dominated by Europe. Appropriately, the bridge was designed, transported and constructed under European supervision. As the locus of economic activity moved towards Avenida Paulista, the city centre fell into decay and the bridge was turned into a pedestrian route. This is how it features in *A Via Láctea*. The bridge sequence is in marked contrast to the rest of the film, which focuses on the collapsing relationship between Heitor and Julia. In flashback, it shows a carefree Julia appearing to take as much pleasure from the anticipation of meeting her lover (alluded to by insertions of images of his favourite books) as she does from watching the cityscape below. The Godard influence is unmistakable: the handheld camera following Julia recalls Jean Seberg wandering the Paris of *À bout de souffle/Breathless* (1960), while the interjection of book covers and lettering has been a constant feature in Godard's cinema. Indeed, true to his playful rejection of classical realism, the bridge sequence confounds our spatial understanding by persistently breaking the rules of continuity editing, first showing Julia walking left to right along the bridge, then cutting to her seemingly walking in the opposite direction. This sense of pleasurable disorientation, reflecting Julia's state of mind, builds up to a climax when she starts running to the place where she knows she will find him: the French bookshop. Appropriately enough, the bridge has carried her toward her own belle époque. **→ *Tatiana Signorelli Heise***

Directed by Lina Chamie
Scene description: Julia crosses a bridge, reminiscing
Timecode for scene: 14:25:01 – 17:15:08

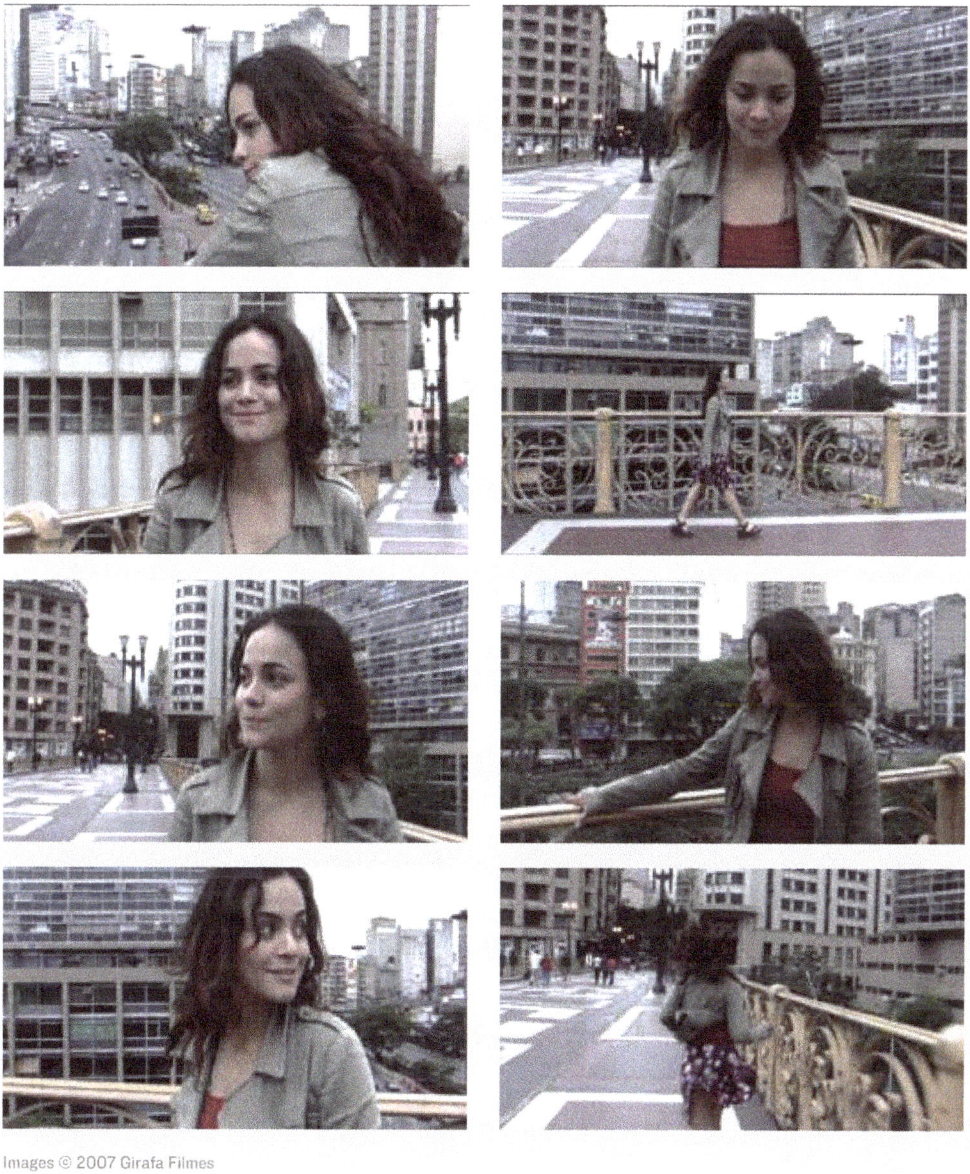

THE SIGN OF THE CITY/ O SIGNO DA CIDADE (2007)

LOCATION *Avenida Barão de Limeira*

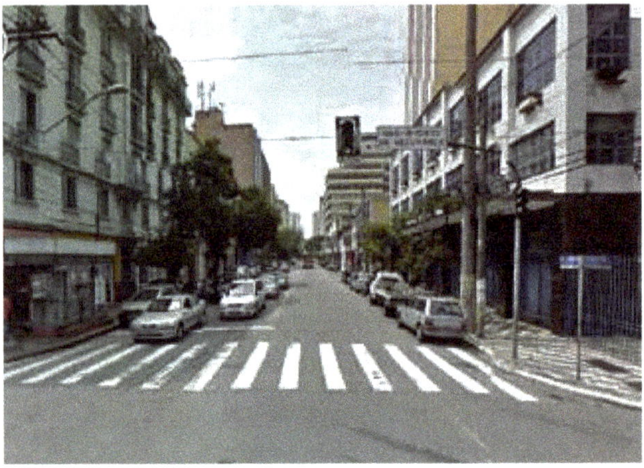

THE SIGN OF THE CITY begins by displaying the signs' formations through the junction of constellations in the sky, followed by a presentation of the city of São Paulo, Brazil. The city lights from buildings and cars are, then, compared to the stars which constitute various signs and astrological charts intertwined inside the metropolis. Teca, Lombardi's character, is an astrologer who provides spiritual home appointments, in addition to having her own radio show. People from the city live their own personal dramas in a plot which is characterized by its psychological focus. Issues such as abortion, sexuality, prostitution, homophobia, violence, depression, suicide and even the city's large number of inhabitants are present, to the point where feelings of emptiness and loneliness overtake each character, immersed in their own personal dramas. In this particular chosen sequence, the city is revealed by a travelling camera. This camera movement denotes Teca's journey through the abandoned historic buildings of São Paulo in the search for Júlia, to convince her to give up on her plan to have an abortion. The graffitied and worn walls subjectively allude to Júlia's and other characters' loneliness. The subsequent shots present the great amount of cars and people in this widely populated metropolis, where the inhabitants feel alone. The relationship developed between the characters and São Paulo, meaning its spaces, dangers and difficulties, unfolds in encounters and disencounters, and functions through the dynamics of the city which, sometimes, operates just like the stars, interfering in the fate of others. ➻***Murilo Gabriel Berardo Bueno, Rafael Mendonça Lisita Pinto and Maria Luiza Martins de Mendonça***

Photo © Google maps

Directed by Carlos Alberto Riccelli
Scene description: Teca walks in the historical centre of São Paulo to help a woman who has performed an illegal abortion
Timecode for scene: 0:34:34 – 0:15:50

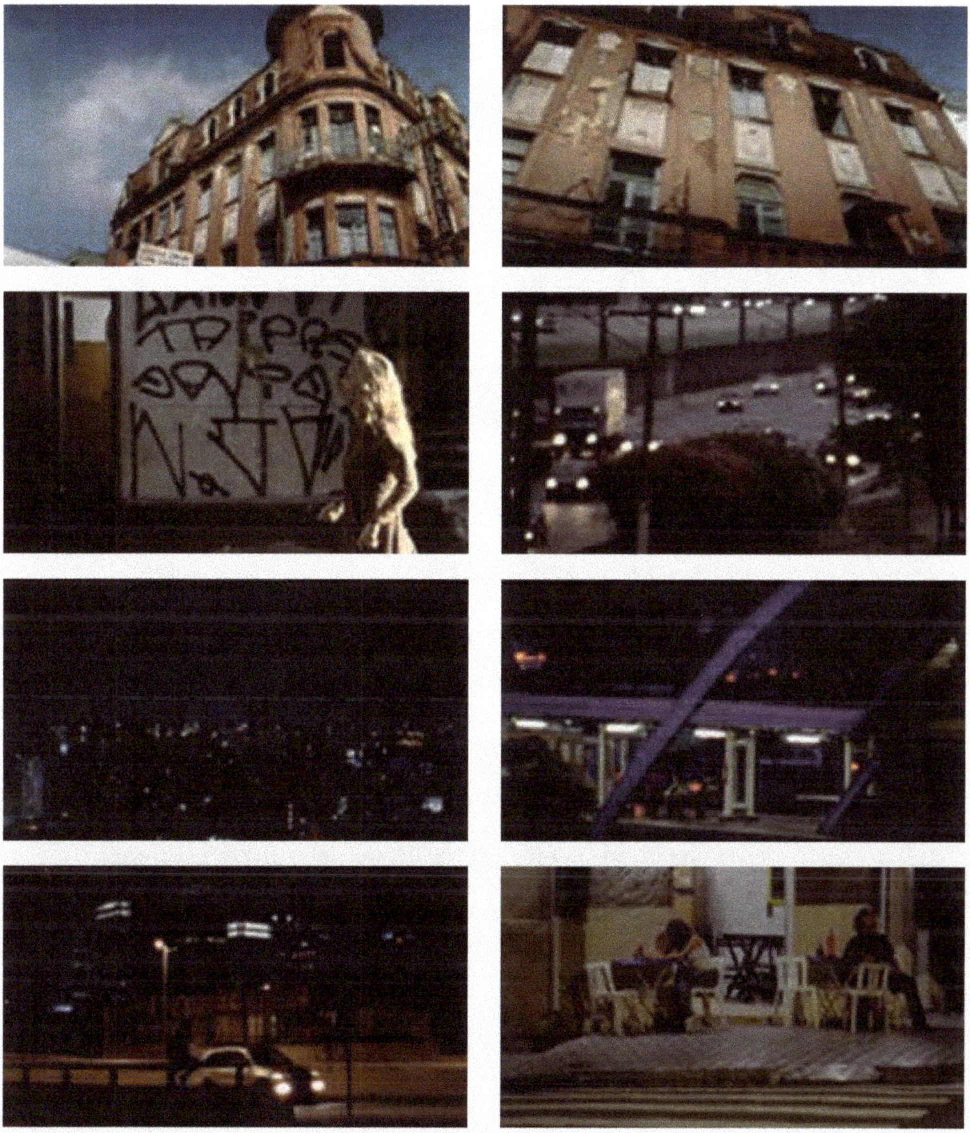

ALICE'S HOUSE/A CASA DE ALICE (2007)

LOCATION *Rua Barão de Itapetininga*

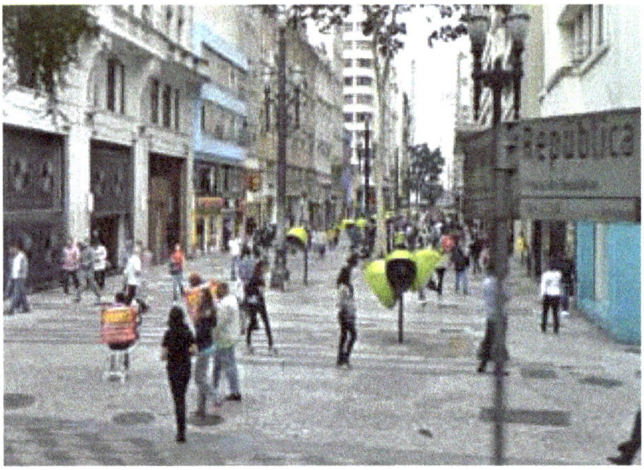

AT THE CENTRE OF THE handful of spaces that serve as the synecdoche for family life in São Paulo is *Alice's House*, where Alice (Carla Ribas), mother of three post-adolescent boys, finds herself emotionally conflicted within the male-dominated universe in which she exists. In order to compensate for the meagre contributions of her unfaithful taxi-driving husband, Lindomar (Zécarlos Machado), Alice paints nails at a beauty salon and contemplates the world that buzzes outside. Only superficially does director Chico Teixeira walk us through the streets of this city and, instead, only by means of close-ups of Alicia's face and POV shots do we get a feel for an urban centre that breathes on the other side of the glass. While the screenshots selected here display the blatant dissolution of Alicia's apartment after she abandons it for her fickle lover and after the grandmother, Dona Jacira Gomes (played by Berta Zemel), is coerced into the nursing home by Lindomar (Jacira, incidentally, is the true owner of the house), the viewer is then invited to honour the literal and figurative sustenance that these two women had provided for their shamefully dependent male counterparts. By enclosing each moment that occurs outside of the apartment within the glass-bound spaces of the salon, city buses and taxis (all of which are areas simultaneously public and private), our sense of the megalopolis is limited by these windows yet enhanced by the perspective of Alicia as she reflects on her private life while surrounded by fellow commuters of this city. ➾***Kyle Black***

Directed by Chico Teixeira
Scene description: Various moments from the film
Timecode for scene: : 0:0:12 – 0:0:56; 1:27:02 – 1:28:01; shots from bus: 0:9:57; 0:50:45; from taxi: 1:02:35; in salon: 1:12:53

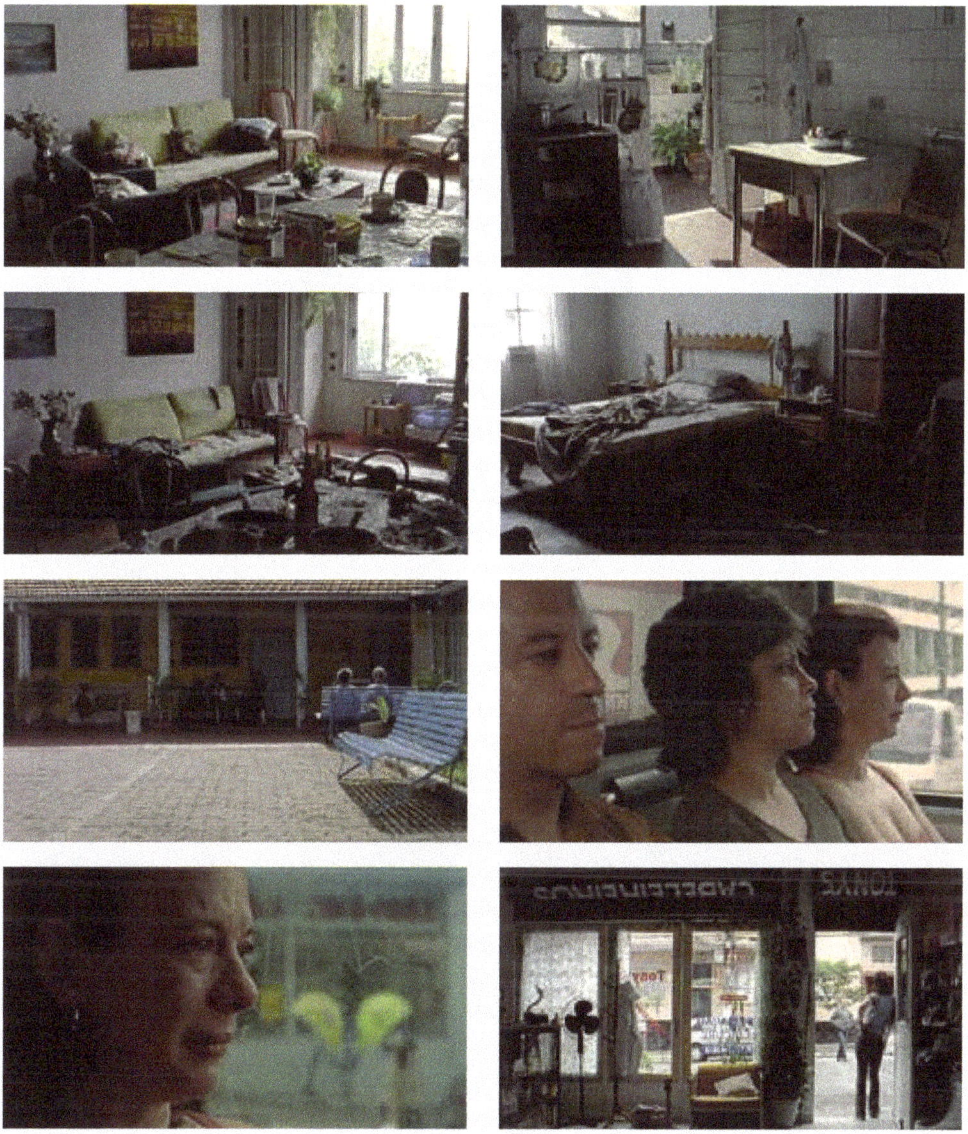

Images © 2007 Superfilmes

BLINDNESS (2008)

LOCATION

City centre, Minhocão (Elevado Presidente Costa e Silva)

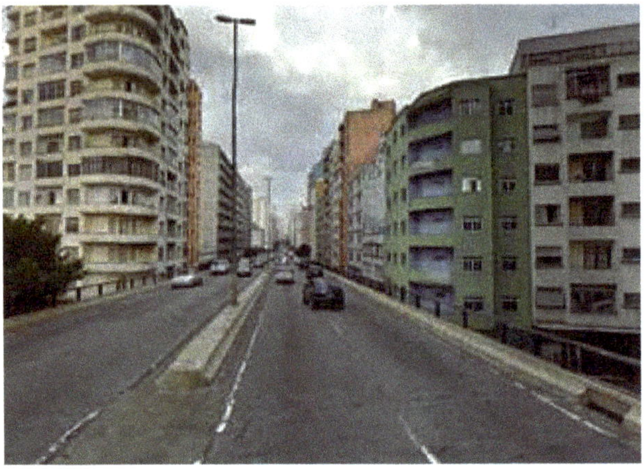

BLINDNESS is based on José Saramago's homonymous novel (1995), in which lack of sight is an allegory for social consciousness. By going blind, a society is thrown into the very condition it has always been living in, only that its blindness now becomes literal. The subsequent fall into complete turmoil offers the chance to gain insight into human behaviour and to recover essential values. Whilst the novel is set in a rather nonspecific city during the 1930s and 1940s, the film designs a contemporary globalized megalopolis in which people from all over the world are fighting individually for their material security. This nameless city is assembled by means of sequences shot in the distinct socio-economic spaces of the co-production partners Brazil, Japan, Canada and Uruguay. Even though filmed in São Paulo, Toronto and Montevideo, the diverse cities are fitted together into one high-tech town since the director mainly shot what is now common to all major cities around the globe: heavy traffic, five star hotels, top of the line clinics, apartments filled with the latest designer furniture, and so on. The scenes set in São Paulo are therefore not easily differentiated. Whereas this strategy actually ignores social differences brutally apparent in São Paulo's landscape, there is one sequence that indicates her urban chaos. Fernando Meirelles chose one of its oddest constructions, the Minhocão, an elevated highway that cuts right through apartment blocks close to the city centre, to stage his citation of Pieter Breughel's painting *The Blind Leading the Blind* (1568). Quite appropriately it is the place where the only character whose sight remains, the wife of the optometrist, conducts her surrogate family through the devastated city. ***Carolin Overhoff Ferreira***

Photo © Google maps

Directed by Fernando Meirelles
Scene description: The blind are guided by the Doctor's wife
Timecode for scene: 1:22:00 – 1:25:47

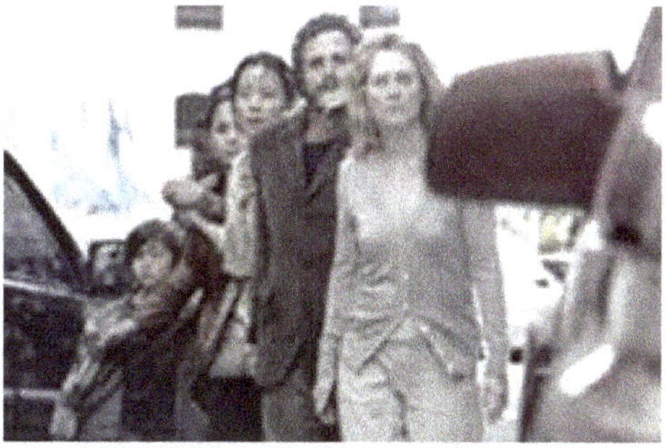

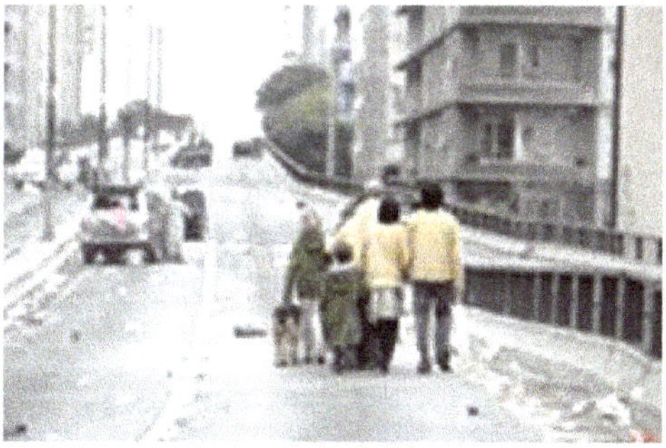

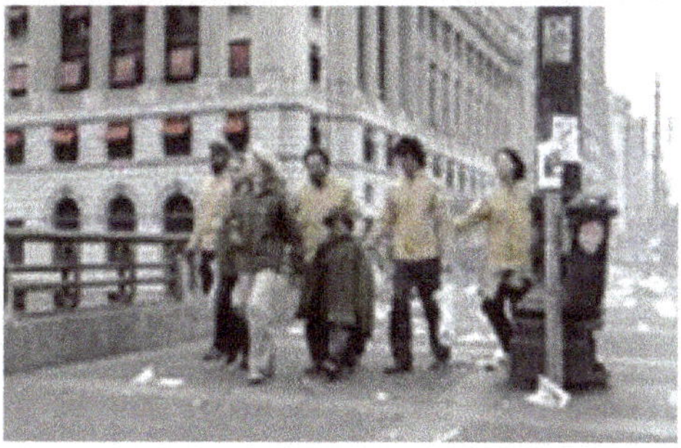

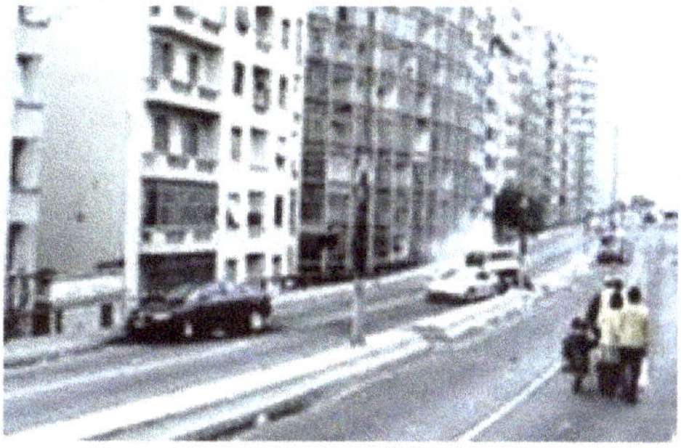

EMBODIMENT OF EVIL/ ENCARNAÇÃO DO DEMÔNIO (2008)

LOCATION *Playcenter amusement park, Rua José Gomes Falcão, 20 Barra Funda*

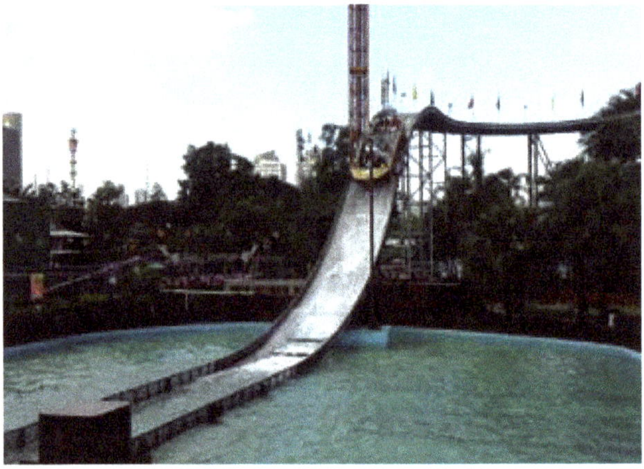

NO FILM-MAKER IN THE HISTORY of São Paulo is as infamous as José Mojica Marins. *Embodiment of Evil* concludes the trilogy of grotesque horror movies devoted to his on-screen alter ego, Coffin Joe (Zé do Caixão), a sadistic undertaker obsessed with ensuring the future of his bloodline by siring a son with a 'superior' woman. In the film's climax, Joe is pursued to São Paulo's famous Playcenter amusement park by police captain Oswaldo Pontes (Adriano Stuart) and the vengeful monk Father Eugênio (Milhem Cortaz), whose father Joe murdered. It is after dark, the park is closed, and the long shadows cast by its few lights create an eerie atmosphere. Joe draws Pontes into the House of Horrors and kills him, but is immediately confronted by Father Eugênio. They fight and Eugênio drives the bladed end of his long metal crucifix into Joe's heart. As Eugênio leaves, one of Joe's acolytes, a young woman named Elena (Nara Sakarê), arrives, opens Joe's trousers and mounts him: as Joe dies, he conceives a child with her. It is fitting that such a profane and iconoclastic character makes his final appearance defiling such a benign, family-friendly place as Playcenter, which was for decades one of the most popular attractions in São Paulo. In 2012, its roller coasters were sold ahead of a proposed re-launch as a more child-centric park. Perhaps, if there is a sequel to *Embodiment of Evil*, we will see the son of Coffin Joe playing there before beginning his own criminal campaign. ➻ ***Scott Jordan Harris***

Directed by José Mojica Marins
Scene description: The Death of Coffin Joe
Timecode for scene: 1:16:43 – 1:25:43

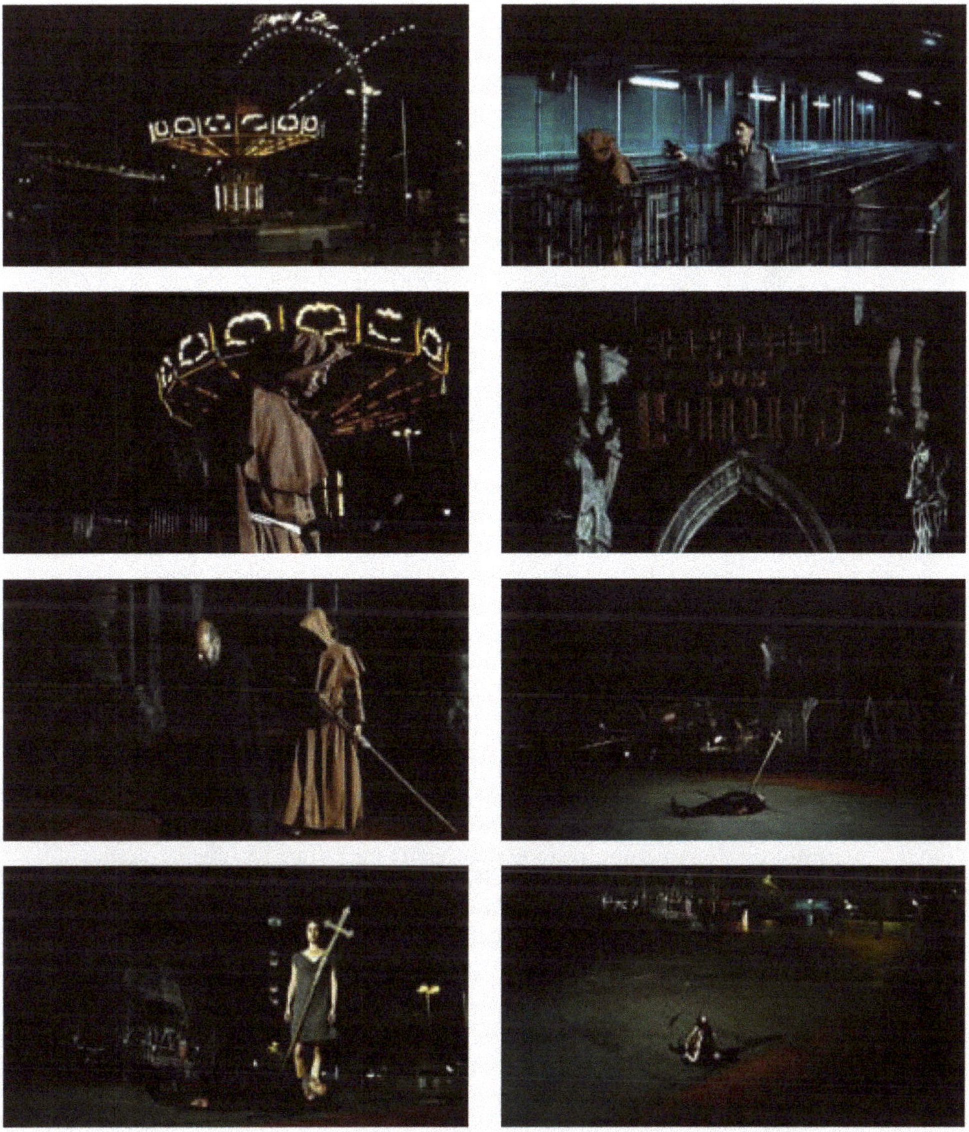

Images © 2008 Gullane Filmes, Olhos de Cão Produções Cinematográficas

LINHA DE PASSE (2008)

LOCATION *Morumbi Stadium, Cidade Líder (East São Paulo), Rodovia Presidente Dutra*

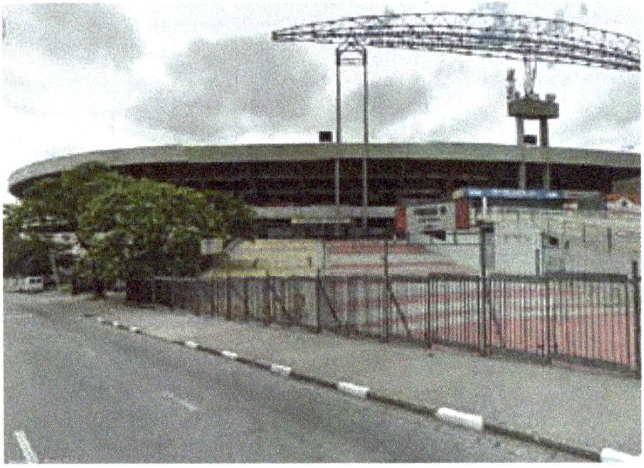

FOUR BROTHERS AND THEIR single mother from the São Paulo periphery try to dribble past the difficulties of life for which they have been destined by their social background. Based on true stories, the family's mother, Cleusa, earns a living as a maid but loses her job because she is pregnant again. Dênis is one of the thousands of motorbike couriers that bypass daily the unbearable traffic on the major highways such as the Rodovia Presidente Dutra. Motorbikes have also become a major means to assault cars and Dênis is always close to getting associated with crime. The oldest brother, Dinho, then again, works at a gas station in their poor neighbourhood in the east part of the city, Cidade Líder, whose only luxury is a panoramic view of São Paulo's chaotic skyline. He tries to stay out of trouble by getting engaged in an Evangelic church, but is also not completely successful. Dario is the hope of the family because social ascension is still mainly related to a career in either show business or sports and he desires to become a soccer player in a junior team. In fact, the almost religious passion for soccer is a key feature in the film and is established at its opening. The introduction of the male characters is juxtaposed with their mother watching a major match between two famous clubs in the Morumbi Stadium: Corinthians, which has Brazil's greatest fan community, and São Paulo. The youngest son, Reginaldo still goes to school but his story also takes us to the labyrinthine highway system since he wants to find his unknown father. Even though this is true for many films, São Paulo is certainly the sixth character in this touching drama about a family that manages to keep the ball in the air without going under. ➺ ***Carolin Overhoff Ferreira***

Photo © Google maps

Directed by Walter Salles
Scene description: Title sequence
Timecode for scene: 0:00:00 to 0:02:20

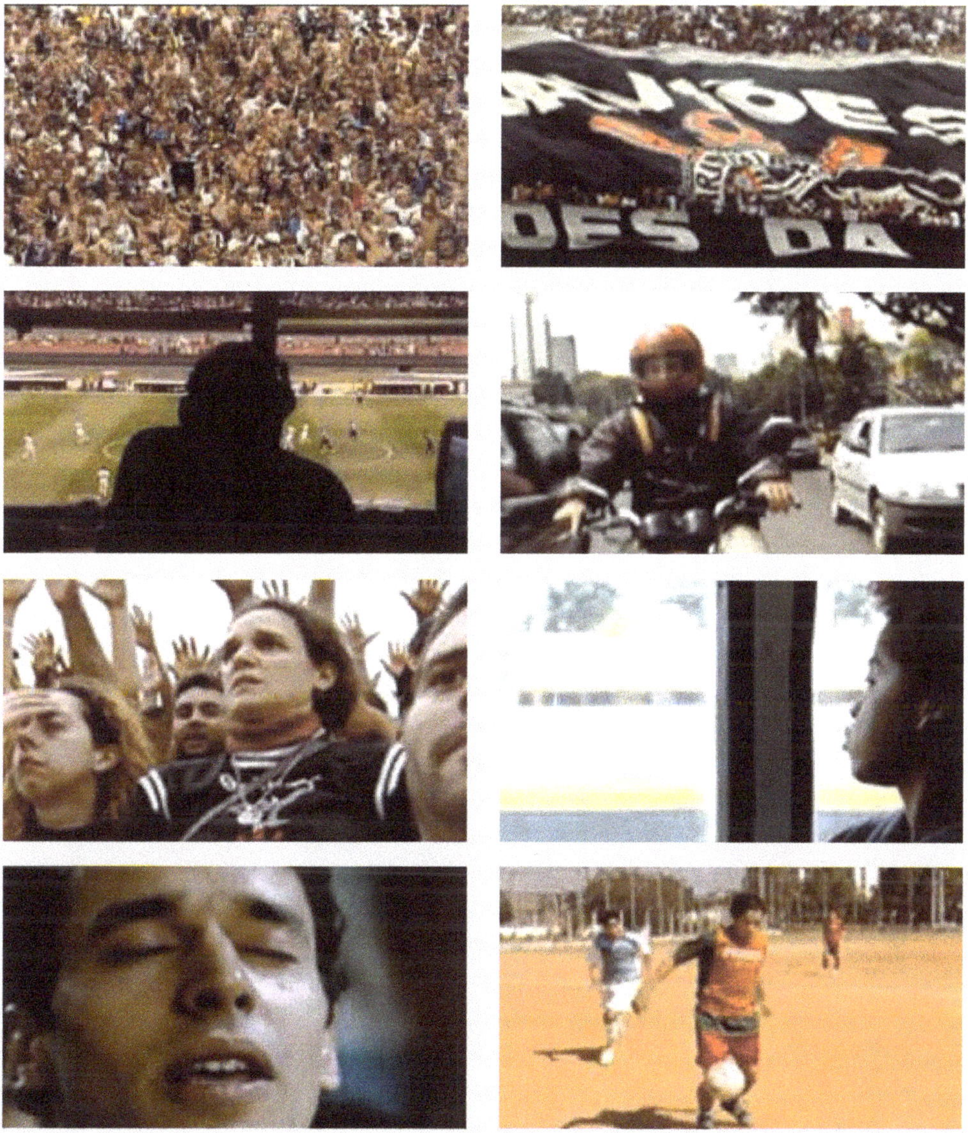

SPOTLIGHT

TRANSNATIONAL MINHOCÃO

The Emblematic Highway

Text by NATÁLIA PINAZZA

ELEVADO PRESIDENTE COSTA E SILVA is an elevated highway also known as 'Minhocão', which translates as 'Big Worm' given its winding shape. It has now become a landmark of the late-capitalist world, thereby transcending its status of an icon solely of São Paulo city. Partly because films that are not entirely set in São Paulo, but also in other cities across the globe such as the international co-productions *Terra estrangeira/Foreign Land* (Daniela Thomas and Walter Salles, 1996), *Blindness* (Fernando Meirelles, 2008), and Kátia Lund's short-film *Bilu and João*, part of the anthology film *All the Invisible Children* (2005), have transformed the Minhocão into a locus where both local and global concerns are negotiated. In the context of the internationalization of the culture industries, which are marked by an increase in cross-border film-making and international film co-production, recent scholarship on 'transnational cinema' explores issues of production, distribution and reception as well as the very use of the constantly problematized term 'transnational'. In light of this ongoing debate on transnational cinema, this essay will address the following questions: first, does the recurrence of Minhocão in films set in São Paulo suggest that the place has acquired a particular allegorical meaning? Unlike the two most recurrent settings in Brazilian cinema, the sertão (the backlands) in the northeast, or the favelas in Rio de Janeiro, Minhocão appears to lack a distinctive and self-evident local colour. Within this understanding, a second question can be raised: is it precisely this aspect of Minhocão that allows film-makers of transnational films to turn this iconic highway into a 'non-place' (Marc Augé, 1992), as is the case with Blindness, in which the location is not even established within the film?. This second question leads to a third and final one: whilst such a refusal to name the metropolis works when aimed at a more diverse and dispersed audience, how does it affect localist readings in which the spectator recognizes Minhocão?

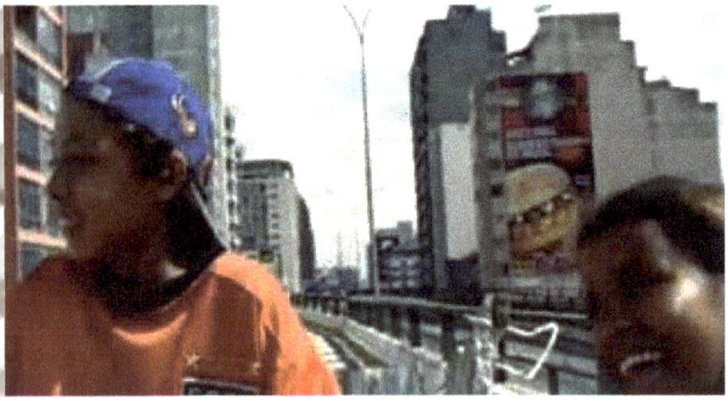

Foreign Land, a co-production between Brazil and Portugal, was made when Brazilian cinema was emerging from years of stagnation in film production, and is more rooted in national concerns than the other films herewith mentioned. The socio-historical background of *Foreign Land* is the economic crisis in the early 1990s that triggered the emigration of the Brazilian middle-class to Europe and, as represented in the film, a consequent fragmentation or even loss of national identity. In this highly allegorical film, which interweaves sequences set in Lisbon and São Paulo, Minhocão functions as a signifier of São Paulo, the protagonist's hometown. The city is introduced by striking images taken during the night and early morning, showing the Minhocão and its billboards whilst the protagonist, off-screen, reads out a quote from Goethe's *Faust*

Opposite *All the Invisible Children* (2005)
Below *Blindness* (2008)

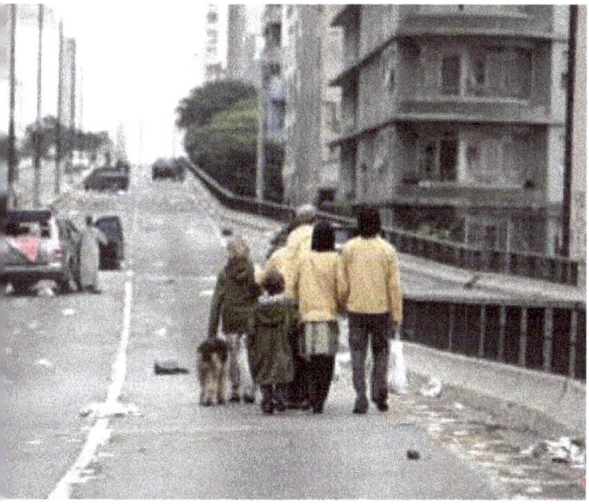

(1808). All the lights in the buildings by Minhocão are out except for one, and so we assume that the person we hear off-screen is there. The spectator only recognizes the connection between text and image in another sequence when the protagonist appears reading in his room and we see Minhocão through the window. *Foreign Land*'s representation of Minhocão and its memorable billboards allow localist readings to associate it immediately with the early/mid 1990s, which emphasizes the allegorical meaning that this viaduct can acquire. In the film, the highway is the setting of a young Paulistano's experiences of a shared national trauma, that is the severe economic measures in 1991, announced on television with actual footage of the speech by the then minister of economy, Zélia Cardoso de Mello. Moreover, scenes set in Lisbon are juxtaposed with scenes set in São Paulo, which is often introduced by the viaduct as if it encapsulated the city. Nonetheless, at the same time that Minhocão can stand for the city and for that specific time in Brazilian history like in *Foreign Land*, its billboards written in English and its urban surroundings also testify to how the highway shares some of the homogenizing tendencies of globalisation.

This 'non-place' characteristic of Minhocão makes it a viable place for the classic sequence from *Blindness* where characters from a variety of nationalities walk closely together without being situated in a specific context. In *Blindness*, no issue that is specifically related to the Brazilian context is addressed and São Paulo remains an unknown metropolis. Of course, a more localist reading of the film would focus on the fact that São Paulo is the hometown of Fernando Meirelles, the director, and it is based on a book by José Saramago, originally written in Portuguese, the director´s mother tongue. *All the Invisible Children*, on the other hand, provides a different approach to the Minhocão. In charting stories of street kids across the globe (Serbia and Montenegro, the United States, Brazil, the United Kingdom, Italy, China and an unspecified country in Africa), *All the Invisible Children* treats the marginalization of children as a concern that transcends the national and even the notion that such problems pertain exclusively to the Third World, a term highly problematic in the context of 'dispersed hegemonies' (Appadurai 1990), which also testifies to Brazil's changing positioning in the global system.

Minhocão is the location of a short yet remarkable sequence where the two child protagonists, Bilu and João, upon having got their own cart, push it through the highway. The representation of these kids is informed by local colour such as samba on the soundtrack, the boy's São Paulo football jersey – he is often referred to as 'São Paulino' (someone who supports the São Paulo football team) – the Formula One video game, which allows him to pretend to be the Paulistano Ayrton Senna, and, most relevant here, the Minhocão that is a landmark in São Paulo. At the same time that this iconic location can be related to such localist reference points, these transnational films show that this elevated highway could be in any urban setting in the world, which is perhaps the main characteristic that attracts directors who wish to engage with global issues to use Minhocão as a location. Considered an architectural mistake by many and transformed into a public leisure space on weekends, Minhocão emerges as a locus where national and transnational boundaries are blurred and local and global issues are addressed simultaneously. To conclude, Minhocão is the setting for stories that communicate to global audiences, at the same time as it allows readings which emerge from its local situation. ⁜

Considered an architectural mistake by many and transformed into a public leisure space on weekends, Minhocão emerges as a locus where national and transnational boundaries are blurred and local and global issues are addressed simultaneously.

N

LOCATIONS MAP

SÃO PAULO

maps are only to be taken as approximates

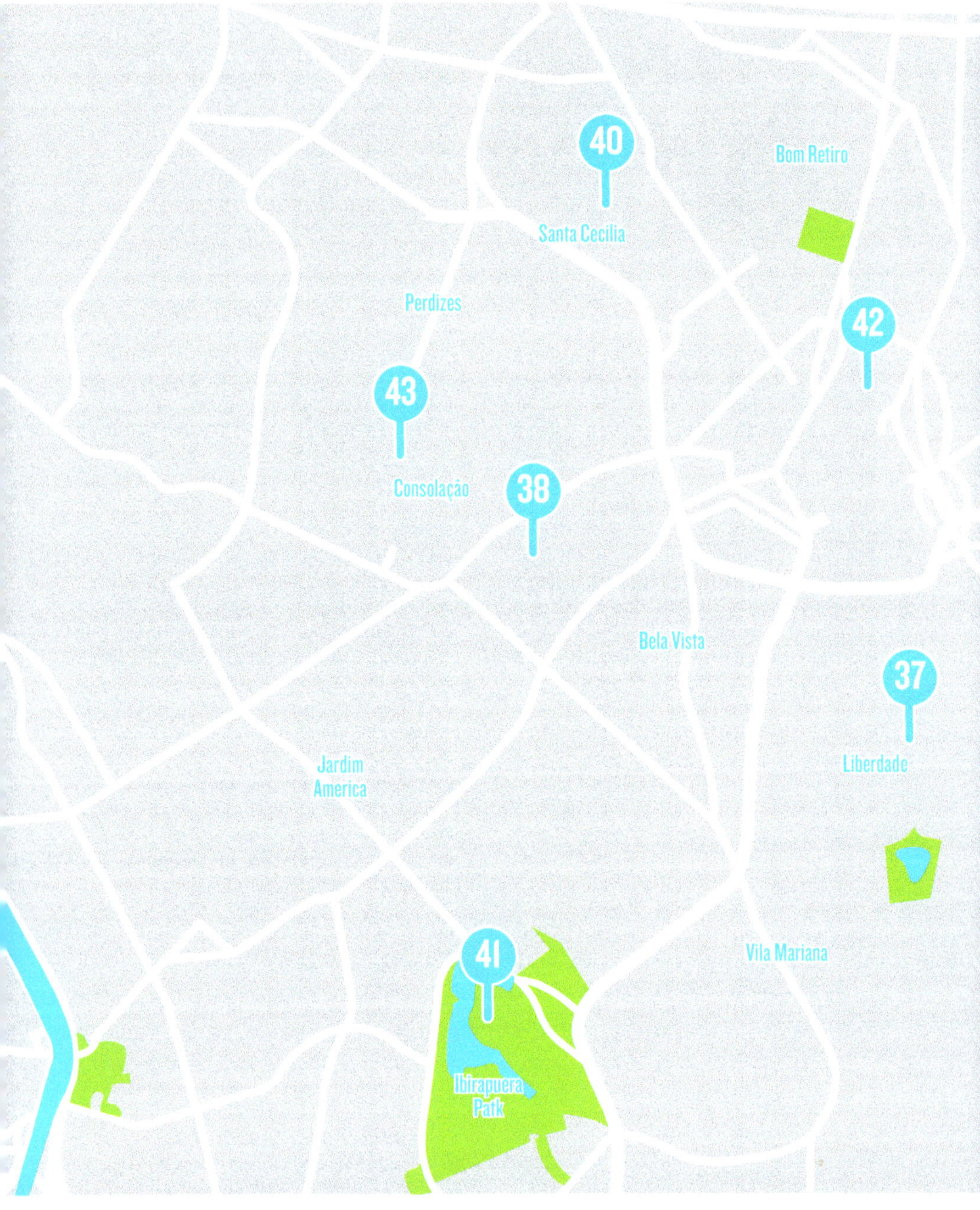

SÃO PAULO LOCATIONS
SCENES 37-43

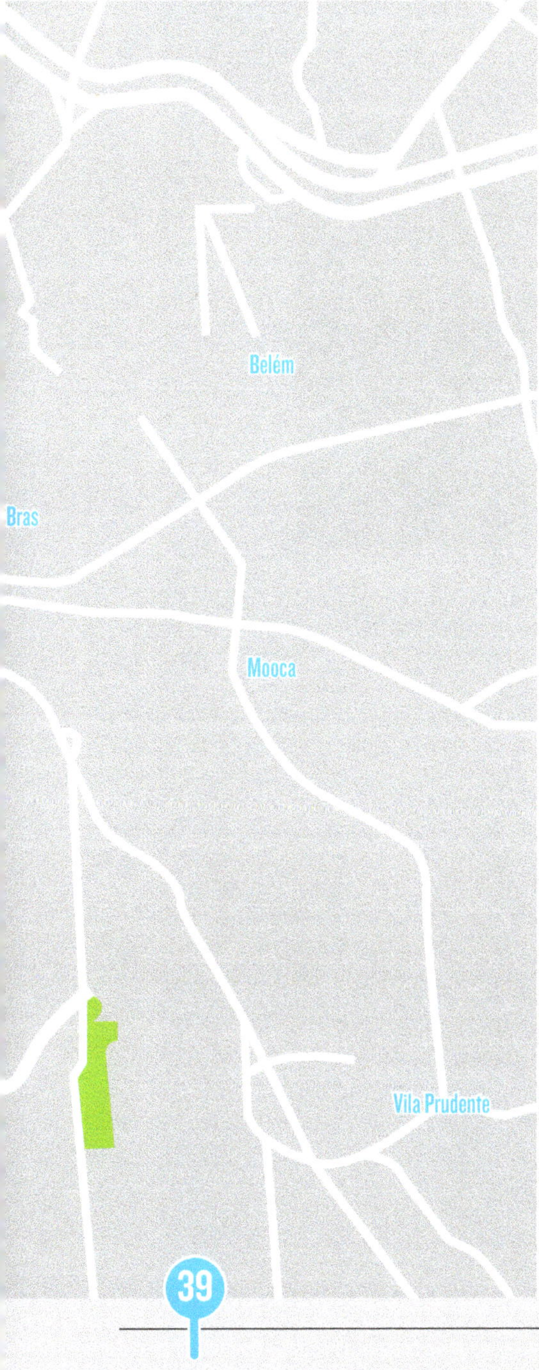

PLASTIC CITY/DANGKOU (2008)

LOCATION *Liberdade District*

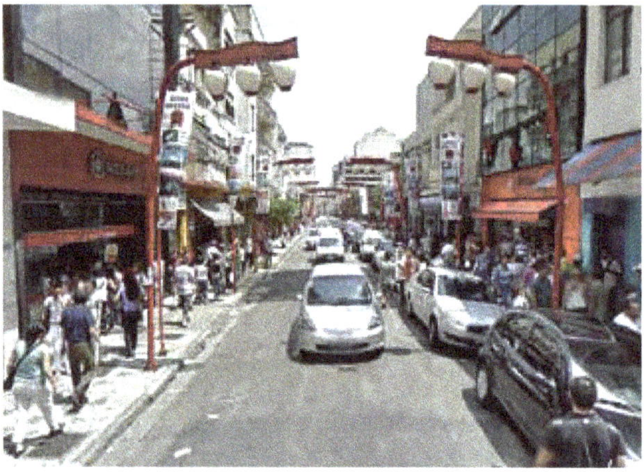

PLASTIC CITY IS A FILM which defies characterization. A fusion of different genres drawing on Chinese, Japanese and Brazilian references, it is the third feature by director and cinematographer Yu Lik-wai, long-time collaborator and partner of Jia Zhang-ke. It tells the story of a Chinese businessman named Yuda and his adopted son Kirin, who together control the smuggling of counterfeit goods in the district of Liberdade, in the centre of São Paulo. Liberdade is originally São Paulo's Japanese district, a distinguishing feature of the city which never had a Chinatown and that in turn has the largest Japanese population outside Japan. In the past ten years, however, the area has become the home of large numbers of Chinese immigrants, who live and work side-by-side with the old Brazilian-Japanese population. In the film's first sequence, Kirin stands open-armed on top of a building and throws money to a group of people below, saying in dubbed Portuguese 'the goods may be pirated, but the money is real'. It is possible to see in these and the following shots the typical Japanese street lights which adorn the streets of Liberdade. The film also features other recognizable locations such as Rua Augusta and its many brothels, Ibirapuera Park and the famous Copan building, but the city of São Paulo is depicted without a trace of realism, and seems more like a fantasy-metropolis where absurd events have a knack of coming true. ➾***Cecília Mello***

Directed by Yu Lik-wai

Scene description: 'The goods may be pirated, but the money is real'

Timecode for scene: 0:02:50 – 0:03:55

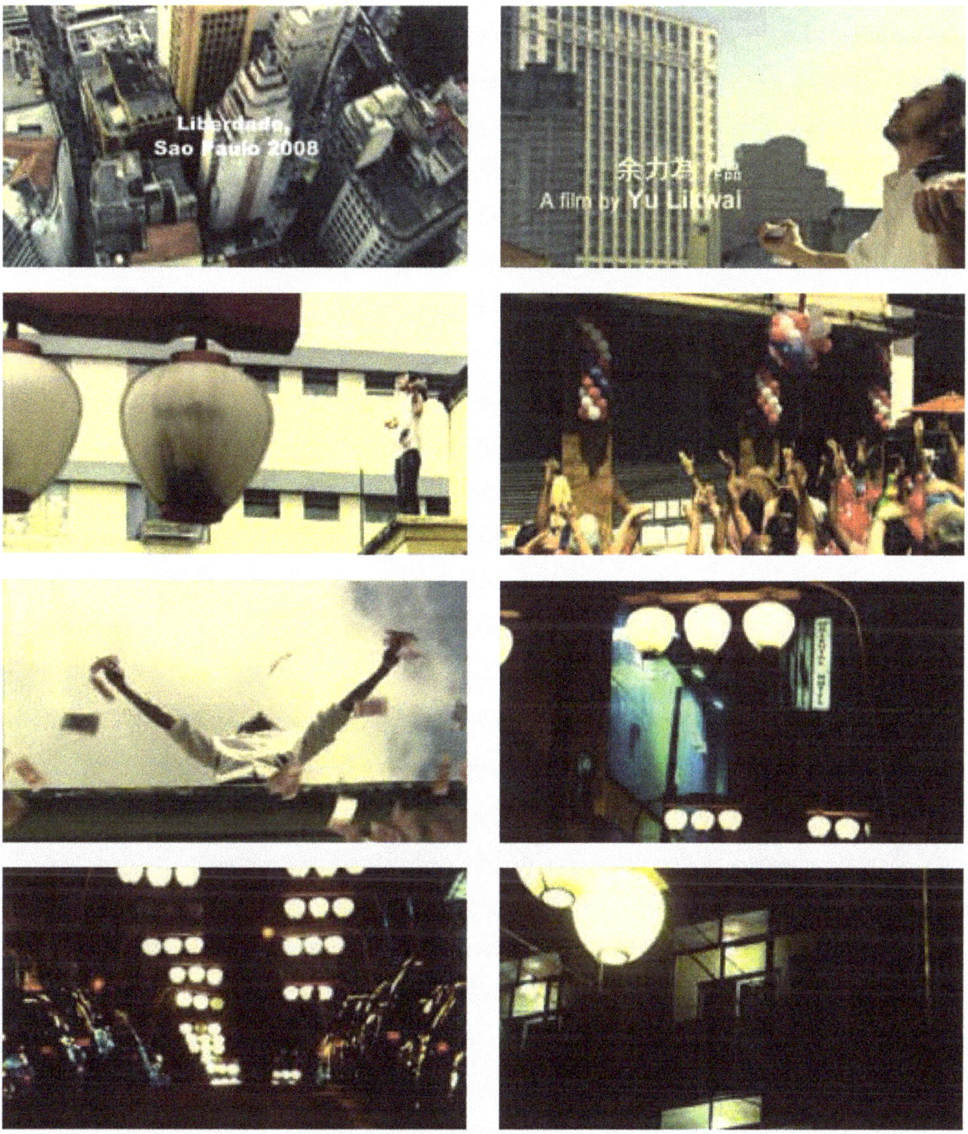

IF NOTHING ELSE WORKS OUT/ SE NADA MAIS DER CERTO (2008)

LOCATION *Baixa Rua Augusta, CEP 01305-000*

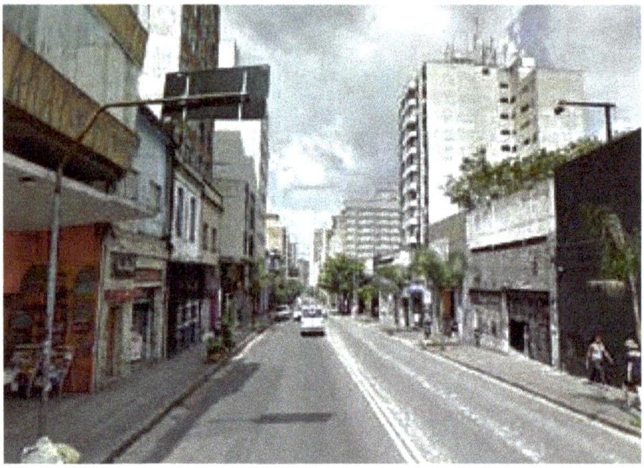

A YOUNG UNEMPLOYED JOURNALIST joins a lesbian drug dealer and a taxi driver in a robbery. Coming from diverse backgrounds, the trio builds a strong bond in a world of moral ambiguity where the border between law and crime is blurred. Refusing a cynical approach, director Belmonte is aware of the ambivalence of moral values in late capitalism and Baixa Rua Augusta is the perfect setting for the social criticism his film puts forward. A study in contrasts, Rua Augusta connects the city centre with luxury-district Jardins. It starts at the now revitalized Praça Roosevelt, a famous meeting point for artists and intellectuals. The region nearer the centre, called Baixa Augusta is well known for its marginal frequenters: drug dealers, prostitutes and transvestites share this space with young hipsters. Marcin and Angela wander through Rua Augusta, butch and femme, middle-class and blue collar, an odd combination that fits perfectly in the diverse *nocturnal fauna* of the street. A site of both luxury and marginality, chaos and order, Rua Augusta allegorizes a universe whose values are unstable, much like in *If Nothing Else Works Out*, but it is also a place where unsuspected bonds of affection can be created and new forms of life can be forged. Belmonte's film finds in Rua Augusta the perfect site for the characters (portrayed through close-ups and frantic camera work) who strive to survive in a world of selfishness and violence but who are still able to foster, in effect, traces of humanity. ➺ ***Ramayana Lira de Sousa***

Photo © Google maps

Directed by José Eduardo Belmonte

Scene description: Marcin meets Leo for the first time, after he saves her from being beaten up by Sybelle, the transvestite who is also a drug dealer

Timecode for scene: 0:10:00 – 0:16:00

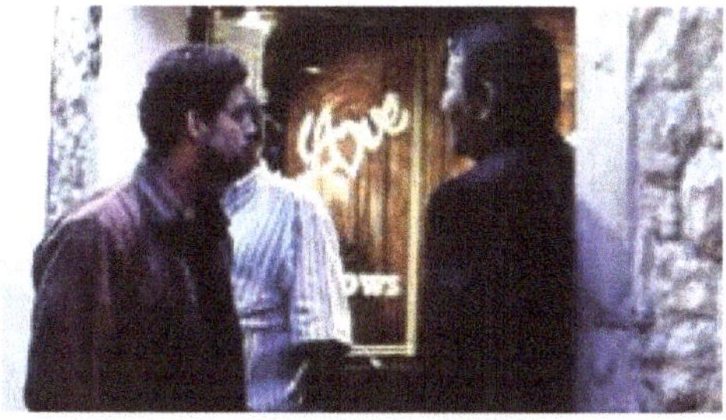

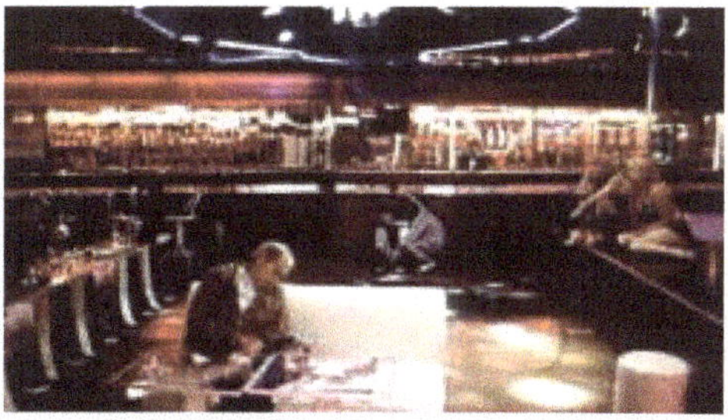

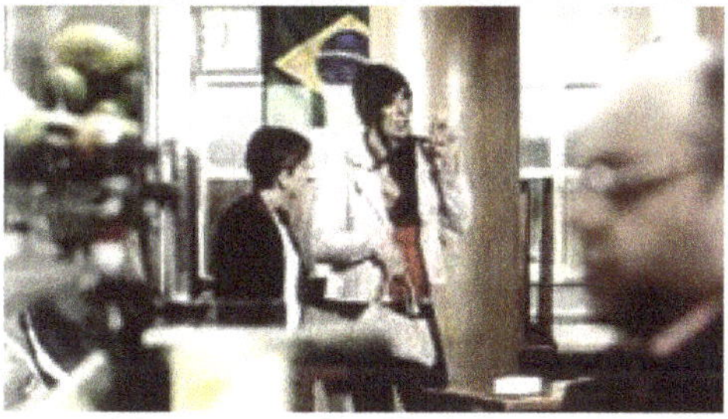

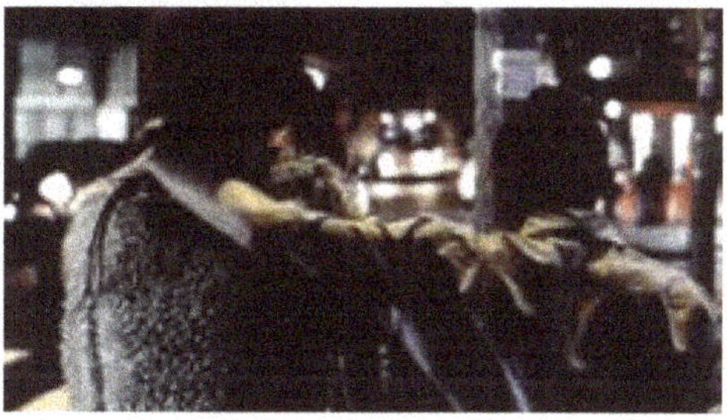

ROTA COMANDO (2009)

LOCATION *Região do Jabaquara, close to Rodovia dos Imigrantes*

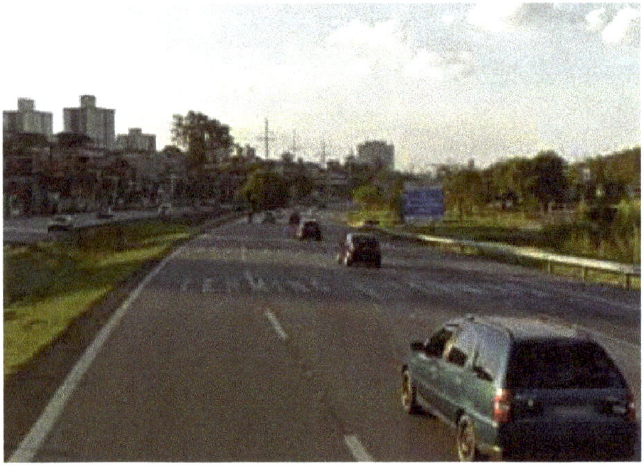

THIS LOW BUDGET FEATURE becomes much more enjoyable when one starts thinking it is not all plot holes and bad acting, but rather an accurate depiction of the fantastical reality that exists in the mind of a ROTA (Rondas Ostensivas Tobias de Aguiar) officer like the ex-captain whose autobiography inspired the screenplay. It is a world in which heroic family men sacrifice themselves in the conflict against truculent outlaws who cannot speak without cursing. Taking such Manichaeism into account, the movie gives a very good feeling of the complexity of organized crime in a big metropolis: most of the time it is impossible to understand what is actually going on. One thing that becomes clear though is that the core work of São Paulo's special police forces is to drive up and down the city's outskirts, stumbling upon suspicious vehicles and helpless victims. As random as this activity seems to be, it is depicted as crucial in the war against the drug empire. In this particular scene, if it weren't for ROTA's serendipitous watch, the security company's ability to track stolen cars using Google Earth would have made little difference to stop crime. These super agents must always be around to give chase to the thugs, taking every case of public–private partnership to a successful conclusion. ➾ ***Gabriel Menotti***

Photo © Google maps

Directed by Elias Júnior

Scene description: After a robbery, the victim asks the police for help

Timecode for scene: 1:27:04 – 1:30:28

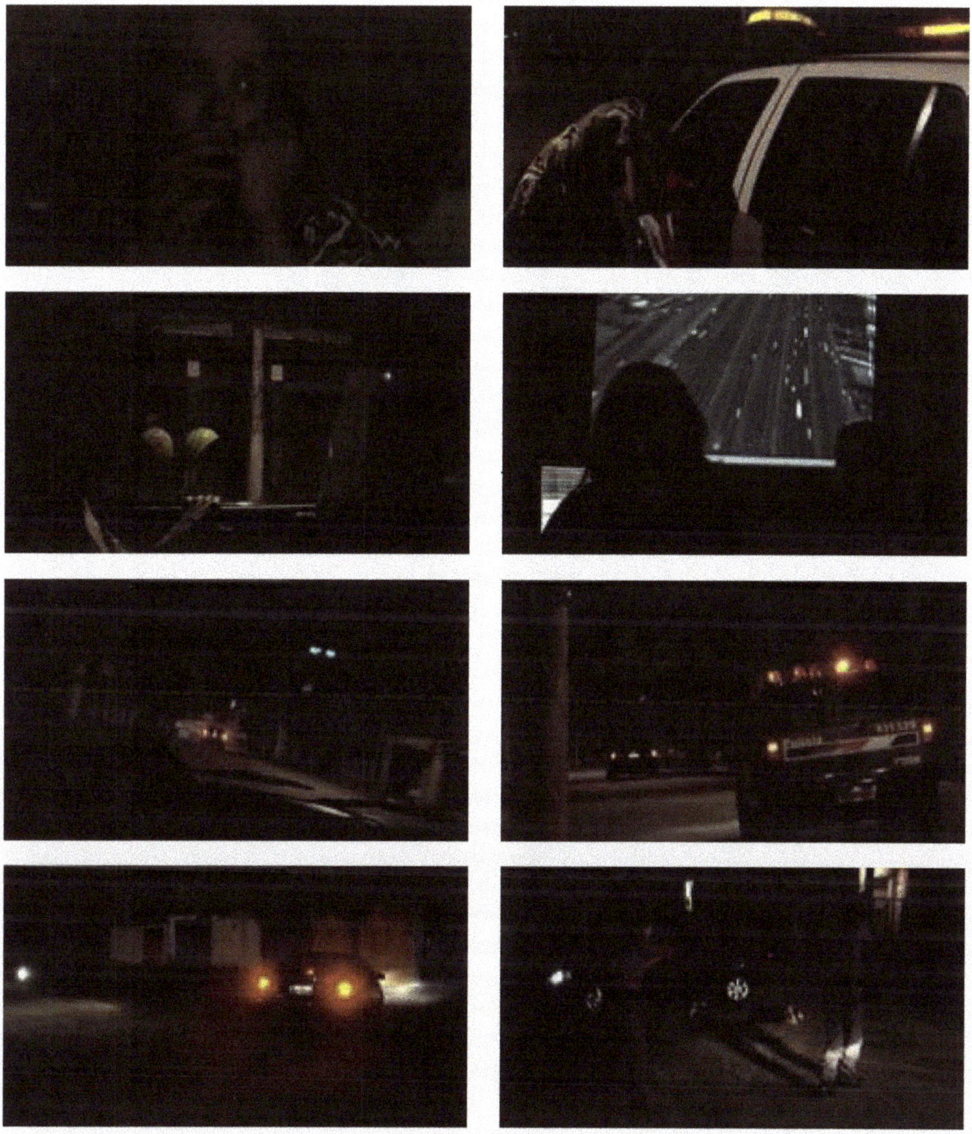

Images © 2009 HDV Studio

BOCA/BOCA DO LIXO (2010)

LOCATION

Aimorés street in Bom Retiro District (actual shooting location was in Rua Comércio, in Santos)

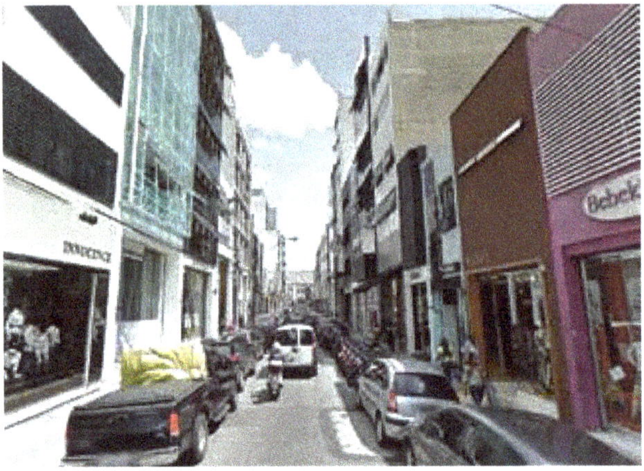

A FREE ADAPTATION of the autobiographical book that gangster, pimp and drug dealer Hiroito de Moraes Joanides (b.1936–d.1992) wrote in prison during the late 1960s (*Boca do Lixo*, 1977), Boca narrates Hiroito's (Daniel de Oliveira) rise and fall as the 'king' of the Boca do Lixo ('trash mouth'), the red light district in the Luz neighbourhood of downtown São Paulo. Without resorting to excessive bloodshed or psychologizing, Boca's intimate focus on Hiroito offers a powerful and stylized evocation of the period, with glossy, saturated colours and sparse dialogue in an action-filled narrative that gradually reveals aspects of the protagonist's personality. Along the way we get a rich and lurid portrayal of a São Paulo underworld of prostitution, strip clubs, drugs, guns and corrupted policemen in the 1950s and 1960s. In one of the film's early scenes we watch a teenage Hiroito (played by Guilherme Seta) visit a prostitute for the first time. His schoolfriend Osmar has taken him to Bom Retiro, and, as an older Hiroito narrates in voice-over, he enjoys the experience so much that he returns to the Aimorés and Itaboca streets whenever he has the necessary five cruzeiros. While the area is already astonishingly different to what it was like in its seedy heyday, contemporary attempts to rejuvenate the area include contentious re-urbanization projects (such as Nova Luz, or 'new light'). In order to recreate the Boca of the 1960s the film-makers used a street in the old town of nearby Santos, which retains the period look, indicated by the characteristic lamp posts, tramlines and cobbles.
→ *Santiago Oyarzabal and Michael Pigott*

Photo © Google maps

Directed by Flavio Frederico
Scene description: Hiroito discovers the red light district
Timecode for scene: 0:02:50 – 0:04:00

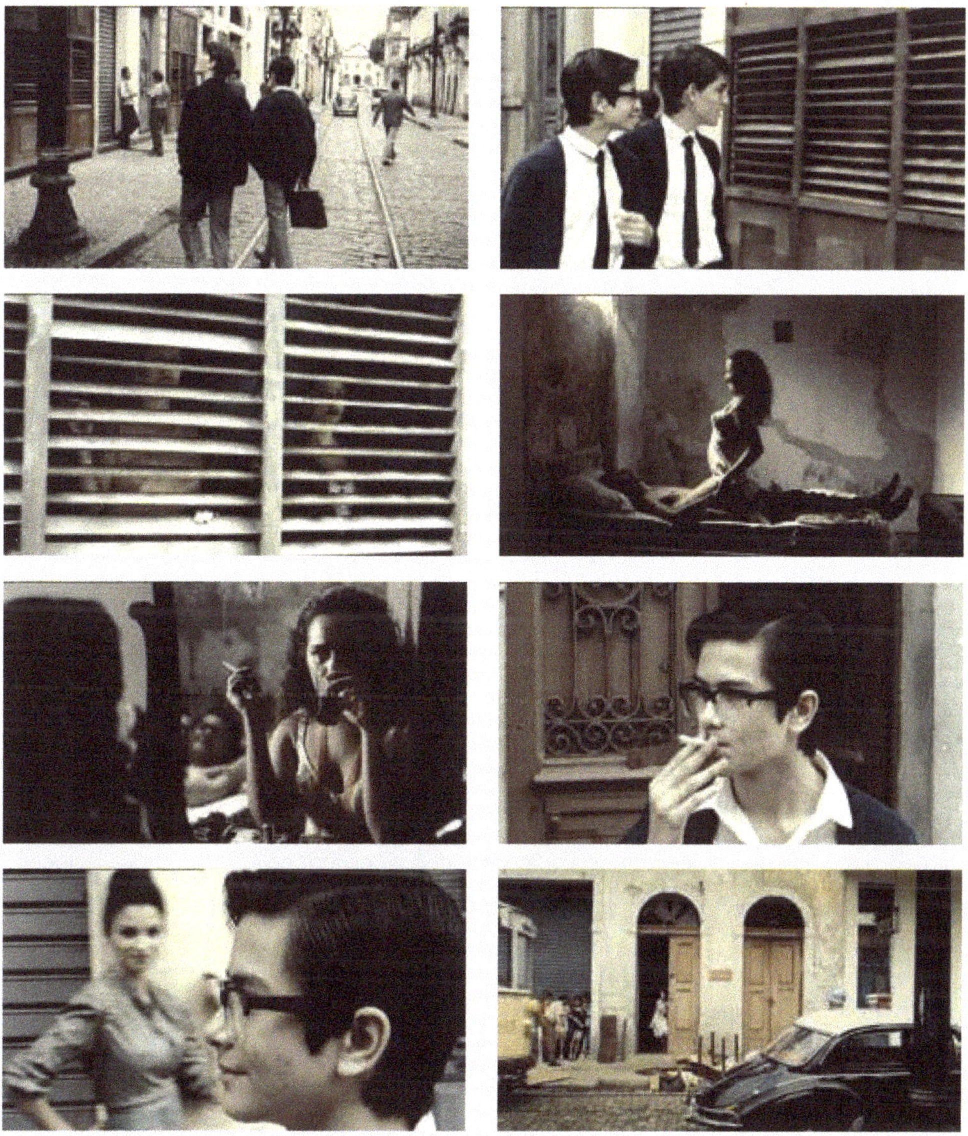

VIDA SOBRE RODAS (2010)

LOCATION *Marquise do Parque Ibirapuera*

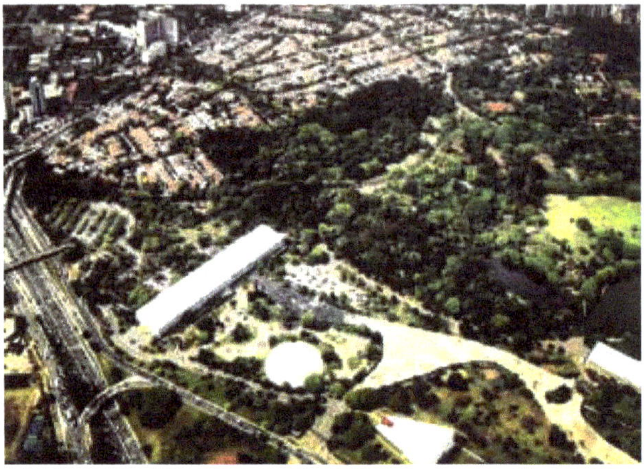

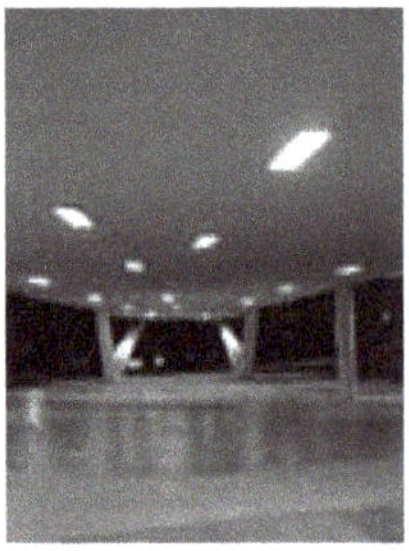

'FERNANDINHO BATMAN' is mentioned in passing, only once in the movie. He is one among many pioneering skateboarders from Brazil who have been turned into the supporting cast of this story, which focuses on the country's current world champions. It is an essential reference, though. With Fernandinho we are introduced to a style of street riding in which every manoeuvre connects to the following one in a sort of continuous stream. Archival footage, taken probably from the *Grito da Rua* TV show, presents a skinny boy in blue jeans and sunglasses sliding across smooth pavement, passing under a curved ceiling, and bouncing off the graffiti-covered walls of the Museum of Modern Art. Tactfully, flowing along such remarkable construction, his movements bring another important historical element to the scene: the Ibirapuera marquee. This large structure of reinforced concrete, designed by the renowned Oscar Niemeyer, lies at the heart of the homonymous park. In *Vida sobre rodas*, it is said to have been one of the main training grounds for skateboarders who couldn't afford to go to the private ramps, thus fulfilling the democratic ideals of modernist architecture – so much so that, later in the 1980s, it would even become the stage of demonstrations for the right to skate. ➺***Gabriel Menotti***

Photos © Gustavo Nagib

Directed by Daniel Baccaro
Scene description: Skateboarders display their talent
Timecode for scene: 0:14:00 – 0:14:33

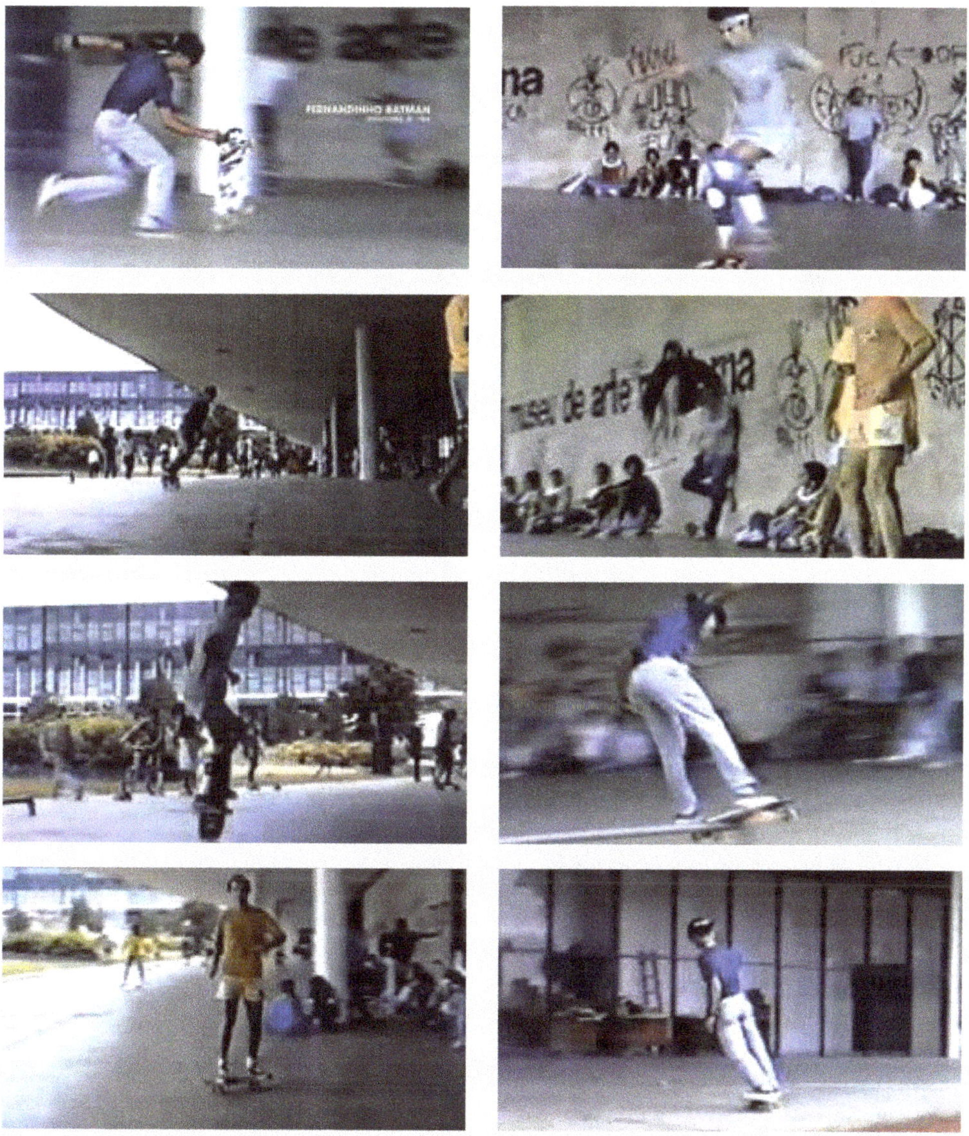

THE GREATEST MOVIE EVER SOLD (2011)

LOCATION *Rua 25 de Março*

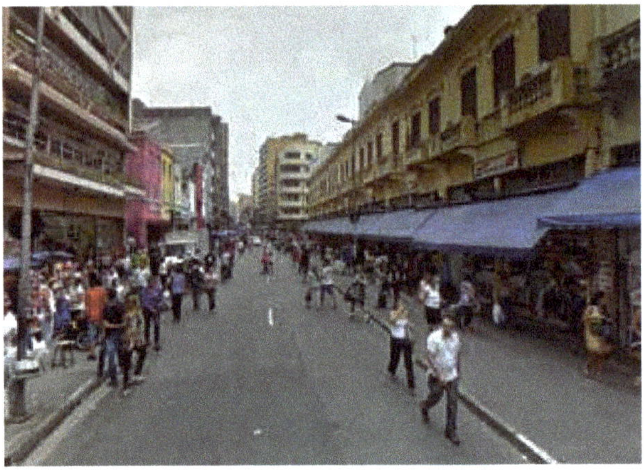

SELDOM HAS THE Rua 25 de Março seemed so empty as when Morgan Spurlock walks through it, trying to find out what the locals think about the ban on outdoor advertisement in the city. The documentary's smooth editing leads us to believe that this is where he meets the only Brazilian interviewee to answer his questions in English: not the mayor or the municipal director of urban planning, but rather the owner of a collectible toy store. In an ad-free São Paulo, the indoor setting of this scene stands as the most visually polluted ever. At this point in the movie, it has become hard to tell whether Spurlock is employing some well-thought rhetorical irony or has simply devised a strategy for snatching freebies while keeping his dignity. Has the trip to Brazil earned the director more than its production costs? Has this interview got him some bonus Transformers®? While I try to brush these petty questions off my mind, the merchant very earnestly says that his business hasn't been harmed, since most customers get to know about it on the Internet or by 'mouth-to-mouth'. The awkward silence before Spurlock corrects him is all it takes to realize that this character's preference for speaking in a foreign language is an impulse not so different from that of indie film-makers – a will to speak directly to the audience, even when you don't get all the expressions right and may sound a little creepy.
→ ***Gabriel Menotti***

Photo © Google maps

Directed by Morgan Spurlock

Scene description: Morgan Spurlock interviews a merchant

Timecode for scene: 0:50:52 – 0:51:44

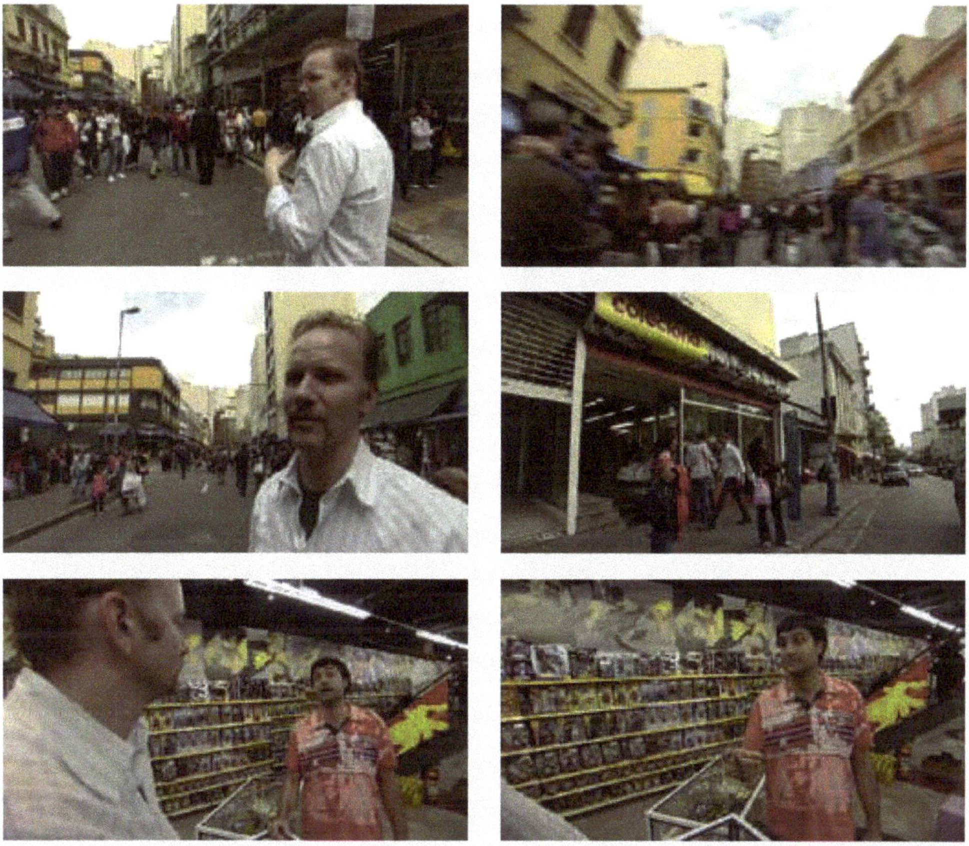

TWO RABBITS/DOIS COELHOS (2012)

LOCATION *Pacaembu Stadium*

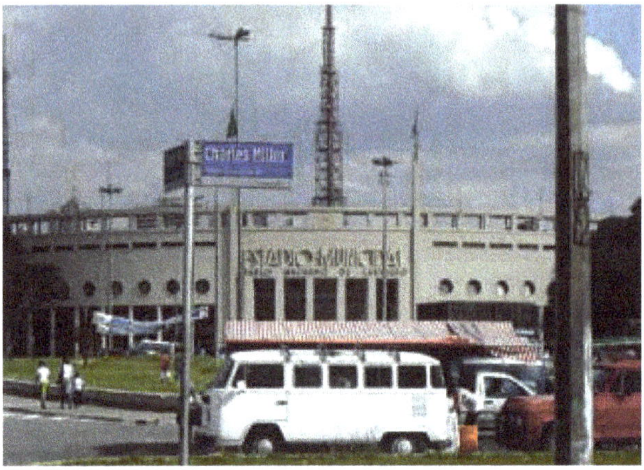

SÃO PAULO, LIKE OTHER BIG CITIES, is fast moving, crowded and full of life. With around eleven million habitants, we could say it doesn't sleep. Afonso Poyart brings these dynamics to the big screen in his film *Two Rabbits*, a title which refers to the popular Brazilian saying, 'to kill two rabbits with a single stroke.' The plot is intertwined with scenes acted in real time alongside nonlinear voice-over, rejecting chronological continuity. Edgar, the main character, and his girlfriend, ambush a crime boss who is also a corrupt politician in order to get two million dollars. The director explores several famous São Paulo locations, synchronizing story and place through heroism, crime and thrills. Poyart uses images of Marginal Pinheiro, Avenida Paulista, Largo do Glicério and Estádio do Pacaembu, often in panoramic aerial shots. The images of Marginal and Avenida Paulista give a feeling that anything could be possible in São Paulo, which is a huge and crowded place. The sequence starts with Edgar following the crime boss. Edgar takes his money and a chase starts. During this sequence aerial shots of Marginal and Paulista combine with close-ups of the car chase. The final scene takes place in front of a famous football stadium, serving as a large real-life stage for their big showdown. Moving from long-shot to medium close-up, the camera closes in on the main characters' faces. The hero becomes a martyr, giving his life to make up for his past mistakes. ➾ ***Fabiana M. Ghiringhello***

Directed by Afonso Poyart

Scene description: Final sequence where characters are in front of the Stadium
Timecode for scene: 1:18:00 – 1:18:16

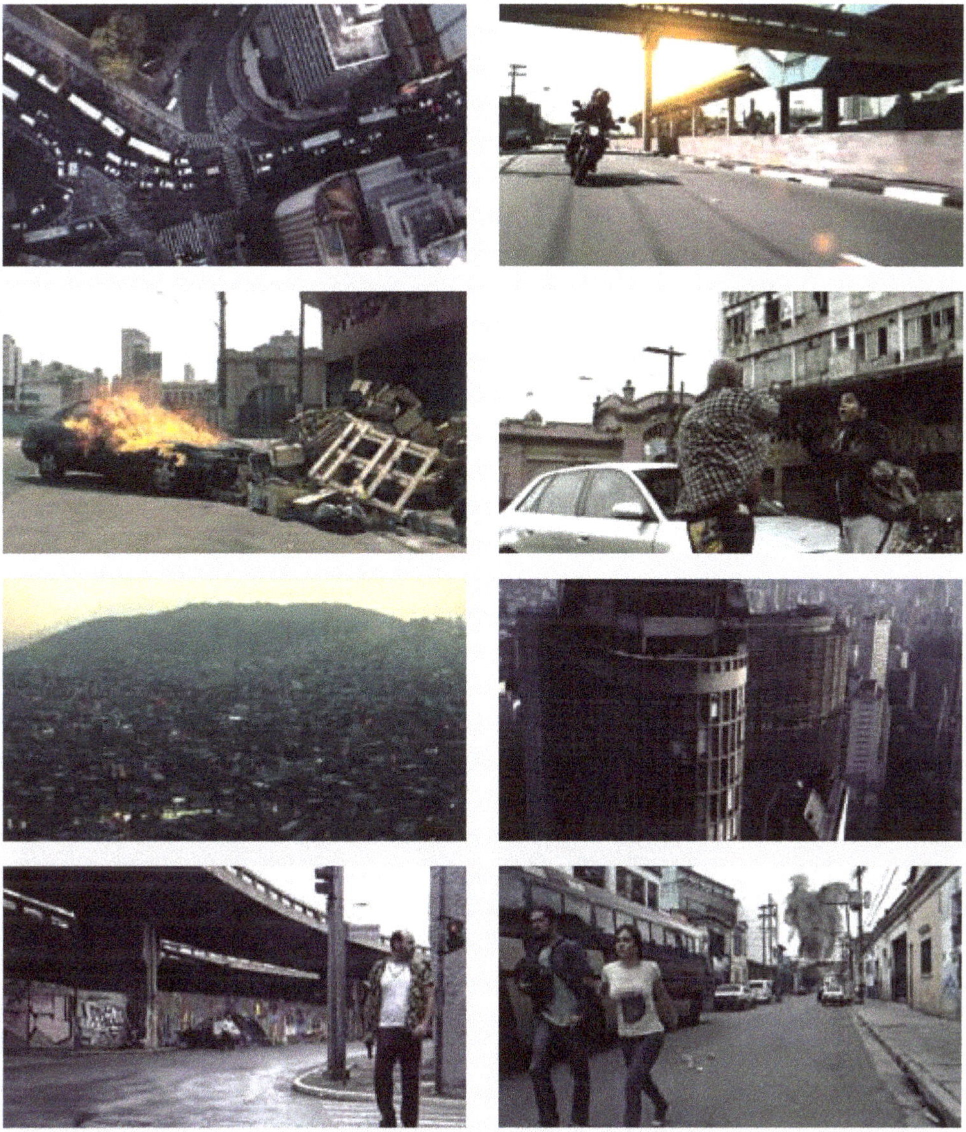

Images © 2012 Black Maria Filme Video Digital, Black Maria

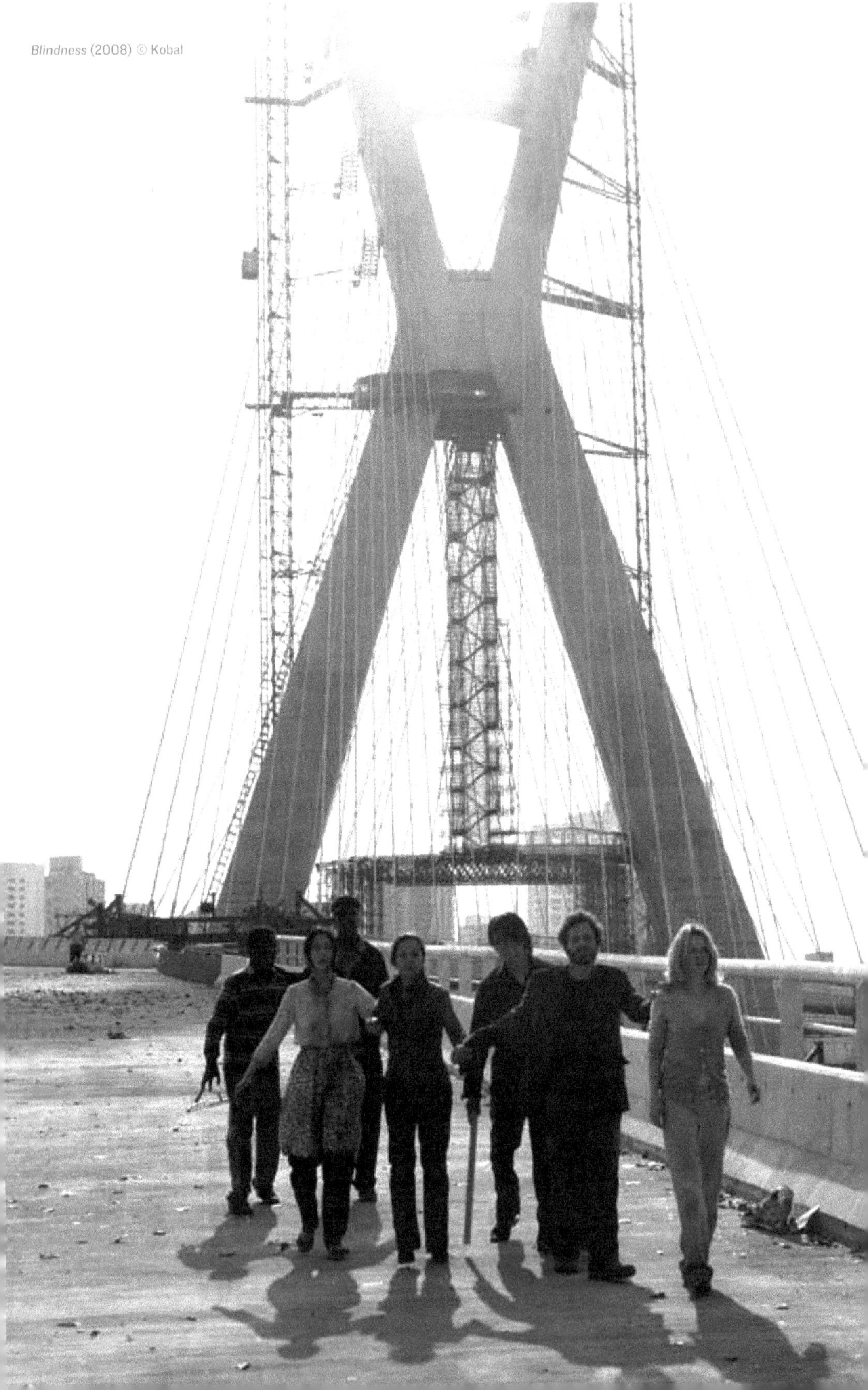

Blindness (2008) © Kobal

GO FURTHER

Recommended reading, useful websites and film availability

BOOKS

São Paulo: Metrópole em trânsito: Percursos urbanos e culturais
ed. by Candido Malta Campos, Lúcia Helena Gama and Vladimir Sacchetta
(Editora SENAC, 2004)

Boca do Lixo: Cinema e classes populares
by Nuno Cesar Abreu
(Editora Unicamp, 2006)

São Paulo: Cidade azul
by Andréa Barbosa
(Alameda, 2012)

O Voo dos anjos: Bressane, Sganzerla
by Jean-Claude Bernardet
(Brasiliense, 1991)

Cinema de invenção
by Jairo Ferreira
(Max Limonad, 1986)

A sombra da outra: A Cinematográfica Maristela e o cinema industrial paulista nos anos 50
by Afrânio Mendes Catani
(Panorama do saber, 2002)

'A Vera Cruz e o mito do cinema industrial'
by Carlos Augusto Calil
In *Projeto Memória Vera Cruz* (Secretaria de Estado da Cultura/Museu da Imagem e do Som, 1987) pp.9-23

Brazilian Cinema
by Randal Johnson and Robert Stam
(Columbia University Press, 1995)

Vera Cruz: Imagens e história do cinema brasileiro
by Sérgio Martinelli
(Abooks Editora, 2002)

Brazil on Screen: Cinema Novo, New Cinema, Utopia
by Lúcia Nagib
(I.B. Tauris, 2007)

Cinema Marginal brasileiro e suas fronteiras: Filmes produzidos nos anos 60 e 70
ed. by Eugênio Puppo and Vera Haddad
(Centro Cultural Banco do Brasil, 2001)

Cinema marginal (1968/1973): A representação em seu limite
by Fernão Ramos
(Brasiliense, 1987)

Um cinema brasileiro antropofágico? (1970–1974)
by Guiomar Ramos
(AnnaBlume, 2008)

São Paulo em preto & branco: Cinema e sociedade nos anos 50 e 60
by Waldir Salvadore
(Annablume, 2005)

O terceiro olho: Ensaios de cinema e vídeo (Mário Peixoto, Glauber Rocha e Júlio Bressane)
by Francisco Elinaldo Teixeira
(Perspectiva, 2003)

Allegories of Underdevelopment
by Ismail Xavier
(Minnesota University Press, 1997)

'Progresso, disciplina fabril e descontração operária: Retóricas do documentário brasileiro silencioso'
by Ismail Xavier
In Eduardo Morettin, Marcos Napolitano and Mônica Karnis (eds), *História e Documentário* (FGV, 2012)
pp. 58–59

Cinema Brasileiro Pós-Moderno: O Neon-realismo
by Luiz Renato Pucci Jr
(Sulina, 2008)

Non-places: Introduction to an Anthropology of Supermodernity
by Marc Augé
(London:Verso, 1995)

ONLINE

http://www.prefeitura.sp.gov.br/cidade/secretarias/cultura/ecine/filmando_sp/

CONTRIBUTORS

Editor and contributing writer biographies

EDITORS

Louis Bayman is an Early Career Research Fellow in the School of Arts at Oxford Brookes University, UK. He has edited the *Directory of World Cinema: Italy* and (with Natália Pinazza, 2013) *Brazil* for Intellect, and (with Sergio Rigoletto) *Popular Italian Cinema* (Palgrave MacMillan, 2013). He is the author of the monograph *The Operatic and the Everyday in Postwar Italian Film Melodrama* (Edinburgh University Press, forthcoming).

Natália Pinazza completed an ORSA-funded PhD at the University of Bath, UK. She graduated from the University of São Paulo before completing an MA (funded by Academic Excellence Awards) at the University of Bath. She teaches at Birkbeck College, University of London and at Regents University of London. She has previously taught at the University of Sheffield, UK and contributed to undergraduate teaching at the University of Bath. She undertook research funded by UNESCO in indigenous visual cultures at the University of Ottawa, Canada. She co-edited the *Directory of World Cinema: Brazil* (Intellect, 2013) and authored *Journeys in Argentine and Brazilian Cinema: Road Films in a Global Era* (Palgrave Macmillan, 2014).

CONTRIBUTORS

Kyle Black is Assistant Professor of Spanish and Latin American culture at Saint Mary's University of Minnesota, where he teaches courses on language, literature, film, and translation studies. His most recent research focuses on Immigrant Cinema from Argentina and Spain and explores issues of global citizenry, racist discourse, the nation-state/border relativity, the dynamics of (im)material production, as well as questions of violence manifesting from gender discrepancies. Black's doctoral dissertation carries the title: Transnational Negotiations in Immigrant Cinema: Dialogic Approaches to the Immigrant Other within Spain and Argentina (Arizona State University, 2012) and, in conjunction with the aforementioned socio-critical themes, the study also examines the realities of this filmmaking within the frameworks of feminist, comedic, and melodramatic genres. Black has traveled extensively throughout Latin America and Europe and attributes his interest in migrating subjectivities to the experiences, research, and friendships made on these journeys.

Alessandra Soares Brandão is Senior Lecturer of Film and Literary Studies for the Graduate Program in Language Sciences – Unisul, Brazil. She was a postdoctoral research fellow at the Centre for World Cinemas – University of Leeds, UK. She has published about Latin American cinema, Brazilian literature and film and co-edited the book *Políticas dos Cinemas Latino-Americanos Contemporâneos* (Editora Unisul, 2012).

Murilo Gabriel Berardo Bueno graduated in advertising. He is specialized in film and education and is Master of Communication at the Faculty of Communication and Library Science – UFG, Brazil. His MA thesis investigates the construction of female archetypes in the filmography of Tata Amaral. He studied in France during his MA and participated in the production of a series of videos for the webtv of the Université Catholique de LOUEST, France. He has experience in communication with an emphasis in direction and production for film and has directed a film called *The Disease of Fabricio*, 2012. He is professor of the advertising course at the Catholic University of Goiás, Brazil.

Reinaldo Cardenuto is a PhD candidate in Media and Audiovisual Process at Escola de Comunicação e Artes - Universty of São Paulo (USP) and lecturer of cinema history at Fundação Armando Alvares Penteado (FAAP), Brazil. He graduated in social sciences from USP and journalism from Pontifícia Universidade Católica (PUC), São Paulo, and was the cinema programmer and assessor for the Secretaria Municipal de Cultura de São Paulo (between 2005 and 2007).

Maria Ignês Carlos Magno is a professor of the MA in Communication at the Universidade Anhembi Morumbi, São Paulo. She has a PhD in Sciences of Communication from Escola de Comunicação e Artes, University of São Paulo, and an MA in Cultural History from Pontifícia Universidade Católica, São Paulo. Her research interests centre on critique, cinema, history, culture and identity.

Márcia Carvalho graduated in social communications (Radio, TV and Web) and has an MSc in Communications and a PhD in Multimedia. She is professor and coordinator in Radio, TV and Internet at the Faculty of Technology and Communication Paulus (São Paulo) and researcher of the history of media and history of film. She has experience in communications, focusing on Brazilian cinema, soundtrack and documentary.

Carolin Overhoff Ferreira teaches contemporary cinema at the Federal University of São Paulo. She is the author of *New Tendencies in Latinamerican Dramaturgy* (Vistas, 1999), *Identity and Difference: Postcoloniality and Transnationality in Lusophone Films* (LIT Verlag, 2012), *Diálogos africanos: Um continente no cinema* (Centro Cultural Banco do Brasil, 2012) and *Cinema Português: Aproximações à sua história e indisciplinaridade* (Alameda, forthcoming). She edited *Terra em Transe: Ética e estética no cinema português* (Martin Meidenbauer Verlags , 2012), *Dekalog: On Manoel de Oliveira* (Wallflower Press, 2008), *O Cinema Português Através dos Seus Filmes* (Campo das Letras, 2007) and *África: Um Continente no Cinema* and *Manoel de Oliveira: Novas Perspectivas sobre a Sua Obra* (both Unifesp, forthcoming).

Fabiana M. Ghiringhello is a journalist with an MA in European Cinema from the University of Bath, UK and specializes in documentary at the Città del Teatro, Italy. She worked for five years as a journalist. Currently, she lives in Pisa where she collaborates with the arthouse cinema Arsenale and works as a coordinator of culture at Association Pisa incontra Brasile.

Scott Jordan Harris is a British film critic and sportswriter. Formerly online arts editor of *The Spectator* and editor of *The Big Picture* magazine, he is now a culture blogger for the *Daily Telegraph*; a contributor to BBC Radio 4's *The Film Programme*; and Roger Ebert's UK correspondent. His work has been published by, among many others, *Sight & Sound, The Spectator, The Guardian*, BBC Online, the *Chicago Sun-Times*, the *Huffington Post, Fangoria*, Film4.com, Turner Classic Movies and the Australian Film Institute. He has contributed to more than a dozen books on film, including *Directory of World Cinema: Brazil* (Intellect, 2013), and is editor of the World Film Locations volumes on New York, New Orleans, Chicago and San Francisco. In 2010 his blog, *A Petrified Fountain*, was named by *Running in Heels* as one of the world's 'best movie blogs'. He is on Twitter as @ScottFilmCritic.

Tatiana Signorelli Heise is Lecturer →

CONTRIBUTORS

Editor and contributing writer biographies (continued)

in Portuguese and Latin American Studies at the University of Glasgow, UK. She writes on Brazilian cinema and film studies more generally. Her latest monograph is *Remaking Brazil: Contested National Identities in Contemporary Brazilian* Cinema (University of Wales Press, 2012). She is currently conducting research for a monograph comparing the political cinemas of Brazil, Chile and Argentina. She is a native Brazilian from São Paulo, where she had a prior career as a journalist.

Tiago de Luca is Lecturer in World Cinemas and Portuguese at the University of Liverpool, UK. He has an MA in Film Studies - UCL, UK (2007) and a PhD in World Cinemas - University of Leeds, UK (2011). He is the author of *Realism of the Senses in World Cinema: The Experience of Physical Reality* (I.B. Tauris, 2013), and his articles have been published in *Senses of Cinema*, *Journal of Chinese Cinemas* and *Cinephile*, among others. He is currently co-editing a volume on *Slow Cinema*, Edinburgh University Press.

Cecília Mello is FAPESP Senior Research Fellow in the Department of History of Art, Federal University of São Paulo, Brazil. Her research focuses on issues of audio-visual realism, cinema and urban spaces, and intermediality. She has co-edited with Lúcia Nagib the book *Realism and the Audiovisual Media* (Palgrave, 2009).

Maria Luiza Martins de Mendonça graduated in public relations and has an MA in Communication from the University of Brasilia, Brazil (1981) and a PhD in Communication Sciences from the University of São Paulo (1999). She received her postdoctorate in audio-visual communication at the Universidad Autónoma de Barcelona (2007). She has participated as a researcher at the University of Quebec in Montreal (UQAM), with a scholarship from the Canadian Embassy. She is a professor in the Faculty of Communication, at the Federal University of Goiás, Brazil.

Gabriel Menotti is a lecturer in multimedia at the Federal University of Espírito Santo (UFES), Brazil. He is the author of *Através da Sala Escura* (Intermeios, 2012), a history of movie theatres from the perspective of VJing spaces. Menotti holds a PhD in Media and Communications from Goldsmiths (University of London), and another from the Catholic University of São Paulo. He has published work in a number of research journals and books, as well as contributed to international events such as the São Paulo Biennial, Rencontres Internationales Paris/Berlin/Madrid and the Transmediale Festival.

Santiago Oyarzabal is a Research Fellow in the Department of Hispanic Studies at Warwick University. His PhD dissertation 'Representations of Social Crisis in Recent Argentine Cinema', focusses on the expression of social and cultural change in the feature films of the 1990s and beyond. He is co-editor of *World Film Locations: Buenos Aires* (Intellect, 2014).

Michael Pigott is Assistant Professor of Video Art and Digital Media at the University of Warwick. He has published articles on world cinema and new media. He is the editor of *World Film Locations: Venice* (Intellect, 2013), co-editor of *World Film Locations: Buenos Aires* (Intellect, 2014), and the author of *Joseph Cornell Versus Cinema* (Bloomsbury, 2013).

Rafael Mendonça Lisita Pinto graduated in advertising at the Catholic University of Goiás, Brazil. He is doing his MA in Visual Culture at the Federal University of Goiás within the research line of visual poetic and creation process, focusing on the study of gender, identity and alterity in filmic language.

Renato Luiz Pucci Jr completed his PhD in Communication Sciences at the University of São Paulo. He is a lecturer in radio and television and teaches the MA programme in Communication at the Universidade Anhembi Morumbi, São Paulo. He is the author of the books *Cinema Brasileiro Pós-moderno: O Neon-realismo* (Editora Sulina, 2008), *O Equilíbrio das Estrelas: Filosofia e Imagens no Cinema de Walter Hugo Khouri* (Annablume, 2001) and of the chapter 'Cinema Pós-moderno' in the book *História do Cinema Mundial* (Papirus, 2006). He is currently researching transformation in fiction in Brazilian television, in particular in terms of postmodern experimentation. He has edited the e-books *Televisão: Formas Audiovisuais de Ficção e Documentário*, volumes 1 (2011) and 2 (2012). He is the coordinator of the panel 'Televisão – Formas Audiovisuais de Ficção e Documentário' at events held by SOCINE – Sociedade Brasileira de Estudos de Cinema e Audiovisual, and is the coordinator of the research cluster 'Inovações e Rupturas na Ficção Televisiva Brasileira' which is associated with OBITEL – Observatório Ibero-Americano da Ficção Televisiva. He is also funded by CNPq – Conselho Nacional de Desenvolvimento Científico e Tecnológico.

Daniel Serravalle de Sá has alternated between long periods of residence in Brazil and Britain. He worked as Graduate Teaching Fellow at the University of Manchester, UK, as Researcher at the Federal University of Santa Catarina (UFSC), Brazil, and as Lecturer at the Federal University of Pará (UFPA), Brazil. He is currently Senior Lecturer at the Federal University of Technology Paraná (UTFPR), Brazil. His research interests incorporate the study of popular culture and the relationship between literature and cinema. In recent years, Daniel has written about the Gothic and its manifestations in different cultural contexts. He has published the book *Gótico Tropical* (2010), co-edited the volume *Gothic: New Directions (2012)* and published many scholarly articles.

Antônio M. da Silva is Associate Lecturer in Afro-Luso-Brazilian studies at the University of Kent, UK. He holds a PhD from the University of Bristol, UK and received an MRes from the University of Leeds, UK, both in Brazilian cinema. His postgraduate research focused on representations of gender and sexuality in Brazilian cinema through depictions of Women in Prison Film (MRes) and the femme fatale (PhD). His main research interests include representations of race, social class, gender and sexuality in Afro-Luso-Brazilian cinema, and their relationship with theories such as feminism, psychoanalysis, colonialism/postcolonialism, and queer: gay/lesbian. At present, his main research projects are on Afro-Luso-Brazilian contemporary female film-makers and on the films of the Brazilian director Cláudio Assis and the Portuguese director João Pedro Rodrigues.

Ramayana Lira de Sousa is Senior Lecturer in film and literary studies for the Graduate Program in Language Sciences, Unisul, Brazil. She was a postdoctoral research fellow at the University of Leeds, UK. Her present research focuses on the politics of affects in contemporary Brazilian cinema. She has published articles and chapters about Brazilian cinema, pornography, gender studies, and literature and co-edited the book *Políticas do Cinemas Latino-Americanos Contemporâneos* (Editora Unisul, 2012).

Alfredo Suppia is a visiting researcher at

CONTRIBUTORS

Editor and contributing writer biographies (continued)

the Department of Cinema, Radio and Television at the University of São Paulo (CTR-ECA-USP). He has lectured in cinema and the audio-visual at the Instituto de Artes e Design, in the MA course in communication at Universidade Federal de Juiz de Fora (UFJF), Brazil.

Fábio Uchôa is a social scientist who graduated from the University of São Paulo. Between 2003 and 2008 he worked and researched at the Brazilian Cinemateca archives. At the Cinemateca he worked with the personal archives of film-makers and intellectuals such as Paulo Emilio Salles Gomes, Glauber Rocha and Francisco Luiz de Almeida Salles. He was also an invited lecturer at the Faculdade de Artes do Paraná, Brazil, where he taught 'cinema underground'. He completed his PhD at Escola de Comunicações e Artes, Universidade de São Paulo ECA/USP and specialized in analysis of film and the representation of the city of São Paulo in the cinema. Since 2012, he has been part of the editorial board of the *Revista Movimento* – a journal that is a part of the Postgraduate Programme 'Meios e Processos Audiovisuais' at ECA/USP.

RECOMMENDED
THE WORLD'S LEADING FILM CRITICS...

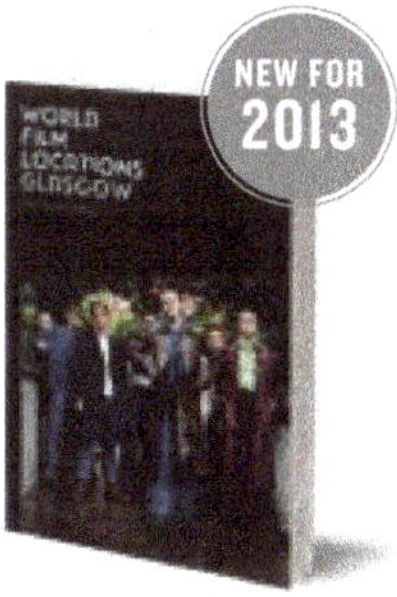

GLASGOW

Edited by
Nicola Balkind
ISBN 9781841507194
PB £9.95 / $18

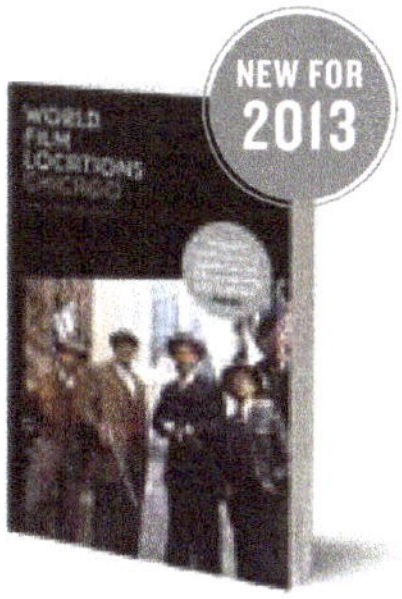

CHICAGO

Edited by
Scott Jordan Harris
ISBN 9781841507187
PB £9.95 / $18

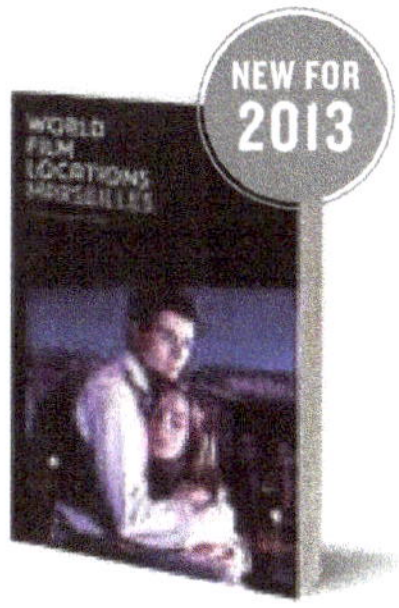

MARSEILLES

Edited by
Marcelline Block
ISBN 9781841507231
PB £9.95 / $18

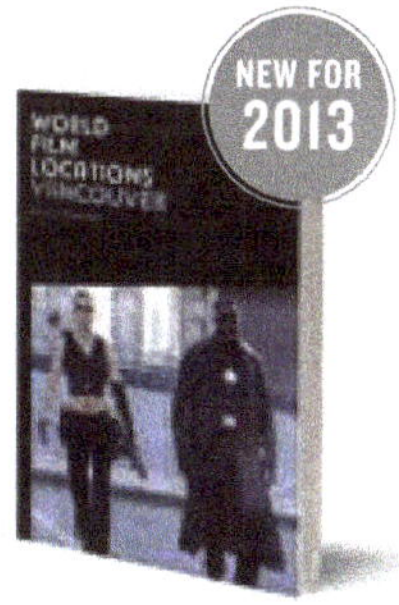

VANCOUVER

Edited by
Rachel Walls
ISBN 9781841507217
PB £9.95 / $18

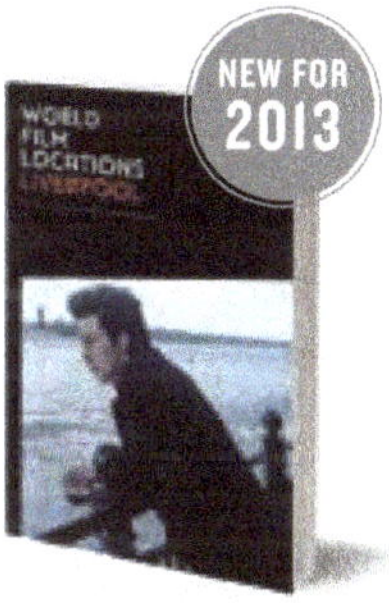

LIVERPOOL

Edited by
Jez Conolly and
Caroline Whelan
ISBN 9781783200269
PB £14.95 / $25

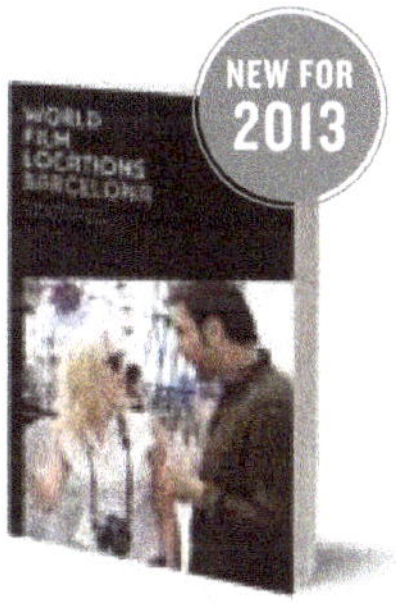

BARCELONA

Edited by
Helio San Miguel and
Lorenzo Torres J.
Hortelano
ISBN 9781783200252
PB £14.95 / $25

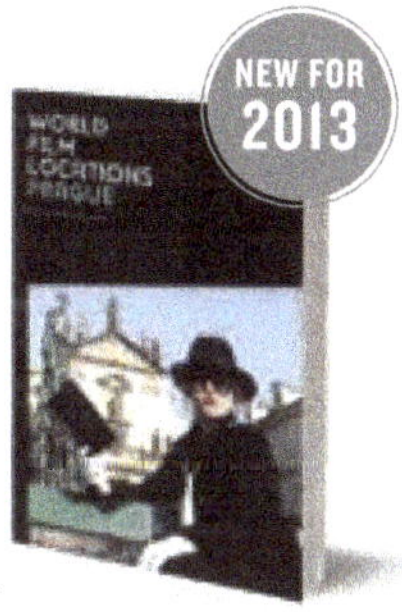

PRAGUE

Edited by
Marcelline Block
ISBN 9781783200276
PB £14.95 / $25

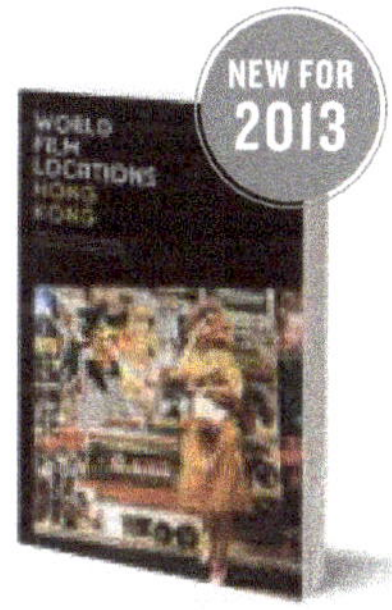

HONG KONG

Edited by
Linda C. Lai and
Kimburley Choi
ISBN 9781783200214
PB £9.95 / $18

LATEST TITLES NOW AVAILABLE FOR AMAZON KINDLE AND OTHER E-READERS + DOWNLOAD THE FREE IPAD APP >>

VISIT THE KINDLE AND ITUNES STORES FOR MORE INFORMATION

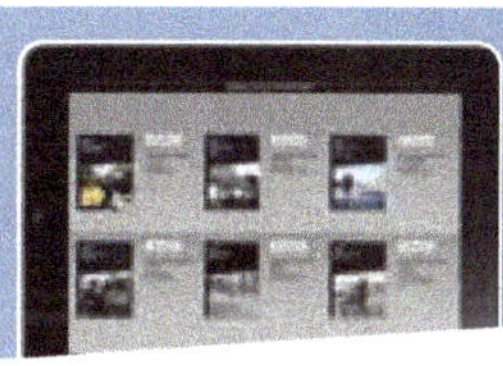

Find us on Facebook For further information and to order books visit: www.intellectbooks.com

FILMOGRAPHY

All films mentioned or featured in this book

Photo by Paulo Silvestrini and Carol Bandeira de Mello

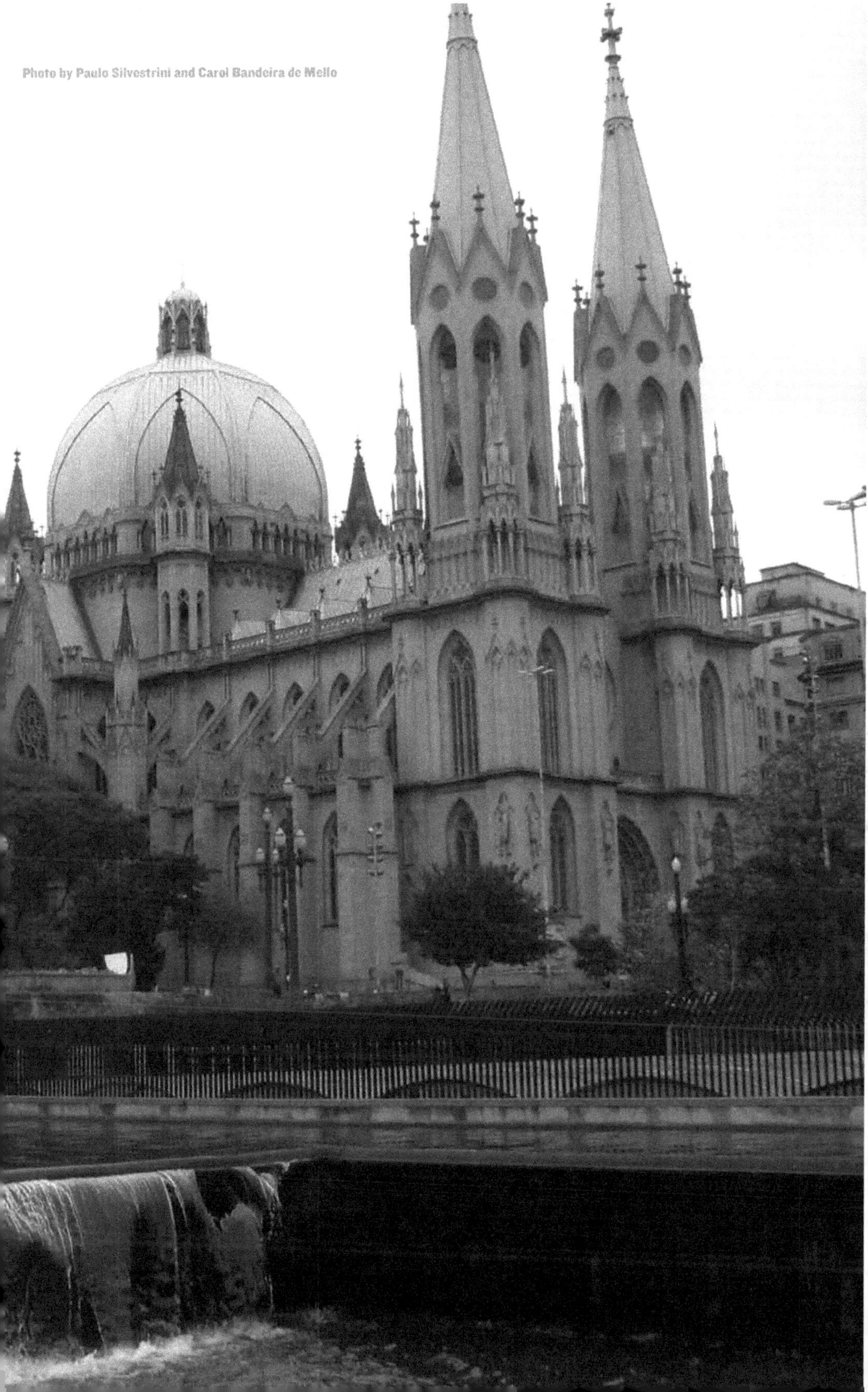

WORLD FILM LOCATIONS EXPLORING THE CITY ONSCREEN

www.intellectbooks.com

www.ingramcontent.com/pod-product-compliance
Lightning Source LLC
LaVergne TN
LVHW051131260826
846232LV00020B/67